"This book unsettles the reader through stories, questions, wonderings, and wanderings; it takes us through a series of encounters into the not-yet-known. The authors invite us to explore, as educators, the emergence of our own capacity to affect and be affected by others—where those others are both human and more-than-human. The multiple and emergent educational encounters that the authors offer us are embodied, and they are grounded in place; and they take us, through new materialist and posthumanist experimentation, into inspiring new ways of knowing-in-being. Together these papers engage in a Baradian ethico-onto-epistemological exploration of pedagogical becomings. They are beautifully written and make a vital and timely contribution to educational thought and practice."

Bronwyn Davies, Western Sydney University, Australia.

"Calling for radical hope, this volume opens potentials for language and literacies research that reaches beyond critique alone and into more just, speculative futures. Toward such futures, the authors develop orientations to language and literacies research that value the 'more than' of experience that affects this sense of radical hope."

Christian Ehret, McGill University, Canada.

TRANSFORMING LANGUAGE AND LITERACY EDUCATION

This book mobilizes concepts associated with new materialism, posthumanism, and relational ontologies with respect to languages and literacies education. With accessible and rich stories about pedagogical practice, the book stimulates other educators to engage in similar "experiments," and assesses how these concepts offer new ways of understanding diverse educational sites.

Kelleen Toohey is Professor Emerita in the Faculty of Education at Simon Fraser University, Vancouver, Canada. Her work in second language education has concerned the teaching of Indigenous languages, "heritage" languages, and English.

Suzanne Smythe is Associate Professor in adult literacy and adult education in the Faculty of Education, Simon Fraser University, Vancouver, Canada. She is currently interested in relational ontologies and new literacies of automation, toward more ethical human-machinic futures.

Diane Dagenais is Professor in the Faculty of Education at Simon Fraser University, Vancouver, Canada. She works in French and English in second language and bilingual education and her research focuses on multilingualism and multiliteracies.

Magali Forte is a PhD student in the Faculty of Education at Simon Fraser University, Vancouver, Canada, and a K-12 teacher in Vancouver. She adopts a socio-material perspective to examine the ways in which multilingual and multimodal processes of identity construction unfold through entanglements of humans and nonhumans in second language education settings.

TRANSFORMING LANGUAGE AND LITERACY EDUCATION

New Materialism, Posthumanism, and Ontoethics

Edited by Kelleen Toohey, Suzanne Smythe, Diane Dagenais and Magali Forte

LONDON AND NEW YORK

First published 2020
by Routledge
2 Park Square, Milton Park, Abingdon, Oxon OX14 4RN

and by Routledge
52 Vanderbilt Avenue, New York, NY 10017

Routledge is an imprint of the Taylor & Francis Group, an informa business

© 2020 selection and editorial matter, Kelleen Toohey, Suzanne Smythe, Diane Dagenais, and Magali Forte; individual chapters, the contributors

The right of Kelleen Toohey, Suzanne Smythe, Diane Dagenais and Magali Forte to be identified as the authors of the editorial material, and of the authors for their individual chapters, has been asserted in accordance with sections 77 and 78 of the Copyright, Designs and Patents Act 1988.

All rights reserved. No part of this book may be reprinted or reproduced or utilised in any form or by any electronic, mechanical, or other means, now known or hereafter invented, including photocopying and recording, or in any information storage or retrieval system, without permission in writing from the publishers.

Trademark notice: Product or corporate names may be trademarks or registered trademarks, and are used only for identification and explanation without intent to infringe.

British Library Cataloguing in Publication Data
A catalogue record for this book is available from the British Library

Library of Congress Cataloging-in-Publication Data
A catalog record has been requested for this book

ISBN: 9781138589353 (hbk)
ISBN: 9781138589360 (pbk)
ISBN: 9780429491702 (ebk)

Typeset in Times New Roman
by Taylor & Francis Books

CONTENTS

List of figures ix
List of contributors xi

Introduction 1
Kelleen Toohey, Suzanne Smythe, Diane Dagenais and
Magali Forte

1 Making and Unmaking Literacy Desirings: Pedagogical
  Matters of Concern from Writers' Studio 18
  Tara Gutshall, Rucker and Candace R. Kuby

2 Practising Place-Thought and Engaging in Critical Place
  Inquiry in a Public Park: Listening, Letting Go, and
  Unsettling Our Writing Pedagogies 32
  Michelle A. Honeyford and Jennifer Watt

3 Becoming Posthuman: Bodies, Affect, and Earth in the
  School Garden 54
  Saskia Van Viegen

4 *Lekta* and Literacy in Early Childhood Education:
  Entwinements of Idealism and Materialism 72
  Liselott Mariett Olsson

5 Rethinking Causality Through Children's Literacies 91
  Jacqueline Barreiro

6	A Rhizomatic Case Analysis of Instructional Coaching as Becoming *Brandon Sherman, Mari Haneda and Annela Teemant*	104
7	"This Documentary Actually Makes Welland Look Good": Exploring Posthumanism in a High School Documentary Film Project *Amélie Lemieux and Jennifer Rowsell*	120
8	Affect Theory as a Lens on Teacher Thinking in Adult Language Classrooms *Monica Waterhouse*	136
9	The Problem and Potential of Representation: Being and Becoming *Margaret MacDonald, Cher Hill and Nathalie Sinclair*	153
10	Exploring Affect in Stop Frame Animation *Gabriele Budach, Dimitri Efremov, Daniela Loghin and Gohar Sharoyan*	175

Index *194*

FIGURES

2.1	Critical place inquiry and place-thought as pedagogical and methodological framework	37
2.2	Check for ticks. We've gone wild.	46
3.1	Image of Asad's story about his migration journey	56
3.2	Students conducting and recording interviews on film	61
3.3	Student rap and dance performance in the garden	61
3.4	Parents and students working together in the garden	62
3.5	Students working in the garden wearing kitchen gloves and using sand shovels from home	63
3.6A–D	Screenshots of video clips chosen by students to showcase their work in the garden	66
4.1	Albert's "old" name	72
4.2	Märta	82
4.3	Presley	83
4.4	Hannah	83
4.5	Denise	84
4.6	Denise	85
4.7	Kelly	86
7.1	Intra-active becoming with Cory Monteith	129
9.1	A triangle constructed on a screen where the vertices can be moved	157
9.2	Representational drawing of the bioreactor used in one of our pedagogical documentations	160
9.3	Rainwarning as rainteacher	162
9.4A	Peach the Tree	166

9.4B	Peach the Tree	167
9.5	Becoming with Peach the tree	169
9.6	Peach the Tree in Mundy Park and her sister tree in fairyland	170
9.7	Being and becoming	172
10.1	Dimitri deeply immersed in conversation and co-creation	182
10.2	Daniela with her bookmark learning how to read	185
10.3	Gohar exploring carrots.	187

CONTRIBUTORS

Jacky Barreiro is a PhD candidate in the Faculty of Education at Simon Fraser University, Vancouver, Canada. Her current inquiry explores the intersection between posthumanist theories, education, and social justice.

Gabriele Budach is Associate Professor in the Faculty of Language, Literature, Education and Arts at the University of Luxembourg. Her research interests include multilingualism, multiliteracies, and learning in contexts of diversity. She has conducted sociolinguistic, ethnographic work in schools and community settings in Germany, Canada, the UK, and Luxembourg. In her recent research, she investigates the creative use of objects and digital technology and their impact on learning and learner identities from new materialist perspectives.

Diane Dagenais is Professor in the Faculty of Education at Simon Fraser University, Vancouver, Canada. She works in French and English in second language and bilingual education and her research focuses on multilingualism and multiliteracies.

Dimitri Efremov is a Master's student at the University of Luxembourg and is currently pursuing his degree in "Learning and Communication in Multilingual and Multicultural Contexts." He has a BA in Economics and Marketing and an MA in Translation and Interpreting. He has work experience as a teacher of English as a second language. His research interests lie within the field of informal learning.

Magali Forte is a PhD student in the Faculty of Education at Simon Fraser University, Vancouver, Canada, and a K-12 teacher in Vancouver. She adopts a socio-material perspective to examine the ways in which multilingual and multimodal processes of identity construction unfold through entanglements of humans and nonhumans in second language education settings.

Tara Gutshall Rucker taught elementary school students for eleven years (first, second, and fifth grades) in public schools in Columbia, USA. Currently, Tara teaches kindergarten in Lee's Summit, Missouri. She received her MA in Curriculum and Instruction through the Teaching Fellows program and an Elementary Mathematics Specialists Certificate both at the University of Missouri. Tara is the co-author of the book *Go Be a Writer!: Expanding the Curricular Boundaries of Literacy Learning* and has published articles in the *Journal of Early Childhood Literacy, Talking Points,* and *Language Arts.*

Mari Haneda is an Associate Professor of World Languages Education and Applied Linguistics at Pennsylvania State University, USA. Her research has focused on equitable classroom interactional practices in K-8 multilingual and multicultural settings that benefit emergent bi/multilingual students and more recently the professional learning of elementary school teachers who work with these students.

Cher Hill is Assistant Professor of Professional Practice and an in-service teacher educator in the Faculty of Education at Simon Fraser University, Vancouver, Canada. Her current research utilizes new materialist theories to make visible the complex relations between human and more-than-human entities within educational contexts.

Michelle A. Honeyford is an Associate Professor in Language & Literacy in the Faculty of Education at the University of Manitoba, Canada. Her research focuses on transcultural and multimodal literacies, writing, participatory learning, and practitioner inquiry in classrooms and in out-of-school learning contexts. She facilitates with teacher candidates an innovative, interest-driven afterschool programme on campus for students in grades 5–10, and is Director of the Manitoba Writing Project, a network for educators interested in writing and social justice.

Candace R. Kuby is Department Chair and Associate Professor of Learning, Teaching, and Curriculum and the Director of Qualitative Inquiry at the University of Missouri, USA. Her research interests are (1) the coming-to-be of literacies when young children work with artistic and digital tools; (2) approaches to qualitative inquiry drawing upon poststructural and posthumanist theories; and (3) pedagogies of qualitative inquiry. Candace is the co-author of several books including, most recently, *Posthumanism and Literacy Education: Knowing/Becoming/Doing Literacies* (Routledge) and *Go Be a Writer!: Expanding the Curricular Boundaries of Literacy Learning* (Teachers College Press). Journals in which her scholarship appears include *Qualitative Inquiry*, the *International Journal of Qualitative Studies in Education*, the *Journal of Literacy Research*, the *Journal of Early Childhood Literacy, Literacy,* and *Language Arts*.

Amélie Lemieux is Assistant Professor of Literacies in Mount Saint Vincent University's Faculty of Education in Halifax, Canada. Her research interests include digitally informed and arts-based literacy learning, maker education, and mapping methodologies.

Daniela Loghin was born in the Republic of Moldova. She obtained a diploma in Accounting from the College of Informatics in Chișinău and a Bachelor's degree in Languages and Translation from the University of Rome "La Sapienza." She completed her MA in "Learning and Communication in Multilingual and Multicultural Contexts" at the University of Luxembourg. Having worked as an English teacher for children, she is interested in multilingualism and alternative teaching methods.

Margaret MacDonald is an Associate Professor at Simon Fraser University, Vancouver, Canada, whose research interests include intergenerational programmes, pedagogical documentation, and innovative curriculum development in early childhood education.

Liselott Mariett Olsson is Associate Professor in Pedagogy at Södertörn University, Stockholm, Sweden. Olsson is originally a preschool teacher, trained in Pedagogy and Educational Philosophy in Sweden and France, and is the author of the book *Movement and Experimentation in Young Children's Learning: Deleuze and Guattari in Early Childhood Education*, published within the Contesting Early Childhood series (Routledge) that she now co-edits together with Professor Michel Vandenbroeck. Olsson has conducted research on early childhood literacy, globalization, and digitalization, has been involved in re-conceptualist movements in ECE in English- and French-speaking academic environments and is currently involved in a trans-disciplinary research project – engaging pedagogy, art, and architecture – concerning the notion of public education and the aesthetic dimension of pedagogy.

Jennifer Rowsell is Professor of Literacies and Social Innovation at the University of Bristol's School of Education, UK. Her research interests include multimodal and arts-based research with young people and digital literacies research; more recent work includes post-humanist and affect approaches to literacy teaching and learning and research on the digital divide.

Gohar Sharoyan is a Master's student at the University of Luxembourg and is currently pursuing her degree in "Learning and Communication in Multilingual and Multicultural Contexts." She holds a BA in Linguistics, Translation and Intercultural Communication from the Yerevan Brusov State University in Armenia. Her particular interest lies in radio. She has been hosting her own show on Radio ARA, a Luxembourgish multilingual radio station, and has been producing podcasts and radio features for the University Campus Radio programme since 2017.

Brandon Sherman is the Research Project Manager for the US Department of Education grant-funded initiative, Partnering for Radical School Improvement. His research interests include critical and sociocultural pedagogies, non-linear theoretical approaches to educational research, and dialogic interaction. His current research focuses on pedagogical coaching, professional learning, and equitable family/community/school partnerships.

Nathalie Sinclair is a Canada Research Chair in Tangible Mathematics Learning at Simon Fraser University, Vancouver, Canada, and a Professor in the Faculty of Education. She is the founding and current editor of *Digital Experiences in Mathematics Education* and has authored several books including *Mathematics and the Body: Material Entanglements in the Classroom*, as well as over seventy journal articles. Her primary areas of research include the role of digital technologies in mathematics education, the teaching and learning of geometry, and the nature of mathematical embodiment.

Suzanne Smythe is Associate Professor in adult literacy and adult education in the Faculty of Education, Simon Fraser University, Vancouver, Canada. She is currently interested in relational ontologies and new literacies of automation, toward more ethical human-machinic futures.

Annela Teemant is Professor of Language Education at Indiana University-Purdue University Indianapolis, USA. Her scholarship focuses on critical sociocultural theory and pedagogy in teacher preparation. She has been awarded five US Department of Education grants that focus on the preparation of general education teachers for multilingual learners.

Kelleen Toohey is Professor Emerita in the Faculty of Education at Simon Fraser University, Vancouver, Canada. Her work in second language education has concerned the teaching of Indigenous languages, "heritage" languages, and English.

Saskia Van Viegen is an Assistant Professor in the Department of Languages, Literatures and Linguistics at York University, UK. Her research interests centre on language in education, particularly plurilingual pedagogies, multiliteracies, and migration issues. Her current projects explore language assessment in K-12 education, resources for learning in multilingual university settings, and language and literacy of youth from refugee backgrounds in secondary education.

Monica Waterhouse is Associate Professor in the Département de Langues, linguistiques et traduction, Université Laval, Canada, where she teaches courses in research methodology, critical perspectives on culture and language education, and English Second Language pedagogy. Her current research project, supported by the Fonds de recherche du Québec, works with the Deleuzian concept of *affect* to study the social and curricular stakes of language learning in newcomer language programs and to explore the potential of arts-based pedagogies in these contexts.

Jennifer Watt is an Assistant Professor in Language & Literacy in the Faculty of Education at the University of Manitoba, Canada. Her research focuses on flourishing and inclusive literacies, multimodal life writing, and well-being and well-becoming in schools. She coordinates a University of Manitoba and Manitoba First Nations Education Resource Centre inclusive language and literacies MEd cohort and is Co-Director of the Manitoba Writing Project.

INTRODUCTION

Kelleen Toohey, Suzanne Smythe, Diane Dagenais and Magali Forte

> Every time we explain how a better future might be built, we redraw the boundaries of the possible. We show that the realm of choice available to us is actually quite large ... We need to school ourselves in the possible, share ideas, imagine outcomes, weigh options. We need to figure out how best to transform the systems we've built ... We need millions of people who are willing to teach the teachable, comfort the disheartened and confront the scoundrels. We need to take our politics public and take on the whole culture of cynical defeatism. On some days, I think we need an optimism uprising.
>
> *(Steffen, 2008)*

American futurist Alex Steffen defined optimism as a political act, seeing cynicism and hopelessness about possibilities for action playing into the hands of those who benefit from the status quo. Many of us who have pointed out and decried the myriad inequities and injustices we see in languages and literacies education have come to agree with Bruno Latour (2004) who observed that "critique itself has run out of steam" and recognized the need to go beyond critique to imagine change, to experiment with possible solutions, and to further optimism and hope about the matters that concern us.

Those of us working in languages and literacies education are therefore seeking hope, something new, surprises, as well as disruptions that move us somewhere different, beyond the striations of low expectations, normed national and international comparisons of skills attainments (e.g. literacy testing of eight-year-olds), language proficiency thresholds for citizenship, and so on. Like Gail Boldt (2019), we are interested in what Gilles Deleuze and Félix Guattari (1987/2005) call haeccities: "potentialities ... that emerge when things come into relation with other things ... that will only ever emerge [through] encounter[s] with something else that acts on [them] so as to energize this potential" (Boldt, 2019, pp. 34–35). The contributing authors of this book each explore in different ways the potential for literacies and languages education in encounters with material, relational, and posthuman concepts. This involves a decentring of literacies and languages as privileged representational practices in a "'mind-independent reality' where things talk back" (DeLanda, 2010, cited in Lather, 2016, p. 125).

Moving across the chapters contained within this book, perhaps as one might from plateau to plateau as Deleuze and Guattari (1987/2005) suggest, we find many evocations of hope, optimism, even "cruel optimism" (Berlant, 2006). Yet Kathleen Fitzpatrick (2019) cautions that optimism and hope can also be stances of privilege. Those who have never benefited from the status quo "have little reason to expect change" (p. 60). Citing Tressie McMillan Cottom's (2016) powerful essay *Finding Hope in a Loveless Place*, she corrects academia's faith in the power of research, theory and good intentions to effect change, noting that for McMillan Cottom (2016), and for other scholars of the Black experience in America, "there is no not knowing what comes next, what comes next is what has always come next except in slightly different forms" (Fitzpatrick, 2019, p. 60). This scholarship does not entail hopelessness, but a "deeper resistance ... a knowledge that the world has long persisted in not changing and indeed may never change, but that you have to make your way in it anyhow" (Fitzpatrick, 2019, p. 59).

In these pages, hope is not a bright horizon; potential is not that of lack or deficit, as in the persistent not-enoughness of Western individualism, and nor is optimism of the variety that erases and tidies up inconvenient details (McMillan Cottom, 2016). In fact, we find ourselves retreating from prevailing assemblages of literacies and languages education that assume and "overclaim" their capacity to make a difference as Patti Lather (2016) points out (p. 125). Rather, we turn toward what Fitzpatrick (2019) offers with Jonathan Lear's "radical hope," the "will to continue working toward a future that seems unimaginable" (p. 61). Reading hope diffractively, the authors and editors of this volume have tried to pose different questions and think-with different concepts to "bring forth a world distinct from what we already are" (Colebrook, 2017, p. 651).

Getting Here

This volume came out of the sensation that dominant perspectives on languages and literacies research and pedagogy have produced recalcitrant and deficient literacy and language subjects. In resistance, we sought out thinkers, texts, researchers, colleagues, and students who were thinking differently and who undid binaries of self/other and identity and subjectivity by attending to sensorial, affective, place-based, political forces (e.g. Barad, 2007; Bennett, 2010; Braidotti, 2011; Coole & Frost, 2010; Deleuze & Guattari, 1987/2005; Taylor & Hughes, 2016). Also enticing were posthuman descriptions of phenomena of children's play in education settings, that asked how languages and literacies come to be (Davies, 2014; Leander & Boldt, 2012; Lenz Taguchi, 2010; Olsson, 2009; Smythe et al., 2017; Toohey, 2018).

Thus, the intention in the first invitations sent to the contributing authors of this book was to generate scholarship, ideas, and concepts created by and for educators, and to contend with the striations, the excesses, and the over-coding of languages and literacies that have been observed by Elizabeth de Freitas (2016) and by Nathalie Sinclair and de Freitas (2019) in the practices of qualitative and quantitative research. These intentions are evoked by Elizabeth St. Pierre, Alecia Jackson, and Lisa Mazzei (2016) as "first, an ethical imperative to rethink the nature of being to refuse the devastating dividing practices of the dogmatic Cartesian image of thought and, second, a heightened curiosity and accompanying experimentation in the becoming of existence" (p. 99). While "experimentation" in educational discourse often connotes a positivistic logic of proof, detachment, and so on, the experimentation that St. Pierre et al., (2016) refer to above is more in line with anthropologist Tim Ingold's (2018) concept of *presencing*: "caring for the world we live in, and for its multiple human and non-human inhabitants ... restoring them to presence ... so we can attend and respond to what they have to say" (p. 28).

Seeing and feeling the world differently, we are becoming aware of how the practices of scholarship are shot through Eurocentric habits of centring white gaze, so that the "new" materiality neglects its indebtedness to Indigenous philosophies (Todd, 2016; Magnat, 2019) that have always thought with entangled agencies of humans and nonhumans, the personal in practices of knowing and inquiry, and humans' relationships and response-abilities with place. During the time of producing this book all four editors were living in, and working, thinking, and writing on the unceded Coast Salish territories of the Səlilwətaɬ (Tsleil-Waututh), Skwxwú7mesh (Squamish), and xʷməθkwəy̓əm (Musqueam) Nations. Like many scholars living in colonized settler states, we are in a time of deeply questioning our scholarly practices within the colonial logics of our institutions. Like Michelle Honeyford and Jennifer Watt, we "find our thinking and writing becoming more entangled in epistemologies, ontologies, and ethics of place" (Chapter 2 in this volume). Writing this Introduction and assembling the book have thus been a process of working out and working on the materiality of our bodies, our writing, the assemblages created, and our responsibilities for this.

The ethics of place is of current concern to many observers in Western Canada, from debates about the construction of a pipeline to carry oil from the tar sands of Alberta through the territories of many First Nations to the Pacific Ocean, to a growing tent city of homeless citizens, camping in a downtown Vancouver park. The tent city grows on the fruits of evidence and policy, or not enough evidence, or the politics of evidence and knowledge that make material deeply unjust relations: "If we refuse to set up washrooms in the tent city maybe these tents will go away." "If we commodify our housing stock to encourage rapid replacement of older housing and the development of new high end homes, the excess in the market will trickle down to affordable housing for our low income citizens." "Literacy and English language education is important to the extent they can be measured and deployed to create more productive citizens who won't need affordable housing." We all bring to our conversations about and contributions to this book flows of anger and indignation, confusion and sometimes hopelessness about how economic and social policy, research in urban geography, other knowledges, and discourses collude and collide to make some people homeless, powerless, and voiceless in their own territories. We find ourselves unable to set aside or bracket from our scholarship the materialities of our lives and the lives of those around us.

Métis/otipemisiw scholar and educator Zoe Todd (2016) expressed her "struggle to situate the material we read in class within the physical realities that we inhabit as student-teacher interlocutors moving through academic and civic spaces" (p. 31). As we learn with and from the efforts and labours of the authors of these chapters, we have become less committed to languages and literacies as subjects of our scholarship, and more attuned to how they are an effect of our scholarly, pedagogical, living-in-a-city, walking-in-parks, place-making practices.

All this has us paying attention to where we write, to what is happening with us and our research participants, to that which seeps into affective flows and concerns and sleepless nights. We are pulled to think and write more slowly and more responsibly, attending to how places and happenings are changing us and those with whom we conduct research. Ingold (2013) reminds us that knowledge of the world inheres in "skills of perception and capacities of judgment that develop in the course of direct, practical and sensuous engagements with our surroundings" (p. 5). Ingold (2014) further argues that we must "attend to persons and things, to learn from them, and to follow in precept and practice. Indeed, there can be no observation without participation – that is, without an intimate coupling, in perception and action of observer and observed" (pp. 387–388). For educational researchers, as Smythe (2018) argued, this involves folding "the stories of [our] learning back into the flow of practice where they matter most" (p. 204). How are we to attend responsibly to persons and things, and intimately couple our perceptions and actions with the humans and nonhumans with whom we think and work? This book gives examples of how diverse researchers in particular localities attempt to live with this responsibility.

The Book: Land, Place, Bodies

Being and knowing, affective and material intra-actions exceed languages and literacies repertoires in pedagogical settings, but also in the writing of book chapters. And here we are now, struggling to assemble an Introduction that can contain these works and our entanglements with/in them. Our own capacities are being stretched and academic writing conventions challenge us (Braidotti, 2011). Editors and authors encountered real-world limits in the formatting requirements of manuscripts, the commercial costs of colour prints, the orthodoxies of margins and linearity that have long governed academic writing. It is precisely these material aspects of languages and literacies that are often ignored (de Freitas & Curinga, 2015; MacLure, 2013; MacLure et al., 2012), but are so vital in how we assemble and share knowledge.

As editors we evoked and enacted our own striations and limits in track changes and questions for clarity, suggestions, and revisions, working and reworking the words within the confines of the screen and the genre. We think about educators and students in classrooms who daily encounter, resist, and surpass what it is possible to be and do and think. The contributors to this volume pushed against and exceeded these confines in poetry and image, drawings and memories, multimodalities of text fonts, stretchy triangles and arms wrapped around trees in the generation of multiplicities of literacies as "each new attainment of literacy introduces difference into what counts as literacy" (Colebrook, 2012, p. x).

Together with Fikile Nxumalo and Jessica Cira Rubin (2019), we considered this book about literacies and languages pedagogies as an assemblage that might map territories beyond the "already-known and easily definable human-centred interpretations of [children's] literacy learning" (p. 205). We invited authors to think/write within their own contexts and with concepts offered by new materialism, posthumanism, and relational ontologies. We wondered if potentialities in languages and literacies pedagogies might emerge as these disparate things encountered one another. As editors, in the process of eagerly reading and responding to authors' texts, we found ourselves thinking/writing with authors and places and spaces, affective flows, their diverse tools, models and heuristics, methods and concepts, stories and vignettes. We saw examples of how standards and exclusions, striations and othering, and the myriad other problems of languages and literacies pedagogies might be countered by paying careful attention to the moments and becomings in lives that are too often swept up and easily erased in universals and generalizations. We became interested in what Elizabeth Grosz (2017) called *ontoethics*: "a way of thinking about not just the world as it is but how it could be, how it is open to change, and above all, the becomings it may undergo" (p. 1). Ontoethics became part of the title of this book because, like Grosz (2017), we believe that we can enhance our understandings of languages and literacies by thinking about the ethical becomings they may undergo, and these chapters do exactly that.

Drawing on Spinoza's *Ethics*, Deleuze (1980) tells us in an oft-quoted passage that "[w]e never know in advance what a body can do," and as the chapters that follow illustrate, languages and literacies education is not about designing "better" curricula or "good teaching strategies." Theories pointing to the unpredictability of assemblages invite us to broaden our gaze and to consider what unanticipated effects may unfold. This path offers a way of imagining pedagogies for languages and literacies as places with/in which many things converge and have an impact on learning. Working and thinking with theories of materiality entails something different from finding universal solutions to problems or proposing approaches for all to follow (Masny & Cole, 2012). It involves an ethical commitment to exploring how assemblages, rather than individuals, have the potential to change the status quo.

> For it is only a question of literacy – or of how modes of writing and reading enable orientations, differences and the creation of minor deflections – that truly enables the possibility of reading and writing *not as modes of replication* (tracing a pattern) but as modes of mapping – marking out new spaces, new dimensions, new lines of filiation.
>
> *(Colebrook, 2012, p. xi, emphasis in the original)*

Throughout the book, the authors shift from such imaginings and lines of filiation to the conventional literacies and languages of classrooms and policies, moving along and then back again, tracing and mapping, yet all the while gradually relinquishing the pretence of control, and accepting that they will encounter uncertainty, the unknowability of "what will happen next."

The Chapters

Tara Gutshall Rucker and Candace Kuby's chapter presents three events that took place in classrooms in which Gutshall Rucker taught, and takes up the concept of *literacy desiring* – a concept which they have been thinking-with for some time (see Kuby & Gutshall Rucker, 2016). Recognizing that theoretical concepts are dynamic because "the world kicks back" as Karen

Barad (1999, p. 2) phrased it, these authors reflect on what they have learned about literacy desiring as they have more experiences with children, classrooms, and activities stimulated by the teacher and researcher's invitation to "[g]o be a writer!" They show how Deleuze and Guattari's (1983, 1987/2005) exploration of the concept of desiring helped them to understand new possibilities inherent in the classroom events they describe. Quoting Deleuzian scholar Daniel Smith (2012), "desire is about something that we perhaps don't know or see yet" (p. 180), Gutshall Rucker and Kuby think about how providing space and materials for literacy desiring to come alive in classrooms might mean foregoing the common notion that students need to have a plan for what their literacy desiring will become, and similarly letting go of the idea that students' writings should always be *finished*. Further (re)reading of Deleuze and Guattari and others, and carefully observing students, similarly prompted the authors to question the notion that writing is solitary and attributable to individuals, and to understand that individual assessments that are widespread in schools deny the importance of relationships with other humans, nonhumans, discourses, and so on. The authors' final description of classroom events stimulated them to think about how writing and literacies are always in flux, and, as they put it, "come into being through/in/with relationships .... [that emerge out of] working-with-materials-discourses-each other" (Gutshall Rucker & Kuby, Chapter 1 in this volume).

Michelle Honeyford and Jennifer Watt take up practices of careful observing and noticing to forge ethical relations of place, what they call *place-thought*, in the context of a summer institute. They ask how might experiences of writing in place "trouble" the deep-rooted, epistemological frameworks inherent in languages and literacies pedagogy? Which practices would unsettle? Which would maintain a tenacious hold? What would they learn, write, and become in the process? They are interested in what thinking *does*. Thinking with Baradian performativity and Ingoldian notions of corresponding or "intimate coupling, in perception and action of observer and observed" they make a shift away from engaging in learning "*about* the world by engaging *in* it directly through practices, doings or actions" (Honeyford & Watt, Chapter 2 in this volume, emphasis added). An urban park in Winnipeg becomes this place-thought, place thinking, as the authors, along with their students, disrupt the margins and conventions of texts and words to also

> create disruptions to the hegemonic power of cultural and cognitive imperialism that have continued to perpetuate (and make invisible) Western colonial and representational approaches to knowledge and knowledge production; and simultaneously, we write (re)cognizing that

our social locations and words continue to be fraught/caught by/within those very relations of privilege and power (Battiste, 2013; Styres, 2017).
(Honeyford & Watt, Chapter 2 in this volume)

Echoing the struggles with hope and "cruel optimism" (Berlant, 2006) that we grapple with in this Introduction, Saskia Van Viegen undoes what could have been the cohesive story of a happy garden, happy children and parents, literacy learned by all, to see a school garden as intensifying the affective forces of loss, ecological disruption, and colonialism. Understood and felt relationally and affectively, literacy becomes a story of land dispossession and climate crisis migrations to-come when we let go of the push to tidy the data and tell a coherent story. Van Viegen leads us to ask what is becoming of the subjectivities and identities of language educators if the ethics of sociality in sociocultural theories are folded with *affective material flows* such as those of environmental change and human migration that are transforming the lives of her students and their families. This is migration not as a backdrop or context but as an affective material force intra-acting with the disciplinary pedagogies of literacy test preparations for this group of eight-year-olds and their families. Van Viegen was inspired by Lather's (2012) critical praxis as a relational methodology that she expanded on to include both bodied and non-bodied others. Van Viegen sought "an alignment between *how* [research participants and researchers] engaged in research and *what* [they] came to know" (Chapter 3 in this volume, emphasis in the original), attending to the often invisible but productive role of the research apparatus in knowledge-making practices. Van Viegen wonders how "ontoethical issues and directions for language and literacy teaching [might become] responsive to [such] circumstances" (Chapter 3 in this volume), coming at an uncomfortable moment in which the very progressive project of literacy disassembles. Quoting Lynne Pearce (2010, p. 151), she further asks "Why, that is, should any of us wish to write or read, a story that does not move its characters – and us – forward in some way?" (Chapter 3 in this volume). Words fail when affect exceeds, for us, for the authors, for learners and teachers.

Liselott Mariett Olsson and Jacqueline Barreiro are both concerned with how children's literacies are entangled with sense and sense-making, with Barreiro reconfiguring, through Barad's (2007) notion of intra-activity, cause-and-effect deficit discourses of minoritized children learning literacies, and Olsson bringing the Stoics' philosophical notion of *Lekta* to the making of "an old E":

> When children write too many lines on an old E, when they exchange the first letter in a name, when they rhyme and sing, when they invent alphabets never before seen, it is possible that they articulate (in often

confusing ways to us adults) the sense that adheres to the material bodies (organic and inorganic) in any given situation.

(Olsson, Chapter 4 in this volume)

Here the usual literacies of development and errors, and of approximating standards are collapsed in favour of writing that exceeds the limits of letters and words as they slither and slide and fly across and off the pages. Ideas of literacy entangle with the materiality of letters and words that sense and play and move.

In her chapter, Olsson helpfully provides a historical account of one of the major debates in languages and literacies education, the "Literacy Wars," showing how proponents on either side accepted reductive and oppositional thinking about what language, knowledge, literacy, and learning are, and how they happen. Characterizing the sides as realism and idealism (as do St. Pierre et al., 2016), she proposes thinking with couplings of materialism and idealism, whereby language might be seen as material acting in the world *and* as the creation of individual and socially constructed meanings. Drawing on her (and others') observations of young children, who are seen to *language* materially (e.g. verbally, corporeally, and extralinguistically), she proposes (following Grosz, 2017) exploring "*also* … the richness of language as an ideational resource" (Chapter 4 in this volume, emphasis in the original), the *incorporeal*. She notes that children use language both materially and ideally, as an imaginative resource to experiment with and make new meanings, and that "children seem particularly interested in exploring the 'rebel becomings' (MacLure, 2016) of language itself" (Chapter 4 in this volume). Drawing on the Stoic philosophical concept of *Lekta* (the "sayable"), she shows how pre-school children explore, as Grosz (2017) puts it, "the ongoing possibility of sense" (p. 38; see also Chapter 4 in this volume) as they write/draw/imagine their names in ways that "*make sense*," and that are creative, original, and joyful.

In her chapter, propelled by her own approach toward *storytelling with theory*, Barreiro reads the sensory, affective forces of literacy-as-sound-and-texture, the sound and shape of an SSSSS, along with the relationship of Mauricito (a young child) with literacy-as-colonial oppression. She offers a different figuration of the tired and striated cause-effect thinking in which Indigenous peoples of the Ecuadorean Andes are enrolled as problematic subjects to be worked upon and improved. Thinking with Barad's (2007) notion of intra-action, Barreiro argues that the way in which causality is theorized, as linear or relational, changes literacy assemblages and literacy subjectivities:

> Thus, Maurisito's literacy becomings are not just in encounters with text, pencil, and paper, or to the occasional time spent at the computer in school, but to a much broader range of affective intra-actions his

body and other bodies engaged in at school, undergoing intensities and flows of affective forces that shape, reshape, and change the rhythm of a body slipping into literacy practices.

(Chapter 5 in this volume)

Similarly to Van Viegen, Barreiro questions if and how education for minoritized children makes a difference in their lives, noting that the relationship between literacy and life is not linear or predictable, but instead intra-acts with the very discourses, materials, volcanoes, pencils, and the tickling sensation of the tongue pushing on teeth as SSSSS emerges in MauriSSSSito, transforming a name, with all its relations, into a new literacy becoming.

The chapter by Brandon Sherman, Mari Haneda, and Annela Teemant concerns one-to-one coaching episodes involving a teacher and an instructional coach. Pointing out the need for "greater theoretical understanding of instructional coaching as a force for change within the complex web of classrooms and schools, to say nothing of students' and teachers' lives" (Sherman, Haneda, & Teemant, Chapter 6 in this volume), the authors build on critical sociocultural perspectives embedded in the pedagogical principles and practices that the coaching sessions were set up to promulgate. The authors also think with rhizomatic concepts and see the instructional coaching sessions (as well as classroom life in general) as assemblages of material humans, objects, and discourses. Noting that much of school classroom life is routine, repetitious, and circumscribed, they see these striations being as overcome, at times, with new ideas and new practices emerging from lines of flight. The newness they describe in this chapter concerns the teacher's explorations (both with her coach and later with her students) of the relationships that students and teachers have with mandated standardized tests. They observe, as do Deleuze and Guattari (1987/2005) and Gutshall Rucker and Kuby (Chapter 1 in this volume), that lines of flight "are neither good nor bad" (Sherman, Haneda & Teemant, Chapter 6 in this volume), and that they can be both creative and destructive. In this case (and in the episodes that Gutshall Rucker and Kuby also describe), the new ideas and practices are presented as creative and productive of learning. As Sherman, Haneda, and Teemant point out, "coaching conversations have the potential to open interstitial spaces to challenge institutional norms, which in turn may change not just isolated pedagogical practices, but the ecology of the classroom as a whole" (Chapter 6 in this volume).

Amélie Lemieux and Jennifer Rowsell use posthumanist concepts to analyse interview data from a videomaking project that they, along with a media artist and an English teacher, conducted with secondary school students. The aim of the study was to develop "a unit ... [in which the students could] express, through documentary/film-making, their [felt perspectives on such issues as] homelessness, anxiety, depression, and Post-Traumatic Stress Disorder" (Lemieux & Rowsell, Chapter 7 in this volume). Students were placed in groups of three or four and worked with iPads to prepare and edit their documentaries using the video editing software iMovie. Following Deleuze and Guattari (1987/2005), the research team aimed to investigate the assemblages of humans and nonhumans involved in the research, and to observe the moments of becoming that unfolded through the documentaries that the students produced, going beyond representational practices as they made "cuts and edits [that] were affectively driven during [this creative] process" (Lemieux & Rowsell, Chapter 7 in this volume).

Lemieux and Rowsell further argue that maker spaces should be regarded as "spaces of being/doing/knowing'" (Kuby & Rowsell, 2017, p 285). Emphasizing the "discursive relationships of becoming" (Kuby, 2017, p. 167) that take place between "interviewer ⟷ interviewee ⟷ topic ⟷ themes ⟷ situations" (Lemieux & Rowsell, Chapter 7 in this volume), they present and analyse several conversations between the researchers and students. Showing how one student struggled with her classmates about how to portray her relationship with anxiety/depression and the themes of their documentary, the authors argue for the importance of opening possibilities for interpretive research on "e/affect" (Kuby et al., 2017, p. 365) in maker education.

Monica Waterhouse contends with the prescriptions and routines of classrooms in her chapter, this time in adult ESL and FSL classrooms where the affective lives of adults newly arrived in Canada are most commonly configured as problems to be contained, managed, deflected, and "fixed," especially when they materialize through emotions such as anger. What if such affective flows could be mobilized to create pedagogies that matter, that engage with the pain and power of migration? Waterhouse puts vignettes ("brief stories or simulations used to elicit responses from participants," as Tierney (2011) defines them) to work to mobilize anger as more than a highly sanctioned and repressed emotion. She suggests that we look at vignettes as *affective text-bodies*, playing their part in assemblages that also involve *teacher-bodies, student-bodies* and *other nonhuman-bodies*, therefore opening up possibilities of *encounters* for educators and learners, opportunities for thinking-with the world, in a Deleuzian sense: "Something in the world forces us to think. This something is an object not of recognition but of a fundamental *encounter*. ... It may be grasped in a range of affective tones: wonder, love, hatred, suffering" (Deleuze, 1994, p. 139, emphasis in the original). Waterhouse goes on to propose that this thinking must engage the imagination, freed from the cognitive constraints of reflective thinking that is so often the cornerstone of teacher training (Hill, 2017), thereby providing "an onto-epistemological basis for inventing new pedagogical realities" (Waterhouse, Chapter 8 in this volume). From this perspective, with each vignette, "each encounter was a singular experimentation; each time a different assemblage was created, it functioned in its own way to produce teacher thinking and the teacher's response" (Chapter 8 in this volume). The encounters afforded as teachers discuss vignettes with researchers, and, potentially, with their students, as well as the affective flows that emerge out of these encounters, provide spaces other than the confines of curricular and cultural constraints and routines.

The chapter by Margaret MacDonald, Cher Hill, and Nathalie Sinclair is intended to highlight the indeterminate, dynamic, entangled, unique, and often untraceable nature of pedagogical encounters, and calls into question the restrictive practices of interpretation and standardized representation that all too often shape and define our common core understandings of knowledge and learning. Through considering typical geometric, pedagogic, and geographic representations, and their typical presentation in instruction, the three authors call attention to how we come to see learning as static, linear, and territorialized. Deleuze and Guattari (1987/2005) invite us to consider the lines of de-territorialization that can be explored in any context in which we might just see segmentarity and territorialization at first. Following this line of thought, MacDonald, Hill, and Sinclair share with us examples drawn from primary school geometry, pedagogical documentation, and forest cartography suggesting that knowledge and knowledge-making can be "delightfully 'unstable' and experimental" (Chapter 9 in this volume), so that students and teachers can create ever newer relations with ideas and materials. Pushing us to go beyond pre-determined questions and comfortable ways of learning/knowing, the authors encourage us to consider the many assemblages we are a part of as we engage in the processes of teaching/learning, and to revise our ontological stance by asking the following question: "Who are we being and becoming, and with whom or what do we come to know?" (Chapter 9 in this volume). For these authors, representations of situations, persons, objects, and learning are temporary staging places, places of discussion among multiple perspectives, so that further experimentation, learning, and representation can be provoked. Thinking with the particular notion of assemblage that Manuel DeLanda (2016) provides, MacDonald, Hill, and Sinclair invite us to pay attention to what emerges, what opens up when we look past the boundaries of conventional ways of knowing/learning.

In their chapter, Gabriele Budach, Dimitri Efremov, Daniela Loghin, and Gohar Sharoyan recall affective intensities and processes of immanence, emergence, and movement that were generated in the creation of stop-motion films during a graduate summer course in Luxembourg. Thinking with the concept of "contact zone" (Pratt, 1991), the four authors chose an object that was meaningful to them, and then proceeded to animate it. As they collaborate in writing and reflecting on this creative and multimodal experience in relation to Deleuzian-Spinozan-inspired work on affect "as the capacity 'to affect and to be'" (Budach et al., Chapter 10 in this volume), they observe how the haptic nature of their engagement with their objects in animation became an immersive and meditative practice, characterized by varying intensities across time, space, and workshop participants, which marks their memories of these events and continues to affect them deeply. Viewing animation as an affective "'bloom-space' (Gregg & Seigworth, 2010) where … projects started to unfold between hands and moving objects in front of a camera lens" (Chapter 10 in this volume), they explore personal lines of flight that emerged in different ways for each of them, tapping into individual memories, feelings, and beliefs that transformed along with their gestures and the films they made (that readers can access online via the information provided by the authors). They draw on Kevin Leander and Gail Boldt (2012), who call into question a static view of literacies education and a premeditated and systematic approach to design, to note how

> [r]ecourse to existing (textual) grammars, their rules and modes of application, for instance to structure a story line, failed, or were at least fundamentally challenged, by a process that seemed to be guided by different forces, that … appeared to defy predictability and structured planning.
>
> *(Chapter 10 in this volume)*

Likewise, we invite readers to see the layout of this book not as a premeditated design that has to be followed, but as a collection offering multiple points of entry and exploration. In an effort to reimagine the traditional format of academic theses in light of challenges to boundary thinking, Honan and Bright (2016) echo Kuby's (2016) and St. Pierre's (2018, 2019) ideas about disrupting traditional ways of conducting research in suggesting the following:

> If we move beyond the structure of method, if we destabilize and deterritorialize the boundaries between and across participant, researcher, sound and silence, voice and movement, then we must also move beyond the boundaries of a textual structure that will not work.
>
> *(Honan & Bright, 2016, p. 738)*

With Nxumalo and Rubin (2019) we looked upon this book *about* literacies and languages pedagogies as an assemblage that might open horizons beyond "already-known and easily definable human-centred interpretations of … literacy learning" (p. 205). Rather than reading the book chapters as bounded windows into literacy and language worlds, we therefore suggest that readers engage in a diffractive reading and visit the chapters that follow as plateaus (Deleuze & Guattari, 1987/2005) "to open to what else might be happening, might be noticed, and might be important" (Nxumalo & Robin, 2019, p. 205). We invite readers to think-with, feel-with, and be-with ascendancies and intensities that flow through the text and are not only contained within it, but also flow as excesses, spilling into our lives and from our lives into our readings of this book.

References

Barad, K. (1999). Agential realism: Feminist interventions in understanding scientific practices. In M. Biagioli (Ed.), *The science studies reader* (pp. 1–11). New York: Routledge.

Barad, K. (2007). *Meeting the universe halfway: Quantum physics and the entanglement of matter and meaning*. Durham, NC: Duke University Press.

Battiste, M. (2013). *Decolonizing education: Nourishing the learning spirit*. Saskatoon, SK: Purich.

Bennett, J. (2010). *Vibrant matter: A political ecology of things*. Durham, NC: Duke University Press.

Berlant, L. (2006). Cruel optimism. *Differences*, 17(3), 20–36. doi:10.1215/10407391-2006-009.

Boldt, G. (2019). Affective flows in the clinic and the classroom. In K. Leander & C. Ehret (Eds.), *Affect in literacy learning and teaching: Pedagogies, politics and coming to know* (pp. 25–42). New York: Routledge.

Braidotti, R. (2011). *Nomadic subjects: Embodiment and sexual difference in contemporary feminist theory* (2nd edn.). New York: Columbia University Press.

Colebrook, C. (2012). Foreword. In D. Masny and D. R. Cole (Eds.), *Mapping multiple literacies: An introduction to Deleuzian literacy studies* (pp. vii–xii). New York: Continuum International Publishing Group.

Colebrook, C. (2017). What is this thing called education? *Qualitative Inquiry*, 23(9), 649–655. doi:10.1177/1077800417725357.

Coole, D., & Frost, S. (Eds.) (2010). *New materialisms: Ontology, agency and politics*. Durham, NC: Duke University Press.

Davies, B. (2014). *Listening to children: Being and becoming*. New York: Routledge.

de Freitas, E. (2016). Karen Barad. In E. de Freitas & M. Walshaw (Eds.), *Alternative theoretical frameworks for mathematics education research* (pp. 149–173). Cham: Springer International Publishing.

de Freitas, E., & Curinga, M. X. (2015). New materialist approaches to the study of language and identity: Assembling the posthuman subject. *Curriculum Inquiry*, 45(3), 249–265. doi:10.1080/03626784.2015.1031059.

DeLanda, M. (2010). *Deleuze: History and science*. New York: Atropos Press.

DeLanda, M. (2016). *Assemblage theory*. Edinburgh: Edinburgh University Press.

Deleuze, G. (1980). *Sur Spinoza*. Cours Vincennes: Ontologie-Ethique. (S. Duffy, Trans.) Retrieved September 4, 2019, www.webdeleuze.com/textes/190.

Deleuze, G. (1994). *Difference and repetition* (P. Patton, Trans.). New York: Columbia University Press. (Original work published 1968).

Deleuze, G., & Guattari, F. (1983). *Anti-Oedipus: Capitalism and schizophrenia*. (R. Hurley, M. Seem, & H. R. Lane, Trans.). Minneapolis: University of Minnesota Press.

Deleuze, G., & Guattari, F. (1987/2005). *A thousand plateaus: Capitalism and Schizophrenia*. (B. Massumi, Trans.). Minneapolis: University of Minnesota Press.

Fitzpatrick, K. (2019). *Generous thinking: A radical approach to saving the university*. Baltimore, MD: Johns Hopkins University Press.

Gregg, M., & Seigworth, G. J. (Eds.). (2010). *The affect theory reader*. Durham, NC: Duke University Press.

Grosz, E. (2017). *The incorporeal: Ontology, ethics and the limits of materialism*. New York: Columbia University Press.

Hill, C. M. (2017). More-than-reflective practice: Becoming a diffractive practitioner. *Teacher Learning and Professional Development*, 2(1), 1–17. Retrieved September 12, 2019, from http://journals.sfu.ca/tlpd/index.php/tlpd/article/view/28.

Honan, E., & Bright, D. (2016). Writing a thesis differently. *International Journal of Qualitative Studies in Education*, 29(5), 731–743. doi:10.1080/09518398.2016.1145280.

Ingold, T. (2013). *Making: Anthropology, archaeology, art and architecture*. London: Routledge.

Ingold, T. (2014). That's enough about ethnography! *HAU: Journal of Ethnographic Theory*, 4(1), 383–395. http://dx.doi.org/10.14318/hau4.1.021.

Ingold, T. (2018). *Anthropology and/as education*. New York: Routledge.

Kuby, C. R. (2016). Emotions as situated, embodied, and fissured: Methodological implications of thinking with theories. In P. Schutz & M. Zembylas (Eds.), *Methodological advances in research on emotion in education* (pp. 125–136). New York: Springer.

Kuby, C. R. (2017). Poststructural and posthuman theories as literacy research methodologies: Tensions and possibilities. In R. Zaidi & J. Rowsell (Eds.), *Literacy lives in transcultural times* (pp. 157–174). New York: Routledge.

Kuby, C. R., & Gutshall Rucker, T. (2016). *Go be a writer!: Expanding the curricular boundaries of literacy learning with children*. New York: Teachers College Press.

Kuby, C. R., Gutshall Rucker, T., & Darolia, L. H. (2017). Persistence(ing): Posthuman agency in a writers' studio. *Journal of Early Childhood Literacy*, 17(3), 353–373. doi:10.1177/1468798417712067.

Kuby, C. R., & Rowsell, J. (2017). Early literacy and the posthuman: Pedagogies and methodologies. *Journal of Early Childhood Literacy*, 17(3), 285–296. doi:10.1177/1468798417715720.

Lather, P. (2012). *Getting lost: Feminist efforts toward a double (d) science*. Albany, NY: State University of New York Press.

Lather, P. (2016). Top ten+ list: (Re)thinking ontology in (post)qualitative research. *Cultural Studies ⇄ Critical Methodologies*, 16(2), 125–131. https://doi.org/10.1177/1532708616634734.

Latour, B. (2004). Why has critique run out of steam? From matters of fact to matters of concern. *Critical Inquiry*, 30(2), 225–248. https://doi.org/10.1086/421123.

Leander, K., & Boldt, G. (2012). Rereading "A Pedagogy of Multiliteracies": Bodies, texts, and emergence. *Journal of Literacy Research*, 45(1), 22–46. doi:10.1177/1086296X12468587.

Lenz Taguchi, H. (2010). *Going beyond the theory/practice divide in early childhood education: Introducing an intra-active pedagogy*. New York: Routledge.

MacLure, M. (2013). Researching without representation? Language and materiality in post-qualitative methodology. *International Journal of Qualitative Studies in Education*, 26(6), 658–667. doi:10.1080/09518398.2013.788755.

MacLure, M. (2016). The refrain of the a-grammatical child: Finding another language in/for qualitative research. *Cultural Studies ⟷ Critical Methodologies*, 16(2), 99–110. doi:10.1177/1532708616639333.

MacLure, M., Jones, L., Holmes, R., & MacRae, C. (2012). Becoming a problem: Behaviour and reputation in the early years classroom. *British Educational Research Journal*, 38(3), 447–471. doi:10.1080/01411926.2011.552709.

Magnat, V. (2019). *The performative power of vocality*. New York: Routledge.

Masny, D., & Cole, D. R. (Eds.) (2012). *Mapping multiple literacies: An introduction to Deleuzian literacy studies*. New York: Continuum International Publishing Group.

McMillan Cottom, T. (2016). *Finding hope in a loveless place*. November 27. Retrieved September 4, 2019, from https://tressiemc.com/uncategorized/finding-hope-in-a-loveless-place/.

Nxumalo, F., & Rubin, J. C. (2019). Encountering waste landscapes: More-than-human place literacies in early childhood education. In C. R. Kuby, K. Spector, & J. Johnson Thiel (Eds.), *Posthumanism and literacy education* (pp. 201–213). New York: Routledge.

Olsson, L. M. (2009). *Movement and experimentation in young children's learning: Deleuze and Guattari in early childhood education*. London: Routledge.

Pearce, L. (2010). Beyond redemption? Mobilizing affect in feminist reading. In M. Liljestrom and S. Paasonen (Eds.), *Working with affect in feminist readings: Disturbing differences* (pp. 151–164). London: Routledge.

Pratt, M. L. (1991). Arts of the contact zone. *Profession*, 33–40. Retrieved August 30, 2019, from www.jstor.org/stable/25595469.

Sinclair, N., & de Freitas, E. (2019). Body studies in mathematics education: Diverse scales of mattering. *ZDM*, 51, 227–237. https://doi.org/10.1007/s11858-019-01052-w.

Smith, D. W. (2012). *Essays on Deleuze*. Edinburgh: Edinburgh University Press.

Smythe, S. (2018). Adult learning in the control society: Digital era governance, literacies of control, and the work of adult educators. *Adult Education Quarterly*, 68(3), 197–214. doi:10.1177/0741713618766645.

Smythe, S., Hill, C., MacDonald, M., Dagenais, D., Sinclair, N., & Toohey, K. (2017). *Disrupting boundaries in education and research*. Cambridge: Cambridge University Press.

Steffen, A. (2008). *The politics of optimism*. March 25. Retrieved September 9, 2019, from www.alexsteffen.com/the_politics_of_optimism.

St. Pierre, E. A. (2018). Writing post qualitative inquiry. *Qualitative Inquiry*, 24(9), 603–608. https://doi.org/10.1177/1077800417734567.

St. Pierre, E. A. (2019). Post qualitative inquiry in an ontology of immanence. *Qualitative Inquiry*, 25(1), 3–16. https://doi.org/10.1177/1077800418772634.

St. Pierre, E. A., Jackson, A. Y., & Mazzei, L. A. (2016). New empiricisms and new materialisms: Conditions for new inquiry. Cultural Studies ⟷ Critical Methodologies, *16*(2), 99–110. https://doi.org/10.1177/1532708616638694.

Styres, S. (2017). *Pathways for remembering and recognizing Indigenous thought in education: Philosophies of lethi'nihstenha Ohwentsia'kekha (Land)*. Toronto, ON: University of Toronto Press.

Taylor, C. A., & Hughes, C. (2016). *Posthuman research practices in education*. London: Palgrave Macmillan.

Tierney, R. D. (2011). *Vignettes as a complementary method in educational research.* Paper presented at the annual meeting of the American Educational Research Association, New Orleans, Louisiana.

Todd, Z. (2016). An Indigenous feminist's take on the ontological turn: "Ontology" is just another word for colonialism. *Journal of Historical Sociology, 29*(1), 4–22. doi:10.1111/johs.12124.

Toohey, K. (2018). *Learning English at school: Identity, socio-material relations and classroom practice.* Bristol: Multilingual Matters.

1

MAKING AND UNMAKING LITERACY DESIRINGS

Pedagogical Matters of Concern from Writers' Studio

Tara Gutshall Rucker and Candace R. Kuby

In this chapter, we return to the concept of "literacy desiring" which we conceptualized based on poststructural and posthumanist scholarship as a way to think about literacies (and literacy processes) as fluid, sometimes unintentional, unbounded, and rhizomatic through relationships with humans, nonhumans, and more-than-humans[1] (Kuby & Gutshall Rucker, 2016). As we wrote in our earlier publications, literacy desiring is oriented toward the present (ever-changing) needs, wishes, and demands of students-with-nonhumans, but also with possible users of literacy artifacts in mind. We began collaborations together in 2010 as co-researchers and co-pedagogues; Tara as an elementary school teacher and Candace as a university researcher. During this time, Tara taught first (6–7 year-olds), second (7–8 year-olds), and fifth grades (10–11 year-olds). When we began, Tara used a Writing Workshop approach to teach (e.g. Wood Ray & Cleaveland, 2004) and shifted to what she called Writers' Studio several years into our partnership to signal a more expansive notion of literacies with artistic and digital tools.

In our previous writings on literacy desirings, we explored the identities of children over the course of a single school year (Kuby & Gutshall Rucker, 2015); the relationships between time, space, materials, and trust in the coming to be of literacy desirings (Kuby, Gutshall Rucker, & Kirchhofer, 2015); various genres of writing such as fiction, nonfiction, personal narratives and literacies that perhaps do not look like writing such as paper airplanes, plastic cube narratives, and paper skateboard parks (Kuby & Gutshall Rucker, 2016); how the first few days of a school year and the invitation to "go be a writer" shape the possibilities of literacies (Kuby & Fontanella-Nothom, 2018); agency from a posthumanist perspective in the coming to be of literacy desirings (Kuby, Gutshall Rucker, & Darolia, 2017); rethinking of the social in the coming to be of literacy desirings (Kuby & Crawford, 2018); and we considered what counts as writing or how literacies are conceptualized as ethical matters of concern (Zapata et al., 2018).

Since conceptualizing the term literacy desiring, we find it on the move as we continue to read post-theories and think about literacy(ies). As writers, we struggle to label (the coming to be of) literacies as "a" literacy desiring. "A" makes literacy desiring sound like an object or noun or a bounded event. We were intentional in using the phrase "literacy desiring" because it is an active verb and resists the notion of being finished. We also find literacy desiring on the move when we read how other educators are thinking-with the term in their own research and teaching. Over time, the more we read, teach, and think together the more we find our understandings of literacy desirings expanding and morphing. Thus, we aren't sure if literacy desiring is really definable. Rather than a linear progression of what it was to us before and what it is now, we see literacy desirings as always being made and unmade in lively relations.

Therefore, we use this chapter as a space to (re)visit this concept several years after we began thinking about/with it. As we "defined" it once, we are now (re)thinking it as we have read more theories and experienced more pedagogical moments in Tara's classrooms. Inspired by Deleuze and Guattari, we see theory and practice as mutually constitutive of each other or theory-practice (Kuby, 2020). Deleuze (2004) writes, "A theory is exactly like a tool box ... a theory has to be used, it has to work" (p. 208). Deleuze and Guattari write that theoretical concepts are always on the move or are intellectually mobile. Concepts are always new, becoming something more to help us think beyond what we already know. Theories are concepts and ideas about the world that are malleable and that change as we think-with them (hence, theory-practice). However, we need to read theories so that, when we think-with them, we have deep understandings of how other authors conceptualize these concepts, but also how they are becoming anew as we plug them into our own thinking/teaching/writing/researching.

In this spirit, we ask: What other or different pedagogies and worlds are possible (even if current realities do not permit them)? We think-with several literacy desirings from Tara's fifth-grade classroom to explore the following matters of concern: Is it okay for students to not finish a piece of writing? Does one ever write alone? What if we saw writing (and literacies more broadly) as unfinished becoming(s)? Each of these matters of concern have implications for how we think about pedagogical practices, especially how to imagine literacies as otherwise, and thus to produce new possible relationalities. In each section below, we share a literacy desiring, discuss the pedagogical matters of concern, and then discuss how thinking about these desirings and (re)reading theories have forced us to unmake and make literacy desirings, or (re)think what literacy desiring(s) is (as if we could clearly define it). Thus, we (re)think new literacy possibilities or theory-practice.

Piggy Scaling the Bookshelf: A Stop Motion Animation

An Extract from Tara's Teaching Notes

Alex and Miguel[2] found Piggy (a stuffed animal) that my daughter had left on a rocking chair in our classroom library. By the end of the week, Piggy had crawled off the chair, climbed up a tall bookshelf, found *Where's Waldo*, climbed back down the shelf, and with the help of Tiger, another stuffed animal, found Waldo! The boys captured all of this on the class iPad which has the Stop Motion app.

When the authors shared the Stop Motion video with the class, the students solicited feedback through a discussion on Schoology,[3] a learning management system. The students loved watching Piggy move up the bookshelf. There were places where he had to hold on tight or belly his way to the next shelf. They also noticed that, towards the end of the video, the photos taken to create the Stop Motion video were rushed, and the story was less clear.

As I reflected further with the authors of the story, they openly shared that they had rushed the end of the story. They wanted to be finished. Isn't that often the case? Recently, I found myself listening to an audio book and for the last thirty minutes I sped it up until it was running at three times the actual speed. I wanted to be finished. This causes me to pose the question, do students have to finish a piece of writing?

The next day, the creators of the Piggy movie continued to use Stop Motion animation, but they also got out the Play-doh. It was clear they did not have a plan. They sat in the middle of the room at the rectangular table, which included a backdrop of yellow poster board folded in thirds. It became a place of play and experimentation.

Over the course of the next two weeks, the boys worked with the Play-doh, capturing its movement in three short animations. They showed the Play-doh moving, flattening, rising (with invisible string), falling, and climbing out of its container. After almost a week of working with the materials, I conferenced with them. They explained that they were learning how Play-doh moves and how to perfect their use of Stop Motion animation. More specifically, they said that when using a piece of string to raise and lower the Play-doh, they tried to take a lot of photos, one of the repeated suggestions from the Schoology discussion, in order to show more precise movements.

During our second conference, I asked the boys what their plan was going forward. In hindsight, I wish I had reworded the question. My question was an honest inquiry, but it was also product oriented or about creating a plan to finish a piece of writing. I suspect the boys didn't have a plan for what was next. They mentioned that they were going to make a story with what they had done so far, but their response seemed more out of compliance, as if they knew what I wanted to hear. The next day, the group dismantled. The Play-doh was put away and the Stop Motion app rested.

In my experience as a writer, it is rare for my initial plan to come to fruition. It changes over and over again. Two weeks ago, when students were synthesizing their learning about our study of America's history, I sat among them to show my learning. A day and a half into our time, I abandoned my work. I wasn't ready to put my thinking/learning to work with the materials or even with pencil and paper. Do I allow students to abandon work or to not know where it is going? Or, if they do, do I trust that their time spent on the piece of (unfinished) writing is just as valuable as the finished product?

In my conference with the boys, what if I had posed different questions, when they were clearly answering my questions, seemingly out of compliance. "What if you didn't write a story, what would you do?" "What other possibilities are there for these materials (Play-doh, string, box) or other materials?" "What could this become?" "Do you need this to become something in order to 'be a writer'?" "If you had to tell your parents/principal why you keep coming back to this, what would you say?"

I'm not sure that the students would have the answers to any of these questions. Unfortunately, at this point, I will never know. However, I do know that when I am writing and am at a standstill, I let it rest and come back to it when I'm ready. And there are some ideas that are still resting. Can I start to trust students to do the same thing?

Pedagogical Matters of Concern: Is It Okay for Students to Not Finish a Piece of Writing?

This literacy desiring prompted us to ask: *Is it okay for students to not finish a piece of writing?* The Stop Motion video, like many other pieces of writing,[4] reminds us that children, or even writers in general, do not always (need to) know what they are going to write. The relationships among the students, the stuffed animals (Piggy and Tiger), the bookshelf, and a familiar book (*Where's Waldo?*) developed over several days. The boys did not know ahead of time how the story was going to develop. It's possible that had Piggy not been on the rocking chair the story would not exist at all. How might we value and give time for in-the-moment happenings to inform students' work as writers? Literacy desirings, as conceptualized by poststructural and posthumanist concepts, are about the relationships coming to be with all materials.

Tara learned that she was comfortable allowing primary school students opportunities to play and the time for their writing to develop over the course of several days or weeks, if not months. We were inspired by scholarship on multimodality, play, and literacies during the early years of collaborating together (e.g. Wohlwend, 2011). However, when she transitioned to fifth grade, Tara (unconsciously) expected fifth graders' literacy desirings to become finished in a timelier manner. After spending time in fifth grade, she realized that her initial thoughts could not be further from what she experienced. Fifth graders need just as much time, if not more, to play in the same rhizomatic way that primary school students do. In some regards, fifth graders have been schooled to do writing in a predetermined way. However, it's not that they don't know how to write. Alex put it this way: "Outside of school there are lots of ways to write, most of the time you don't even know you are writing, you are just doing something you enjoy." How can we trust children of all ages and give them time to *be* writers (playful writers), knowing and expecting that they will leave some of their writing unfinished?

As noted in the vignette, this prompted Tara to wonder what might have happened had she asked the boys different questions during the conference. She was focused on how their work would come together as a finished piece of writing (and even that wondering is rooted in an assumption that the Playdoh and the Stop Motion app should work together in order to be validated in school). This reminds us of other writers we've encountered. For example, after watching Edward cut out several snowflakes, Tara almost asked him to map out a writing plan. Instead, she stood back, trusting him to be a writer. Over a period of time, he wrote a collection of memories about different emotions he had experienced in the snow (see Gutshall & Kuby, 2013). Another example is when a group of second graders started to create a play based on Robin Hood several weeks before the school year ended. We knew there wasn't time for the group to complete their work at school, but we didn't hold back when they brought in trash bags of costumes and props days before school was dismissed for summer (see Kuby, 2017). From these literacy desirings, we ponder if one must know where writing is going before beginning, and we have come to believe that unfinished writing is valuable in and of itself.

Unmaking and Making Literacy Desiring(s): Literacies as Relational Desirings

The example of Piggy (and Tiger and the boys and the iPad and ... and ... and ...) influenced pedagogical thinking for us. And as theory-practice are mutually constitutive of each other, it also forced us to (re)visit our conceptualization of literacy desiring(s). We set out to (re)read writings by Deleuze and Guattari on desire, as a DeleuzoGuattarian notion of desire was central to our thinking on literacies originally in our collaboration.

A DeleuzoGuattarian notion of desire is described as affirmative and productive. For example, Deleuzian scholar Smith (2012) writes that desire is affirmative and is "something that we perhaps do not know or see as yet" (p. 180). Therefore, "desire is no longer defined in terms of *lack* (I desire something because I do not have it), but rather in terms of *production* (I produce the object because I desire it)" (Smith, 2012, p. 318, emphasis in the original). However, we do note that while DeleuzoGuattarian notions of desire are affirmative and productive, they can also be destructive and result in the undoing of bodies and relationships and/or diminish their capacity to act. In other words, DeleuzoGuattarian notions of desire aren't about producing binaries such as good and bad, or positive and negative, but rather a "both/and," producing positive *and* negative a/effects.

These producing notions of desire help us to think about literacies such as Piggy and the Stop Motion animation. The realness of literacies. Or said another way, the ontological aspects of literacies. Literacies, the relationships of literacies coming to be, are ontological (focus on reality[ies]), not simply epistemological (focus on knowledge). As Piggy, an unexpected material left by Tara's daughter, became part of a literacy desiring, realities and relationships were produced. And new literacies were produced. As Smith (2012) writes, desire is about something that we perhaps don't know or see yet. This radically shifts how we think about literacies because often we find ourselves asking children "what are you making?" or "what are you writing?" If we believe that desiring isn't (always) a pre-planned, intentional act, then we have to shift how we think about literacies and the coming-to-be of them as relational and unpredictable. And if we believe that desire is affirmative and productive – we have to ask for whom? The students? Teachers? Both? The world? For us, it is sometimes hard to provide curricular spaces for children to engage in literacy desirings because of the uncertainty of it and the pressure to have children create an end product validated by schools. However, we have to trust students in their desirings with *materials* and *engage* with them in learning about new literacies.

In sum, we see literacy desirings about the relationships (of humans, nonhumans, more-than-humans) coming to be with each other and all materials – in the moment. "If desire is productive or causal, then its product is itself *real*" (Smith, 2012, p. 187, emphasis in the original) or put another way, "If desire produces, its product is real" (Deleuze & Guattari, 1983, p. 26). As educators, we cannot discount the playing-with-materials as not important or not literacy (learning). Rather, we see the example above as literacies – or literacying (see Kuby, 2019) – an active making, producing, coming to be of literacies in material-discursive relationships.

Trouble Land: A Game of Kings and Dungeons

An Extract from Tara's teaching notes

"Mrs. Rucker, we're ready to play!" A group of four boys sat at the round table with the game, Trouble Land. As I sat down next to them, I learned that they hadn't played the game yet; they were ready to test it out with Donte. This was also the first time I saw Donte engage with Trouble Land.

Andrew, Fadel, and Adam made the game. They started with a piece of cardboard from the recycling bin. They covered it with paper, made a path of black and white squares and then added many details, such as a trap door, rivers (flowing backwards), ladders (leading forward), and a king's castle with a dungeon. The caps of dried-out marker pens acted as the four players and a red cap signified the presence of the king sitting on his throne in the castle.

I was surprised to see Donte sitting at the table. He had been working with another student on a Stop Motion video for two weeks. It now lay abandoned. To someone only observing, one would think he was one of the creators of the game. The rest of the group didn't seem affected by Donte joining them; rather, they seemed to welcome having a new person to test out the game. It was Donte who explained to the group that they needed to revise the game to make it clearer and more user-friendly.

Over the course of the next week, the group played the game, made revisions to the rules, game cards and the game board. They also shouted out every time someone was appointed the new king (winner of the game). By Friday, I noticed that Andrew and Adam, two of the three original game makers, had left the round table and started a new literacy desiring. It seemed they had moved on. Donte and Fadel had not. They recruited a crowd of students that I helped to narrow down to four in order to play the (four-player) game.

As I stepped back, I was struck by these encounters. It was unclear who owned the game. Donte acted as if he'd been a part of the group since its inception, even though he didn't have any part in making the game. He came in when it was time to test it out. The notion of ownership was fluid, as were the literacy desirings.

I wondered whether we value what it means to *be* a writer. Or have schools created a process that is far from the reality of truly being and desiring? In my first-, second-, and fifth-grade classrooms, students know how to *be* writers. Is their understanding hidden by administrators and teachers' interpretations of standards, curricular resources, or even the need to be in control? What if we intentionally sat back and gave students the time that *all* writers need, in addition to space and trust. What would happen?

My gut feeling is that students would lead us to encounter many rhizomatic literacy desirings.

Pedagogical Matters of Concern: Does One Ever Write Alone?

This literacy desiring prompted us to ask: *Does one ever write alone?* Over time it became clear that no one person owned Trouble Land. We think this is also true of literacy desirings. Literacy desirings are unbounded and open possibilities for entering and exiting. As with this vignette, we see three boys conceptualize a game and create the structure for it. However, when it came to testing-it-out, Donte and eventually others, if not the whole class, became part of the desirings as they played the game and offered new suggestions. Even more so, as the students were being-with-the-game, new possibilities emerged. Just as Tara thought that Andrew and Adam had permanently removed themselves from the literacy desiring, Adam revisited the game to make further revisions based on feedback that he heard others sharing outside of writing time. And later when Andrew was at a standstill with another writing piece, he went back and added more to the setting (the tree) on the game board. The relationships between the creators-game board-directions-users-testers were fluid and constantly changing.

This raises the questions: What if we accepted that there was no owner? What if we didn't expect students to stay with one piece of writing at a time? In Tara's first years of teaching, students wrote independently. She expected students to write their *own* stories. Through our collaboration, we explored ways to open up spaces to be a writer. As Tara invited students to "go be a writer" students naturally began to form partnerships and share their writing. Students didn't always pull out their *own* piece of writing. Nor did students always write within the same genre at the same time. When told to "be a writer" students often considered how to negotiate their time. This often included seeking out their partnership(s) and making a plan for the day or week. Writers shared and collaborated, even copied and borrowed ideas in the spirit of collaboration.

For example, one year in second grade, Miley wrote a book entitled *Monkey's Vacation*. The rest of the class enjoyed her book so much that a group of students started writing sequels, including a puppet adaptation of the series (see Kuby, 2018). The book-chapters were written and shared among many students. Sometimes we even had to pause the whole class and ask who had possession of each chapter. Instead of taking offence at others using her idea, over time Miley took on the role of an editor, managing the authors and the organization of the books. These same boundaries, or lack thereof, were present with Trouble Land. It isn't one person's game or piece of writing. There is fluidity among students, ideas, materials, and … and … and …

Unmaking and Making Literacy Desiring(s): Subjectivity as and ... and ... and ...

This literacy desiring around Trouble Land makes us pause and think about subjectivity, DeleuzoGuattarian notions of subjectivity. When thinking about ownership, we have to stop and consider who is an "I." Is there an "I" anymore in DeleuzoGuattarian thinking? How does this shape how we think about literacies? Deleuze and Guattari (1980/1987) write, "To reach, not the point where one no longer says I, but the point where it is no longer of any importance whether one says I" (p. 3). Thus, it is not that they say there isn't an "I," a subject, but rather we get to the place where we no longer think of people as individual "I"s. In other words, we are always already entangled with others (humans, nonhumans, more-than-humans, discourses). We are already and ... and ... and ...

In the opening to *A Thousand Plateaus*, Deleuze & Guattari (1980/1987) write "The two of us wrote *Anti-Oedipus* together. Since each of us was several, there was already quite a crowd" (p. 3). This reminds us that we are never writers alone, but rather we are always already entangled with other people, times, spaces, discourses, and materials. We think about how this inspires our conceptualizations of writing. We know as co-thinkers/readers/teachers/researchers/writers that when the two of us write, we often can't remember or identify who wrote what. Our writing becomes one or, as Deleuze and Guattari write, we are a singularity full of multiplicities. Trouble Land, too, appears to be a singularity, a game board. However, when looking at how it came into being and what it continues to produce, we see many multiplicities entering in and exiting out, in flows and forces of desirings. There isn't "an" owner of Trouble Land, nor does there need to be, as students have learned in Tara's classroom that writing is a collaborative space of making and unmaking literacies. This has implications for how we think about literacies, curriculum, and assessments. Inspired by Deleuzo-Guattarian ideas of subject, how do we get to a place where we no longer need individualized assessments (i.e. "I") but rather where we can see literacies as always already and ... and ... and ...? In our book, *Go Be a Writer!* (Kuby & Gutshall Rucker, 2016) and in other writings, we've tried to not use a name or pronoun with "literacy desiring," a subtle yet deeply theoretical way of signalling that "it" doesn't belong to a person. Rather, desiring is always on the move, in the making, with/in relationships. How do we take up this same logic of thought in pedagogical decisions?

Cat versus Fox: Puppets Travelling Home

An Extract from Tara's Teaching Notes

Three girls worked on a poem, scenery, cat and fox stick puppets, and a script for nearly two weeks. The characters unfolded based on the girls' favourite animals. In their story, Cat tried to keep Fox from drinking all the water from the pond in the middle of the forest. After Spring Break, they completely abandoned the work. The script was misplaced and they had new interests to pursue. I questioned, "Is this okay?"

I scheduled a conference with the girls so that they could share what they were currently working on and why they decided to leave the story unfinished. Their reason to stop working on it made sense. They felt it was as complete as it could be, and each of them had other writing they wanted to pursue. As they shared, I wondered what would happen if someone new *used* their scenery and puppets as writers. Could someone undo (or redo) their unfinished work?

One of the three girls, Elizabeth, took the group's writing home to her younger brother. Afterwards, she explained that he first tried to guess their story and act it out with the stick puppets. But then he made up his *own* stories. She admitted some of his were better than theirs ... and he didn't have a script! "It's funner [sic] ... without a script!" she explained.

Later that same day Elizabeth shared this experience with the class. The group unanimously agreed that it is more fun without a script. It allows for more imagination and ideas to emerge. You or the user can say what you want or figure out what you want to say along the way. Elizabeth indicated that, with a script, you have to say something (what is written down) and it is difficult to add your thinking.

The following day, Zara took the group's stick puppets and the scenery home to her younger sister. Her sister agreed with Elizabeth's brother. She even asked for an extra night to play with the story and make up more stories.

Pedagogical Matters of Concern: What if We Saw Writing as Unfinished Becoming(s)?

This literacy desiring prompted us to ask: *What if we saw writing (and literacies more broadly) as unfinished becoming(s)?* The vignette builds on the previous two sections and considers the notion of being finished and ownership. Although the girls had finished, their writing became reimagined when it was handed to different people. Their siblings took up the writing and imagined new possibilities with the stick puppets and scenery. It was rhizomatic and unpredictable in nature. As the siblings worked with the puppets-scenery-poems-(misplaced) script, it became unclear who the owner of the literacy desiring was. The story itself also became anew. The story went in different and new directions. The original authors concluded that the story was even "funner" than their initial ideas.

In this literacy desiring, Tara's role is present as she gave students an opportunity to rework their desirings by sharing it with their siblings. In the moment of the conference with the girls, Tara suggests that they share the unfinished and misplaced writing with others. By imagining new possibilities alongside students and not enforcing deadlines, students see that literacies are constantly on the move and changing. For example, at the end of this school year, Daniela imagined new possibilities for several poems she wrote several months earlier after reading a couple of books about perseverance. She decided to revise several of her poems to coincide with the books and encouraged her classmates as they headed to middle school next year. Zara, who had written very little poetry throughout the year, followed Daniela's lead and added new poems to the collection.

These vignettes also cause us to think more broadly about what counts as writing and the teacher's role in it. How a teacher conceptualizes literacies influences students. Many times, students look to Tara for permission, literally with their eyes and/or by asking verbally. Tara often answers their "Can I/we ...?" with "Be a writer" in an effort to not hinder literacy desirings. The physical space and materials made available to students play a role in this. Tara provides blank paper for students to use because she's noticed that blank paper opens up many possibilities for writers. She also provides notebooks, pre-stapled booklets, and a variety of lined paper, some with boxes. However, the list could go on and on as students also access coloured paper, yarn, stencils, pipe cleaners, computers, glue, markers, paints, iPads, staplers, tape, and ... and ... and ... to create with in Writers' Studio. In other words, throughout the year, Tara offers students uninterrupted time to explore a range of materials, technologies, and partnerships during Writers' Studio. In doing so, students see writing as a space for their literacy desirings (that Alex suggested students already have outside of school) to become.

Unmaking and Making Literacy Desiring(s): Ethico-onto-Epistemologies of Literacies

Deleuze and Guattari were not explicitly concerned with knowing, knowledge, or epistemologies. Rather, their project was about ontologies – realities or the production of being and becoming. However, as Barad (2007) writes, our knowing and being are entangled and cannot be separated. And, this knowing and being are always already entangled in relationships (and ethics). These relationships are sometimes referred to as ethico-onto-epistemologies

(Barad, 2007). The cat vs. fox literacy desiring we have described above causes us to wonder what if writing is about becoming anew and therefore always already unfinished? How might our pedagogies change if we think that writing (and literacies) don't pre-exist but rather come into being through/in/with relationships? We cannot predict what happens when children are working-with-materials-discourses-each other. Or as Barad (1999) writes, "the world kicks back" (p. 2). This means that as children work with materials (and materials work with children) in/of the world, they kick back or are a part of the world coming to be.

This brings us to the "ethico," or the ethics, relationships, and axiology (ies) of literacies. What is our response-ability (or our abilities to respond) to the literacy relationships we find ourselves a part of? How do we respond? What are the ethics and consequences to the world coming to be when we tell children what counts as literacy or writing (and what does not)? How do we hinder the possibilities of new literacies? New relationships? New knowledges? Our decisions as teachers – our talk, gestures, body language, use of class time, invitation to engage with certain materials, and so forth – all matter in how *and* what literacies are produced. Smith (2012) writes that "Deleuze's own philosophy of desire [focuses on] the conditions for the production of the *new*" (p. 188, emphasis in the original). This begs us to consider our response-abilities in (co)creating conditions for the production of new literacies.

(Un)finishing Our Writing

In an effort to materialize our thinking on writing as unfinished becomings, we end this chapter in an unfinished kind of way. We don't have a list of implications and/or how-tos to create spaces for literacy desirings in your classroom. Rather, we invite you to consider some of the questions we pose in relation to each literacy desiring above. For us, it is a matter of ethics when we conceptualize what *and* how literacies come to be. We invite you to ponder and wonder: What other or different literacy pedagogies (or worlds) are possible (even if current realities don't permit them)?

Going back to Alex's quotation, we hear the voices of teachers with whom we've interacted ask: How does this (literacy desiring) happen? How do I make it happen in my classroom? We believe it is not so much about us as teachers (although it is to some extent as we've discussed above) but about following children/materials' desirings. A both/and. Teachers *and* children *and* materials *and* discourses working with each other in creating new literacies.

And so, as we come to the end of this chapter, we have not figured out what exactly literacy desirings are. In fact, this writing opens up more questions for us to consider. Figuring it out isn't the point, as that would finish what literacy desiring is. Rather, thinking/writing about literacy desirings is also a process, an unfinished becoming for us. Our desiring is affirmative and productive. As Deleuzian scholar Goodchild (1996) writes:

> Desire does not belong to us – it comes from outside self and other, and is given to us in an event of crisis, liberation, and relation. Desire is grace. Desire gives itself as an event that always transforms our entire mode of existence, the very meaning of our Being.
>
> *(p. 65)*

Transforms. Crisis. Liberation. Relation. Grace. Being. Inspired, we will continue to make and unmake literacy desirings in our collaborations together. And we invite you to do so as well.

Notes

1 The terms human and nonhuman signal bodies that identify as human and nonhuman (e.g. plants, rocks, discursive bodies, policies, animals, art tools, and so forth). For us, more-than-human signals the notion that animals, plants, and landforms are just as necessary as humans are to the ongoing flourishing of the world. More-than-human also signals the non-representational dimensions of life.
2 All student names are pseudonyms.
3 For more information about Schoology, see www.schoology.com.
4 We realize that some readers might not consider Stop Motion animation as writing. We think and write elsewhere about how the ways we define or conceptualize writing shapes the possibilities of what writing (literacies) might be(come) (see Kuby & Fontanella-Nothom, 2018; Kuby & Gutshall Rucker, 2016; and Zapata et al., 2018).

References

Barad, K. (1999). Agential realism: Feminist interventions in understanding scientific practices. In M. Biagioli (Ed.), *The science studies reader* (pp. 1–11). New York: Routledge.

Barad, K. (2007). *Meeting the universe halfway: Quantum physics and the entanglement of matter and meaning.* Durham, NC: Duke University Press.

Deleuze, G., & Guattari, F. ([1980] 1987). *A thousand plateaus: Capitalism and schizophrenia.* (B. Massumi, Trans.) Minneapolis: University of Minnesota Press.

Deleuze, G., & Guattari, F. (1983). *Anti-Oedipus: Capitalism and schizophrenia.* (R. Hurley, M. Seem, & H. R. Lane, Trans.) Minneapolis: University of Minnesota Press.

Deleuze, G. (2004). *Desert Islands.* Los Angeles, CA: Semiotext(e).

Goodchild, P. (1996). *Gilles Deleuze and the question of philosophy.* London: Fairleigh Dickinson University Press.

Gutshall, T. L., & Kuby, C. R. (2013). Students as integral contributors to teacher research. *Talking Points,* 25(1), 2–8. Retrieved April 29, 2019, from www.ncte.org/journals/tp/issues/v25-1.

Kuby, C. R. (2017). Why a paradigm shift of "more than human ontologies" is needed: Putting to work poststructural and posthumanist theories in Writers' Studio. *International Journal of Qualitative Studies in Education*, 39(9), 877–896. doi:10.1080/09518398.2017.1336803.

Kuby, C. R. (2018). Rhizomes and intra-activity with materials: Ways of disrupting and reimagining early literacy research, teaching, and learning. In J. M. Iorio & W. Parnell (Eds.), *Disrupting by imagining: Rethinking early childhood research* (pp. 146–165). New York: Routledge.

Kuby, C. R. (2019). Literacying: Literacy desiring in Writers' Studio. In B. D. Hodgins (Ed.), *Feminist research for 21st-century childhoods: Common Worlds Methods* (pp. 147–159). London: Bloomsbury Academic.

Kuby, C. R. (2020). Knowing/be(com)ing/doing literacies: (Re)Thinking theory-practice with a personal narrative game board. In K. Lenters & M. McDermott (Eds.). *Affect, embodiment, and place in critical literacy: Assembling theory and practice.* New York: Routledge.

Kuby, C. R., & Crawford, S. (2018). Intra-activity of humans and nonhumans in Writers' Studio: (Re)imagining and (re)defining 'social'. *Literacy*, 52(1), 20–30. Retrieved April 29, 2019, from https://onlinelibrary.wiley.com/doi/10.1111/lit.12120.

Kuby, C. R., & Fontanella-Nothom, O. (2018). Reimagining writers and writing: The end of the book and the beginning of writing. *Literacy Research: Theory, Method, and Practice*, 67, 310–326. doi:10.1177/2381336918786257.

Kuby, C. R., & Gutshall Rucker, T. (2015). Everyone has a Neil: Possibilities of literacy desiring in writers' studio. *Language Arts*, 92(5), 314–327. Retrieved April 29, 2019, from www.jstor.org/stable/24577589.

Kuby, C. R., & Gutshall Rucker, T. (2016). *Go be a writer!: Expanding the curricular boundaries of literacy learning with children.* New York: Teachers College Press.

Kuby, C. R., Gutshall Rucker, T., & Darolia, L. H. (2017). Persistence(ing): Posthuman agency in a Writers' Studio. *Journal of Early Childhood Literacy*, 17(3), 353–373. doi:10.1177/1468798417712067.

Kuby, C. R., Gutshall Rucker, T., & Kirchhofer, J. M. (2015). "Go be a writer": Intra-activity with materials, time, and space in literacy learning. *Journal of Early Childhood Literacy*, 15(3), 394–419. doi:10.1177/1468798414566702.

Smith, D. W. (2012). *Essays on Deleuze.* Edinburgh: Edinburgh University Press.

Wohlwend, K. (2011). *playing their way into literacies: Reading, writing, and belonging in the early childhood classroom.* New York: Teachers College Press.

Wood Ray, K., & Cleaveland, L. B. (2004). *About the authors: Writing workshop with our youngest writers.* Portsmouth, NH: Heinemann.

Zapata, A., Kuby, C. R., & Thiel, J. J. (2018). Encounters with writing: Becoming-with posthumanist ethics. *Journal of Literacy Research*, 50(4), 478–501. doi:10.1177/1086296X18803707.

2

PRACTISING PLACE-THOUGHT AND ENGAGING IN CRITICAL PLACE INQUIRY IN A PUBLIC PARK

Listening, Letting Go, and Unsettling Our Writing Pedagogies

Michelle A. Honeyford and Jennifer Watt

Writing is often an unsettling process. This chapter has been no exception. We have produced (at least two) material forms of this chapter that felt (at least temporarily) like final drafts. At the time of writing, the two-week summer writing institute that was (and is) the focus of this critical place inquiry (Tuck et al., 2014; Tuck & McKenzie, 2015) was two seasons behind us. The park, once green, was covered in brown and yellow leaves, and is now blanketed with deep, white snow. We have been stuck and tempted to stay there, but our hearts, minds, bodies, and souls continue to be moved: by the ways place-thought has been taken up by the educators in the institute with their own students and colleagues; by how we continue to reference this experience to illustrate the rich learning experiences our renewed curriculum calls for in teaching language arts (Manitoba Education and Training, 2017); by the Truth and Reconciliation Commission of Canada's Calls to Action (2015) to develop culturally responsive curricula (Call #10, Subpoint 3, p. 321), to build capacity for intercultural understanding, empathy, and mutual respect (Call #62, Subpoint 3, p. 331), and to develop professional learning experiences and resources for teachers in these areas (Call #6, Subpoint 2, p. 331)[1]; by our own desire to nourish the learning spirit in students, teachers, and communities (Battiste, 2010, 2013); and by the invitation of this book to embrace "indeterminacy and emergence" (Leander & Boldt, 2012, p. 32) in pedagogical narratives that seek to open language and literacy becomings through storied and relational epistemologies, ontologies, and ethics.

And so we write, with/in theoretical and pedagogical orientations to place that might create disruptions to the hegemonic power of cultural and cognitive imperialism that have continued to perpetuate (and make invisible) Western colonial and representational approaches to knowledge and knowledge production; and, simultaneously, we write (re)cognizing that our social locations and words continue to be fraught/caught by/within those very relations of privilege and power (Battiste, 2013; Styres, 2017). In this space of friction, writing with humility and vulnerability, we've found our writing taking different forms: assemblages of new and found poetry, prose, stories, questions, wonderings, and wanderings.

(Un)settling Acknowledgements: Locating Ourselves

> Acknowledgement: Acceptance of the truth or existence of something
> *(Oxford Dictionary of English, n.d.)*

We live, teach, and write on Treaty One territory, which is located on original lands of Anishinaabeg, Cree, Oji-Cree, Dakota, and Dene peoples, and on the homeland of the Métis Nation. We are both immigrants to the province of Manitoba, having moved here from other parts of Canada via teaching and life experiences in the USA and internationally. Over the years we have been here, we have come to deeply appreciate and respect how

Manitoba has always been
a place of activity, change, and struggle –
movements that illustrate the harshness and beauty of life.
From time immemorial,
ancestors of Aboriginal communities now known as the Anishinaabe,
Assiniboine, Cree, Dene, Inuit, Métis, Oji-Cree, and Sioux
inhabited,
migrated to, and
settled
throughout these lands.
They made homes,
held ceremonies in sacred spaces, and
forged relationships among themselves and
with beings
throughout the environment.
They established traditions
that extend into today.
Much of this involved
an intricate use
of oral and written expressions

> chang[ing] and adapt[ing]
> with the environment
> over time.
> *(Sinclair & Cariou, 2012, pp. 2–3, formatting changed for emphasis)*

It is important to contextualize curricular and pedagogical place-work in the long history and ongoing realities and legacy of Indigenous and non-Indigenous relations in Canada. For more than a century, Canada's Aboriginal policy was the cultural genocide[2] of Aboriginal peoples (TRC, 2015, p. 1). The government's project was an attempt to assimilate and eradicate Indigenous peoples through the seizure and occupation of land, the fraudulent and coercive negotiation of Treaties, the elimination of Indigenous peoples' governing structures, the banning of Indigenous languages, the disempowerment of Indigenous women and persecution of Indigenous leaders, and the outlawing of Indigenous cultural and spiritual practices. The "pass system" confined Indigenous people to their reserves. The residential school system in Canada had devastating consequences for First Nations, Inuit, and Métis peoples, families, and communities, and for the collective capacity of Indigenous and non-Indigenous peoples to listen, learn, and live in reciprocity and relationship (Styres, 2017, p. 24; Battiste, 2013; TRC, 2015).

> **Settler Colonialism**
> The specific formation of colonialism
> in which the colonizer comes to stay.
> The violence of invasion
> is not contained to first contact
> or the unfortunate birthpangs of a new nation,
> but it is reasserted each day of occupation.
> Both a historical *and* contemporary
> matrix of relations and conditions
> that define life in the settler-colonial nation-state.
> For settlers to live on
> and profit from land,
> they must eliminate Indigenous peoples, extinguish
> historical, epistemological, philosophical, moral, and political
> claims to land.
> Land, in being settled,
> becomes property.
> Whiteness and settler status
> are made invisible,
> only seen when threatened.
> Settler colonialism is typified by
> practiced epistemological refusal;

the covering of tracks.
(Found in[3] Tuck & Gaztambide-Fernández, 2013, pp. 73–74)

Education and literacy are not "benign processes," but have served as instruments of settler colonialism, "tragically diminish[ing] Indigenous languages and knowledges" and contributing to "the discontinuity and trauma Aboriginal peoples continue to experience" (Battiste, 2013, p. 26). It is essential that Indigenous worldviews are (re)centred in education as "holistic, lifelong, purposeful, experiential, communal, spiritual, and learned within a language and culture" (Battiste, 2010, p. 15). As we engage with Indigenous artists, writers, speakers, activists, scholars, and students in our teaching and scholarship, we have been moved to "more fully consider the implications and significance of place in lived lives" (Tuck & McKenzie, 2015, p. 1), and we find our thinking and writing becoming more entangled in epistemologies, ontologies, and ethics of place.

Critical Place Inquiry: Context and Questions of a Place-Thought Experiment

Place-Thought
The non-distinctive space
Where place&thought were never separated
(because they never could or can be).
Based upon the premise:
Land is alive and thinking.
And humans and non-humans derive agency
through extensions of these thoughts.
(Found in Watts, 2013, p. 21)

Our desire to focus the summer writing institute as an inquiry into writing in/with place was partly inspired by Daniel Coleman's 2017 book, *Yardwork: A Biography of an Urban Place*. As a newcomer to Hamilton, Ontario, Coleman's backyard on the edge of the Niagara Escarpment (which he showed us when we Skyped him during the course) became a site of inquiry into the ecology, environment, and history of the area. From following the flow of water to the migratory patterns of birds and wildlife, from tracking species of trees and plants to the complex history of Indigenous-settler relations, the inquiry yields for him deep understandings of the interrelationships and inter-dependence of human and non-human in place.

Our backyard was King's Park, an urban park that was an approximately twenty-minute walk from campus and bordered the Red River. The park features soccer and sports fields, a large pond and waterfall, bridges and a paved walking trail, a "transplanted" Chinese pagoda and labyrinth honouring the Canadian writer Carol Shields, picnic and fire pit areas, a rose garden, an off-leash dog park, and a dirt bike trail. The park attracts a variety of visitors and inhabitants, human and non-human, wild and domesticated. We hoped that, weather permitting, we could walk to the park almost every day, allowing students time to write, to meet with their writing groups, and, possibly, to participate in park-based teaching demonstrations (for those keen to teach in an outdoor setting). We could see the potential for the park to become a powerful catalyst for writing and critical place inquiry, and thus to offer a unique experience for our students (teachers and administrators in the province, as well as international students and educators) who enrol in the institute seeking to develop their capacity to write and teach writing. Thus, we contacted those registered for the six-credit, two-week intensive courses –which can be applied toward the completion of a post-baccalaureate diploma (at the 5000-level) or a graduate program (at the 7000-level) – to share our plans and prepare them, both pragmatically (e.g. a packing list) and conceptually (a pre-reading list of articles exploring writing and place from multiple perspectives).

Place-Thought Experiment
Designing a course, is,
in many ways,
a thought experiment.
And so,
"the question
of whom to think-with
is immensely material."
(Found in Haraway, 2016, p. 43)

In selecting course texts and readings, inviting guest speakers, and designing an initial set of writing invitations, we sought out multiple perspectives to "think-with" (Haraway, 2016, p. 43) living/writing/being in/with place differently. The concept of *place-thought* (Watts, 2013) acted as a centring "creative force," a "learning device" (Jackson & Mazzei, 2012; St. Pierre, 2017) to think-with pedagogically to see "what newness might be incited" (Jackson & Mazzei, 2012; see also Lenz Taguchi & St. Pierre, 2017); and to open up possibilities for *critical place inquiry* (Tuck & McKenzie, 2015), raising important epistemological, ontological, and ethical questions for our pedagogical practice (see Figure 2.1). We engaged in this multi-dimensional conceptual inquiry into the course as it was designed by us and as it unfolded in assemblage: students, guest speakers, readings, activities, moments, practices, places, conversations, lived experiences, memories, encounters, identities, material and embodied realities. In our becomings as writers and

Place-Thought and Critical Place Inquiry 37

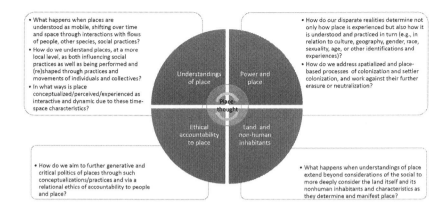

FIGURE 2.1 Critical place inquiry and place-thought as pedagogical and methodological framework

writing teachers, what would be produced by *"hold[ing] open space for one another"* (Haraway, 2016, p. 38, emphasis added)? What would place teach us about writing – and our relationships and responsibilities as writers and educators – if we opened new pedagogical spaces for becoming- and writing-with one another?

Understandings of Place

Tuck & McKenzie (2015) argue for understandings of place as dynamic and mobile, "shifting over time and space and through interactions with flows of people, other species, social practices" (p. 19). Readings for the course included *Manitowapow: Aboriginal Writings from the Land of Water* (Sinclair & Cariou, 2012), an anthology of Indigenous literature by Indigenous authors in this province. Place has always played a powerful role in writing, and, as Sinclair & Cariou (2012) point out, "systems of writing have been used in Manitowapow since time immemorial. Often employed alongside oral traditions, these texts record interactions among people and express connections to animals, spirit beings, and other creatures" (p. 7). Rock petroforms and pictographs "represent the complex ecological and spiritual systems embedded in particular places … [and] illustrate a network of intellectual and physical pathways Aboriginal people travelled and how the trading of stories and information took place alongside goods and resources" (Sinclair & Cariou, 2012, p. 8). As Erdrich (2014) describes, the words for "books" and "rock paintings" in Ojibwemowin share a root word, *mazin*, that is "the root for dozens of words all concerned with made images and with the substances upon which the images are put, mainly paper or screens" (pp. 2–3). Writing has always been "culturally negotiated, embodied and material" (Comber, 2016, p. 37).

Writing in the context of the colonially named King's Park served to provide a local way of experiencing "places as both influencing social practices as well as being performed and (re)shaped through practices and movements of individuals and collectives" (Tuck & McKenzie, 2015, p. 19). Sinclair and Cariou's (2012) *Manitowapow* (re)acquainted students with Indigenous writers, places, and events, "a broad history" encompassing "many incredible struggles," opening up "Aboriginal understandings of what has happened in this place over time," giving "voice to Aboriginal cultural values of community, sharing, respect for the land, and honour for the ancestors"; and providing diverse "responses to this place, Manitowapow, in its many manifestations" (pp. 5–6).

Manitowapow illustrates how place- and life-writing provide possibilities for powerful pedagogical inquiries into "what we *not yet are* and a future that we do *not yet know*" (Lenz Taguchi & St. Pierre, 2017, p. 645, emphasis in the original). Coleman et al. (2012) point out that at its roots the word curriculum means "to change, to move, to flow" (p. 152). Situating our institute in a dynamic space, our place-thought was susceptible to weather and elements beyond our control, as well as to the changing nature of our questions and understandings, and to provocations by other writers. Even then, there were students who struggled to write or connect to the park, and we worked to assure them that place-thought was not constrained to writing about a specific place, but becoming open to the inquiries place prompts in us. As Comber (2016) reminds us, "there is no need to romanticize place, or to privilege the local, or to assume that people automatically feel a sense of belonging where they live, or that communities are united or homogeneous" (p. 36). Any inquiry into place needs to acknowledge that "'the local' … needs to be understood relationally" (Comber, 2016, p. 37). For some, it was sitting with a particular reading in the park; for others, it was something a guest said, or a particular intra-action, sensation, memory, or feeling through which relationships grew – in unexpected ways and rhizomatic directions – so that place became "interactive and dynamic due to these time-space characteristics" (Tuck & McKenzie, 2015, p. 19).

> Writing attunes us
> "not through some visceral belonging,
> But through *practising* place,
> negotiating intersecting trajectories;
> place as arena
> where negotiation is
> forced upon us."
> *(Found in Massey, 2005, p. 154, emphasis in the original)*

Power and Place

Critical place inquiry is a stance for research (and pedagogy) that "recognizes that disparate realities determine not only how place is experienced but also how it is understood and practised in turn (e.g. in relation to culture, geography, gender, race, sexuality, age, or other identifications and experiences)" (Tuck & McKenzie, 2015, p. 19). We began our first day, and first visit to the park, sitting in a circle with an Anishnaabe Elder who spoke about the power of place in the Ojibway language, contrasting the stories of learning from the land and her experiences as a residential school survivor. The next day, we met with a local city councillor at the park. Prior to a career in politics, she had participated in a grassroots community group to raise funds to rehabilitate and revive King's Park in an effort to contribute to a sense of belonging and connection in a rapidly growing area that attracts immigrant families owing to its proximity to the university and schools. Other guests who inspired very different place-thinking and ways of practising place included an entomologist who studies wild bees, a city archivist and archival studies professor, a master gardener, and a professor in mindfulness and well-being who helped us to become more attentive to our bodies and minds in relationship to place. Through writing we were discovering how

> the power of language ...
> enables us to open up
> the not-yet-known
> while at the same time
> work out of the materiality
> of our bodies &
> of the places around them.
> *(Found in Davies, 2011, p. 29)*

Putting place at the centre of our curriculum and pedagogy, and exploring place from Indigenous, political, economic, ethnographic, historical, environmental, ecological, and well-being perspectives required our students (from Manitowapow and all over the world) to negotiate very different "relations of place" (Styres, 2017).

> "becoming-with each other" (Haraway, 2016, p. 4)
> in our relations with social & natural worlds
> learning to appreciate interconnectedness
> how "[w]e live because everything else does" (Wagamese, 2016, p. 36)
> our understandings
> "always situated, someplace and not noplace
> Entangled and worldly."
> *(Found in Haraway, 2016, p. 4)*

Land and Non-Human Inhabitants

Critical place inquiry calls for understandings of place to "extend beyond considerations of the social to more deeply consider the land itself and its nonhuman inhabitants and characteristics as they determine and manifest place" (Tuck & McKenzie, 2015, p. 19). Place highlights "how and why we must understand in an integral way the roles of human and nonhuman, material and discursive, and natural and cultural factors in scientific and other practices" (Barad, 2007, p. 25). We need to continue to expand and diversify the epistemological, ontological, and ethical practices and perspectives we take up in education. How we come to know, who we come to be, and how we live is shaped in ethical relationship not just with humans, but with more-than-humans – with the forces of nature and the agency of animals, wind, plants, and water, for example. From an agential realist perspective, Barad (2007) argues for a shift from social constructivist approaches to learning that emphasizes knowing through social constructs and representations, to performative approaches to learning about the world by engaging in it directly through practices, doings, or actions (p. 28).

To prompt such a shift for our students, we located much of our writing and peer teaching demonstrations in the context of the park. We also introduced them to the concept of *intra-action* as a theory to think-with. In shifting our language from "interactions" with place to "intra-actions" with place, we signified "the mutual constitution of entangled agencies" in place (Barad, 2007, p. 33). It is in the moment of an intra-action that relational agency emerges; for example, in the moment that the doe and the writer in the woods look one another in the eye (see the poem that follows). The concept of intra-action changes *"how* these factors [material, discursive, natural, and cultural] work together, and how conceptions of materiality, social practice, nature, and discourse must change to accommodate their mutual involvement" (Barad, 2007, p. 25; emphasis in the original).

Intra-action has been a generative concept for language and literacy researchers exploring human and material relations in writing, place inquiry, silence, and media-making, for example (Kuby et al., 2015; Somerville, 2016; Akama, 2015; Ehret et al., 2016). A challenge in this work is avoiding "writ[ing] matter and meaning into separate categories" or "forcing them together, collapsing important differences between them, or treating them in the same way," but instead "allowing any integral aspects to emerge (by not writing them out before we get started)" (Barad, 2007, p. 25). Place-thought is a way of practising place-writing in a way that "enables us to theorize the social and the natural world together, to read our best understandings of social and natural phenomena through one another in a way that clarifies the relationship between them" (Barad, 2007, p. 25).

In the moment of intra-action
relational agency emerges:
In the moment the doe
& the writer in the woods
look one another in the eye.
The encounter simultaneously sets in motion
the writer's apology
for disrupting,
understanding she is causing the doe
to calculate the risk
for the fawn beside her.
Mother-to-mother, the writer understands
when
a moment later
with a nod and flick of the tail
the doe takes a graceful leap,
the fawn following her lead
to safety.

Ethical Accountability to Place

Critical place inquiry calls for scholarship to "further generative and critical politics of places through such conceptualizations/practices [of place] and via a relational ethics of accountability to people and place" (Tuck & McKenzie, 2015, p. 19). The capacity and obligation to live in respectful relationship, "to respond to the other" (Barad, 2007, p. 392), is a "response-ability" (Haraway, 2016) taught through living and learning more closely with the land. Richard Wagamese (2016) wrote beautifully about learning to be inclusive of "all our relations": every person, and every "rock, mineral, blade of grass, and creature," for "[w]e live because everything else does. If we were to choose collectively to live that teaching, the energy of our change of consciousness would heal each of us – and heal the planet" (p. 36). As Clayton Thomas-Muller of the Mathais Colomb Cree Nation in Northern Manitoba has argued, "Our greatest power as the peoples of Mother Earth is in maintaining our sacred responsibility to protect her and to speak to those animal and plant relations that cannot speak for themselves" (as cited by Mosionier, 2011, p. xvi).

We can consider then how practising place through writing holds open space to "become-with each other" in relation to the social and natural worlds, learning to appreciate the intra-connectedness of those relationships and the ways that understandings are "always situated, someplace and not noplace, entangled and worldly" (Haraway, 2016, p. 4). Some of the initial appeal of the manicured lawns and green spaces in King's Park was lost when the constant drone of a commercial lawn mower invaded our quest for quiet, and later was further problematized ecologically by the concept of "green deserts" introduced to us by wild bees. Our two weeks in the park – and increasing capacity to notice the ecological, political, cultural, economic, and historical tensions in the environment – moved us as writers and teachers "beyond the fixities and limitations of the present moment [by turning] our attention to what we are made of, our material continuity and ontological co-implication with others, including non-human others, and [to] open ourselves to multiple points of view" (Davies, 2011, p. 30).

> July 3
> only one long weekend away from the last days of school
> exhausted, 24 educators,
> heads and hearts still immersed in their school spaces,
> unsure how to be (in the) present when
> "writing" conjures up report cards, emails, year-end evaluations, and school literacy
> plans,
> where "writers" are other people

> Not us, sunscreen-scented, water bottles dripping,
> with newly gifted writing notebooks in earth tones
> (made of recycled materials) tucked in backpacks
> clumping out of the air-conditioned classroom,
> into the hall, down the staircase, through the door.
> Jen leading, Michelle bringing up the rear
> taking a circuitous route through parking lots, past the
> edible garden, metal shop, and the wild chaos of giant flowers and
> plants against
> the brick agriculture building.
> Looking out of place on the quiet residential street,
> ducking tree branches, overgrown bushes
> pushing us off the sidewalk
> adults on a field trip, first day of summer camp
> celebrating our arrival with selfies at the cactus-shaped sign,
> Pit stop at the restroom.

> We pause in the parking lot
> uncertain how to approach, proceed
> How do we get to know one another? What if we have nothing to say?

Learning to Listen and Notice Differently

In the sections that follow, we pull together threads of place-thought and critical place inquiry as they entangle us and move us in new practices of place. During the first few days in the park, we learned to listen and notice differently, and we became more aware of the complex web of relationships in King's Park. As Coleman (2017) wrote about studying his backyard, "The more I lean in to these everyday voices of this exact place, the more familiar they become, and the more my being and longing come together" (p. 11).

We began by learning how to listen to one another. For example, on our first day, we collectively created a "text rendering" of an article on nourishing the learning spirit (Battiste, 2010). We stood in a circle, shoulder-to-shoulder, in the same spot in the park where we had listened earlier to the teaching of an Elder. In a "spirit reading," we shared the words and phrases that had especially resonated with us, adding to the oral text by speaking when we were comfortable or when we heard a connection to something spoken by someone else. We had to listen carefully to one another: to our pauses, to multiple voices overlapping, to our bodies and breaths, to a community in the early stages of becoming.

We learned quickly that human voices are only one dimension of listening in place. Wind, lawn mowers, other park visitors and inhabitants (e.g. squirrels, birds, and insects), an ever-running generator – all competed for our ability to attend to and even physically grasp sounds. Wanting not to "blunder in" (Kimmerer, 2013) to the park, we invited an Elder to open the course by sharing teachings about the Land. The Elder's voice was gentle and her soft-spoken stories and words of wisdom reached those sitting closest to her in the circle, creating an intimate listening experience for them, but those further away strained to hear. We could see our students shift their bodies and move their heads to try to catch more of the sounds that were being spoken by her and less of the noises muffling her voice. The students all remained attentive, challenged to listen in ways that went beyond audible words and explicitly discernable meanings. As a way to further respond, acknowledge, and begin to name this different kind of listening, we read the picture book *The Other Way to Listen* (Baylor & Parnall, 1997) – a beautiful text that explores ways of listening to the landscape.

As the participants began to practice new ways of listening in their individual writing time (most often situated in the park), they also became more experimental in their writing. After a morning spent learning how to find, net, and identify wild bees, a participant wrote an insightful (and scathing) review of the park from the perspective of a bee. Another writer, prompted by the story the city councillor told about the red pagoda that had been "transplanted" from another park in the city that no longer wanted it, embarked on a daily practice of observing, photographing, drawing, and engaging in experimental writing about/with/as the pagoda. In the end, he wrote a poetic narrative through multiple voices as a tribute to the pagoda's somewhat surprising history, relationships, and roles with the park's human and non-human visitors and inhabitants. Another student, initially aggravated and distracted by the angry chirping of a squirrel whenever she sat to write at a picnic table, experienced a breakthrough when she began to imagine that the squirrel was urgently offering life advice.

Thus, as we developed the capacity to listen and notice differently, we heard different voices and perspectives, sometimes those that troubled (Haraway, 2016) or indicted us in our ignorance or complicity. For instance, when we took a "moss-eye view" of the park to consider what weeds or bees can "show us about worlds," we learned that nature can lead us on "unexpected journey(s)" to "worlds worth caring about" (Tsing, 2018, p. 74). We couldn't look at the park, or ourselves, in the same way, for "in the space of that hearing/seeing/breathing, we came to know our own selves differently, to know, in that assemblage, an intensity" of sounds and sites/sights we didn't know before (Wyatt et al., 2014, p. 408). Some acknowledged a "species loneliness" (Kimmerer, 2013) that the time in the park was awakening in them; others became frustratedly aware of how little they knew about plants and wildlife around them. Kimmerer's (2013) indictment rang true: "Most people don't know the names of these relatives; in fact, they hardly even see them" (p. 209). Several students began using apps on their phones to photograph and identify flora more specifically (and scientifically) in their writing, while others used keen observation and drawings to let the plants suggest their own descriptive names and stories.

In practising place through writing, the intradependence of living things became more evident. As Davies (2011) describes, "Human, animal, earth and other matter – all exist, and exist in networks of relationality, dependence and influence" (p. 30). The sound of the lawn mower attuned us to the environmental impact of maintaining fields of green grass; we came to learn that the drone of the generator was a political response to residents' aesthetic priorities to have a full pond despite the dry spring; and one morning, we recognized (much too late) that the low-flying plane distracting us during a teaching demonstration was in fact spraying insecticide. In turn, listening attuned our writing. Like Coleman (2017), some of us found that amid the "imbalance of our acquisitive, aggressive times, the work of belonging may require more listening than speaking, more contemplation than action, more intuitive immersion than bold assertions" (pp. 11–12). Others felt compelled to write with urgency, courage, boldness, and passion. Students expressed surprise at "where they went" in their writing, to the stories, memories, places, perspectives, and possibilities that emerged through encounters with place and how place compelled them to think and write respons-ive/ably.

Learning to Let Go and Write Wild

During our first visits to the park, most of the participants were finding their way within many places – the place of the park, the place of the course within their programme of studies, the place of themselves as learners after the hectic pace of being teachers, and the place of writing in their lives. This was a process of complex orientation: they needed to navigate the layout of the park, the expectations of the course, and the shift in identity of seeing themselves as a writer among writers and being among beings (rather than perhaps a teacher among teachers, a student among students, or a human among humans). Perhaps because of all the emotional, cognitive, and physical demands of this wayfinding, many of the participants stayed relatively close, confined, and controlled during the early days of individual writing time. Although we invited students to go anywhere they felt like, most stayed within eyesight distance of others, mainly remaining within the manicured spaces bounded by the paved walking path through the central areas of the park. Some participants found moments of inspiration to write in meaningful ways within these maintained spaces, while others commented that they felt too pressured to produce writing that "captured" the place, especially since they knew that they would be sharing this writing with others. For many in the class, there seemed to be a heightened need to control and craft writing in the first few days of the course in an attempt to produce a certain level of polished readiness.

As instructors, we noticed that we were also experiencing a pressure to write *about* place and to assert our own personal agency onto both the place and our writing (one of the authors noticed herself abandoning her writer's notebook to weed one of the maintained garden spaces in the park). We decided by the fourth day of the institute that we needed to let go of the routine we had established. Without even fully understanding our own intentions (or perhaps the intentions of the place), we planned a "six-word, six-minute, six-stop poetry hike" that took us off the asphalt walkway, past the "Danger: Unstable River Bank" sign and into the wild growth along the dirt trail maintained mostly by deer and dirt bikers. Six times along the way, we stopped (in a long line or in a circle), took six steps in any direction, photographed what we saw and wrote about it in six words (Figure 2.2 shows an image and one of our compositions). Many participants included the images and six-word poems in their writing portfolios.

Several participants talked about this experience being a turning point for them in the writing institute. As we crouched over writing notebooks and took photos in single file on a path just wide enough for one, walked through spider webs that clung to our faces and burrs that attached themselves to our socks, stepped over fallen logs and ducked under tree branches, the agency of place began to work on and through us. We let go of our

FIGURE 2.2 A six-step image and a six-word poem:
Check for ticks.
We've gone wild.

perspectives of the park as an expansive green desert and our assumptions that humans can or should shape, control, and design natural spaces. We also let go of assumptions that the best writing is always the most crafted writing. Instead, within their improvisational sparseness, many participants recognized and reflected on how these wild, six-word poems seemed to write themselves. The participants stopped, noticed, and let go of their writerly agency enough so that place and non-human beings could write to and through them. The poems and photographs had an agency of their own, taking the writers into wilder places, connections, conversations, and imaginings than they expected.

On other days, following wild bees and tracking weeds challenged us to write wild and let go of our only-from-a-human perspectives. As we became intimate with our wild fellows, we began to see, think, and feel differently about the constraints of environmental power and control; to reconsider beauty, brevity, and precarity; to admire resilience, difference, diversity, and interconnectedness. For example, although we had co-existed with wild bees throughout our lives, it was through being-in-place with them, intimately close to them in the flowering bushes, that we became aware of how little thought, consideration, or care we had given these creatures, and in turn, many other non-human organisms that may disappear before we ever get the chance to come to know them. Our guest gardener sent us on a scavenger hunt for weeds, then seduced us into appreciating them for their medicinal properties; soil erosion control; sustenance of human and non-human life; stories of place; colour, texture and variety; and ubiquity. We became sheepish, contrite, and then critical about our obsession with weed-free lawns and gardens. We realized a new appreciation for weeds as a "library of nature," a (free) teaching resource, wherever we might be – on a city sidewalk, school playground, or in a park.

Writing wild embodied play –
imaginative and humorous wordplay & craft
as human and non-human collaborators
offering words, sounds, sights, smells & encounters.

Place moved us to practice –
forest bathing, tree climbing, bee catching,
bodies contorted, eyes closed, sweat dripping,
wind flipping pages in notebooks.
Writing wild released imaginations –
cultivated risk-taking, creativity, pleasure & joyfulness.

Writing wild encouraged writers–
to let go of things held close.
Writing (for many) became a practice
described as therapeutic.
In the space of the park,
in the side-by-side conversations
sustained while walking,
in close circles on the ground

or around a picnic table,
we could let go of some
of our heaviest stories,
most-pressing worries,
& previously held assumptions.

By writing wild, we could become better listeners–
to all the human & non-human beings
in which we were in relation
more attentive to complexity & multiple perspectives,
more mindful & self-compassionate
about what & how & where & why to let go.

Unsettling Practices: Writing/Living/Becoming in a Relational Ethics of Accountability to People and Place

Indigenous scholar and educator Naadli Todd Lee Ormiston (Northern Tutchone, Tlingit) describes how "paddling is pedagogy" (Ormiston, 2019), learning from the land on a fifty-five day canoe trip on the Eagle, Bell, Porcupine, and Yukon rivers, spanning the traditional territories of the Tlingit peoples. Excerpts from the journal kept during the trip are woven into the story and teachings as a Canoe Journey narrative, an experience of "new beginnings, survival, 'coming-to-know' and transformation" (p. 39), a framework "for thinking about and living decolonization ... an opportunity to consider the power of traditional teachings for their epistemic range and the hope for creating change" (p. 39), a guide "toward Yan gaa duuneek, a Tlingit word which means to walk with dignity" (p. 39).

Our appreciation of intertwining
ethics, knowing, & being (Barad, 2007) with place
emerging through writing & learning in place.
We are becoming more aware
of the significance
of writing as a practice of place.
Awakening to the idea that
"each intra-action matters,
since the possibilities
for what the world may become
call out in the pause
that precedes each breath
before a moment comes into being
and the world is remade again"
(Found in Barad, 2007, p. 185).

> In this call and response,
> we are attuning to how
> "the becoming of the world is a deeply ethical matter"
> (Barad, 2007, p. 185).
> Writing is an ongoing,
> ethical practice
> unsettling our relationships
> with the world.

On the seventh day of the institute, we stayed on campus with the intent of modelling how our everyday school spaces can also become significant contexts for critical place inquiry. Through our "writing in all directions" activity, we extended an invitation to each writing group to choose a quadrant of campus through which to walk slowly and mindfully, and to see/hear/feel anew this place (which for many was quite familiar). We invited them to take materials (e.g. chalk, index cards, pipe cleaners) to create temporary "pop-up" writing installations that would act as invitations to write for those walking by. We hoped our students would come to practise place beyond the boundaries of the park, and to consider how knowledge creation on a university campus might become less about acting upon the world and more about learning and teaching in collaboration with the world.

While everyone creatively embraced the challenge, responses to the invitations varied. Some of our students felt the sting when their invitations were erased, ignored, or removed without a trace. In less than 24 hours, the weather, time, and direct human activity intervened unexpectedly (e.g. the tree on which a writing invitation had been tied was chopped down overnight; the chalk writing at the entrance of a building, protected by a large overhang, was scrupulously cleaned). The activity taught us about language and the power of erasure. It also raised questions about the "generative and critical politics of places" (Tuck & McKenzie, 2015, p. 19) and mechanisms of control and censorship.

Place-thought has revealed the limitations and harm of our Western lenses and challenged us to question assumptions about our presen(t)ce and future. Place-writing has opened our eyes to see in new ways, our ears to listen in new ways, our hearts to feel in new ways, and our voices and actions to be in the world in new ways. This can be unsettling, but it is far overdue for settlers to be unsettled. Critical place inquiry must be enacted in the pedagogies of the everyday – the work of unsettling language and literacy education through the full recognition that the ontological, epistemological, and ethical positions from which settler colonial education have operated have deeply wounded students and communities. We have been on "the wrong ground" (Barad, 2007, p. 381).

On the tenth and final day of the course, we set out on our final journey to the park carrying gifts: plants, tobacco, and thank-you notes and poems (written on non-bleached cotton paper with soy ink so as to be as compost-friendly as possible). We also carried a shovel, trowel, and an email from the city councillor granting us permission[4] to gift the park with several native-to-Manitoba plants – Little and Big Bluestem grasses and a variety of prairie sages, which are also considered a sacred medicine by many First Nations. Our guest gardener and entomologist had suggested these as hardy and resilient plants that would need no human intervention in order to thrive in this place, and that would attract wild bees and help them to thrive as well. After our planting ceremonies, we gathered in a circle to celebrate our writing, to share with one another selections from our collective anthology of place-writing. Our "paddling" with the park was a journey, too, and the stories and writing that emerged have created new becomings for us as well, as writers, educators, and as settlers who have more to learn, who wish to make

> a commitment to journeying – a seeking out and coming to an understanding of the stories and knowledges embedded in those lands, a conscious choosing to live in intimate, sacred, and storied relationships with those lands and not the least of which is an acknowledgement of the ways one is implicated in the networks and relations of power that comprise the tangled colonial history of the lands one is upon.
>
> *(Styres, 2019, p. 29)*

And so, the writing is revised yet again, still unsettled
But with the awareness that the time has come,
Place confronts us, urges us to (re)new relationships
To (re)learn in humility and respect, to get to know one another
To listen to all that needs to be said.
                                      Of that we have come to understand,

                                      Powerfully, deeply, and more

        certainly.

Notes

1 The Truth and Reconciliation Commission of Canada (TRC) was organized in 2008 as an outcome of the Indian Residential Schools Settlement Agreement. The TRC was intended to reveal the truth about Canada's residential school system and lay the groundwork for reconciliation between Canada's Indigenous and non-Indigenous peoples. The mandate of the TRC included collecting relevant documents from church and government entities, hosting national events, statement

gathering and truth sharing, establishing a National Research Centre, and publishing a final report (Moran, 2015/2017).
2 The Final Report of the National Inquiry into Missing and Murdered Indigenous Women and Girls (MMIWG) was released on June 3, 2019, as our chapter was in the final editing stages. *Reclaiming Power and Place* gathered oral testimonies and undertook detailed archival research to understand "the root causes of Canada's staggering rates of violence against Indigenous women, girls and 2SLGBTQQIA people" (MMIWG, 2019). The findings of this Inquiry led the commissioners to conclude that this violence amounts to "race-based genocide" (MMIWG, 2019, p. 1). The use of the term "genocide," rather than "cultural genocide" to refer to the effects of Canada's settler colonial policies and activities toward Indigenous peoples, has provoked considerable discussion, drawing attention to both the legal and the social dimensions of Canadian colonial genocide (Woolford & Benvenuto, 2017, p. 3). Importantly, the Inquiry produced 231 Calls for Justice that are the subject of close study and consideration among Canadian civil society, scholars, and educators.
3 Throughout this chapter we have engaged in poetic inquiry through the production of both found and original poems. The found poems draw upon the practice of "literature-voiced research poetry," a method first used by Prendergast (2004) and described by Leavy (2009). Our found poems align with how Walsh et al., (2015) define found poetry as "poems found in the environment, composed from words and phrases in previously existing texts" (p. 2). At the end of each found poem, we indicate its genesis through a citation to the authors' original work in parentheses. Poems that originated from our own writing are indicated through the omission of a citation or end parentheses. The poems (both found and original) are purposefully placed in various, sometimes unexpected, spaces on the page (right-justified, left-justified, centred). The place of the poem on the page is another way to disrupt, startle, or invite pause for the reader.
4 We acknowledge how even a permission note is fraught with contested notions of land, property, and ownership.

References

Akama, Y. (2015). Being awake to *Ma*: Designing in between-ness as a way of becoming with. *International Journal of CoCreation in Design and the Arts*, 11(3–4), 262–274. doi:10.1080/15710882.2015.1081243.

Barad, K. (2007). *Meeting the universe halfway: Quantum physics and the entanglement of matter and meaning*. Durham, NC: Duke University Press.

Battiste, M. (2010). Nourishing the learning spirit. *Education Canada*, 50(1), 14–18. Retrieved May 29, 2019, from www.edcan.ca/wp-content/uploads/EdCan-2010-v50-n1-Battiste.pdf.

Battiste, M. (2013). *Decolonizing education: Nourishing the learning spirit*. Saskatoon, SK: Purich.

Baylor, B., & Parnall. P. (1997). *The other way to listen*. New York: Aladdin.

Coleman, D. (2017). *Yardwork: A biography of an urban place*. Hamilton, ON: Wolsak & Wynn.

Coleman, D., Battiste, M., Henderson, S., Findlay, I. M., & Findlay, L. (2012). Different knowings and the Indigenous humanities. *ESC: English Studies in Canada*, 38(1), 141–159. Retrieved May 29, 2019, from https://journals.library.ualberta.ca/esc/index.php/ESC/article/view/20878.

Comber, B. (2016). *Literacy, place, and pedagogies of possibility*. New York: Routledge.

Davies, B. (2011). An experiment in writing place. In M. Somerville, B. Davies, K. Power, S. Gannon, & P. de Carteret (Eds.), *Place pedagogy change* (pp. 29–44). Rotterdam: Sense Publishers.

Ehret, C., Hollett, T., & Jocius, R. (2016). The matter of new media making: An intra-action analysis of adolescents making a digital book trailer. *Journal of Literacy Research*, 48(3), 346–377. doi:10.1177/1086296X16665323.

Erdrich, L. (2014). *Books & islands in Ojibwe country: Traveling through the land of my ancestors*. New York, NY: Harper.

Haraway, D. J. (2016). *Staying with the trouble: Making kin in the chthulucene*. Durham, NC: Duke University Press.

Jackson, A. Y., & Mazzei, L. A. (2012). *Thinking with theory in qualitative research: Viewing data across multiple perspectives*. New York: Routledge.

Kimmerer, R. W. (2013). *Braiding sweetgrass: Indigenous wisdom, scientific knowledge, and the teachings of plants*. Minneapolis, MN: Milkweed Editions.

Kuby, C., Gutshall Rucker, T., & Kirchhofer, J. (2015). "Go be a writer": Intra-activity with materials, time and space in literacy learning. *Journal of Early Childhood Literacy*, 15(3), 394–419. doi:10.1177/1468798414566702.

Leander, K., & Boldt, G. (2012). Rereading "A pedagogy of multiliteracies": Bodies, texts, and emergence. *Journal of Literacy Research*, 45(1), 22–46. doi:10.1177/1086296X12468587.

Leavy, P. (2009). *Method meets art: Arts-based research practices*. New York: Guilford Press.

Lenz Taguchi, H., & St. Pierre, E. A. (2017). Using concept as method in educational and social science inquiry. *Qualitative Inquiry*, 23(9), 643–648. doi:10.1177/1077800417732634.

Manitoba Education and Training (2017). *Draft English Language Arts document to support initial implementation*. Winnipeg, MB: Manitoba Education and Training.

Massey, D. (2005). *For space*. Thousand Oaks, CA: Sage.

Moran, R. (2015/2017). Truth and reconciliation commission. *The Canadian Encyclopedia*. Retrieved May 29, 2019, from www.thecanadianencyclopedia.ca/en/article/truth-and-reconciliation-commission.

Mosionier, B. (2011). Foreword. In N. K. Sinclair & W. Cariou (Eds.), *Manitowapow: Aboriginal writings from the land of water* (pp. xv–xvi). Winnipeg, MB: Highwater Press.

National Inquiry into Missing and Murdered Indigenous Women and Girls (2019). *Reclaiming our power and place: Executive Summary of the Final Report*. Retrieved July 18, 2019, from www.mmiwg-ffada.ca/wp-content/uploads/2019/06/Executive_Summary.pdf.

Ormiston, N. T. L. (2019). Haa Shageinyaa: "Point your canoe downstream and keep your head up!". In L. Tuhiwai Smith, E. Tuck, & K. W. Yang (Eds.), *Indigenous and decolonizing studies in education: Mapping the long view* (pp. 38–49). New York: Routledge.

Oxford Dictionary of English (n.d.). Oxford: Oxford University Press. Retrieved May 29, 2019, from https://en.oxforddictionaries.com/definition/acknowledgement.

Prendergast, M. (2004). "Shaped like a question mark": Found poetry from Herbert Blau's The Audience. *Research in Drama Education*, 9(1), 73–92. doi:10.1080/1356978042000185920.

Sinclair, N. J., & Cariou, W. (2012). *Manitowapow*. Winnipeg, MB: Portage & Main Press.

Somerville, M. (2016). The post-human I: Encountering "data" in new materialism. *International Journal of Qualitative Studies in Education*, 29(9), 1161–1172. doi:10.1080/09518398.2016.1201611.

St. Pierre, E. A. (2017). Haecceity: Laying out a plane for post qualitative research. *Qualitative Inquiry*, 23(9), 686–698. doi:10.1177/1077800417727764.

Styres, S. (2017). *Pathways for remembering and recognizing Indigenous thought in education: Philosophies of lethi'nihstenha Ohwentsia'kekha (Land)*. Toronto, ON: University of Toronto Press.

Styres, S. (2019). Literacies of land: Decolonizing narratives, storying and literature. In L. Tuhiwai Smith, E. Tuck, & K. W. Yang (Eds.) *Indigenous and decolonizing studies in education: Mapping the long view* (pp. 24–37). New York: Routledge.

Truth and Reconciliation Commission of Canada (TRC) (2015). *Final report of the truth and reconciliation commission of Canada*, Vol. 1, *Summary*. Winnipeg, MB: Truth and Reconciliation Commission of Canada.

Tsing, A. L. (2018). Getting by in terrifying times. *Dialogues in Human Geography*, 8(1), 73–76. doi:10.1177/2043820617738836.

Tuck, E., & Gaztambide-Fernández, R. A. (2013). Curriculum, replacement, and settler futurity. *Journal of Curriculum Theorizing*, 29(1), 72–89. Retrieved May 29, 2019, from http://journal.jctonline.org/index.php/jct/article/view/411.

Tuck, E., & McKenzie, M. (2015). *Place in research: Theory, methodology, and methods*. New York: Routledge.

Tuck, E., McKenzie, M., & McCoy, K. (2014). Land education: Indigenous, post-colonial, and decolonizing perspectives on place and environmental research. *Environmental Education Research*, 20(1), 1–23. doi:10.1080/13504622.2013.877708.

Wagamese, R. (2016). *Embers: One Ojibway's meditations*. Madeira Park, BC: Douglas & McIntyre.

Walsh, S., Bickel, B., & Leggo, C. (2015). *Arts-based and contemplative practices in research and teaching*. New York: Routledge.

Watts, V. (2013). Indigenous place-thought & agency amongst humans and non-humans (First Woman and Sky Woman go on a European world tour!). *Decolonization: Indigeneity, Education & Society*, 2(1), 20–34. Retrieved May 29, 2019, from https://jps.library.utoronto.ca/index.php/des/article/view/19145.

Woolford, A., & Benvenuto, J. (2017). *Canada and colonial genocide*. Abingdon: Routledge.

Wyatt, J., Gale, K., Gannon, S., Davies, B., Denzin, N., & St. Pierre, E. A. (2014). Deleuze and collaborative writing: Responding to/with "JKSB". *Cultural Studies ⇄ Critical Methodologies*, 14(4), 407–416. doi:10.1177/1532708614530313.

3

BECOMING POSTHUMAN

Bodies, Affect, and Earth in the School Garden

Saskia Van Viegen

> I wrote a poem about the sun comes: "The clouds open. There is something yellow coming out. And the sun came, and everybody smiles."
>
> *(Harshani,[1] 8 years old)[2]*

Sitting in a circle on the carpet in their Grade 3 classroom, Harshani described the banana trees that grew on her family's farm: "three children can fit under a banana leaf ... when it rains, we use it as an umbrella." The conversation turned to the kinds of plants that the children had grown in their home countries. Each building on the comments of the child before, the children talked about dates and pomegranates, lemon and apple trees. Atif told about the horses he had cared for, about riding them with his father. Two boys explained how you save tomato seeds, drying them carefully to plant the following year.

The fieldnotes above were written during a collaborative inquiry project (Stille, 2013) involving students at the elementary level, which was designed to promote equity and inclusion for bi/multilingual children from immigrant and refugee backgrounds who had been displaced, either voluntarily or not, from their country of origin. Together with the teacher and students as collaborators over a period of six months from January to June 2010, I explored the ways in which classroom practices could incorporate funds of knowledge (González et al., 2005; Marshall & Toohey, 2010) from students' families and communities, drawing upon their cultural and linguistic resources, diverse histories, and multiple modes of representation, in order to connect them with school curriculum learning, and to support English language and literacy development. The project employed Lather's (2012) critical praxis methodology to generate data. A fundamental aspect of praxis-oriented research is that it is constituted relationally, through involvement with others, working together to understand and transform conditions of experience. However, as I revisit the project today, I realize that my praxis encompasses both bodied- and non-bodied others – human and earth, bio- and plant life, tools and spaces. This chapter explores my shift to understanding these others not as separate, but as entangled, enmeshed in a network where material objects and the forces among them act and shape participation. Broadly, this new materialist perspective and relational ontology is prompting a new approach to my teaching and learning activities.

Many of the families of children in the class had come to Canada from politically unstable, war-affected countries. Within these contexts, violence and conflict from ongoing civil war had interrupted the children's access to safe schools, and the children's reflections on and perceptions of these circumstances demanded our attention. For instance, as I was getting to know the children, Monira (9 years old) shared about her family, "Because we are coming here because the security not good. Another guys, they say they don't want the students to go to school … They don't have schools, they closed the schools, and everybody can't go to school." Representations of violence and conflict also appeared in the children's drawings and stories about their home countries. As an example, Asad (9 years old) drew a picture that illustrated his experiences of migration when writing a dual-language digital story about his home country (see Figure 3.1). Asad's drawing suggests how weaponized objects manifest in his realities and feelings of security; notably, the drawing called our attention not only to the social, but also to the material and flows of activity in the children's lives (Toohey et al., 2015).

Taken together, these considerations raise questions concerning how to understand and frame the complexity of meanings and representations that emerged from our work. I went into the project seeking an alignment between *how* the research participants and I engaged in research and *what* we came to know, and we thought about the theories of knowing and being that underpinned our efforts. For instance, recognizing students' rich cultural and linguistic backgrounds and the diversity of their linguistic repertoires, we questioned the binary between so-called native and non-native speakers on which English language teaching is often predicated; a dualism which tends to reproduce social and linguistic hierarchies and assumptions about particular kinds of bodies (i.e. human, migrant, racialized, Others). Accordingly, we engaged in activities to challenge our thinking and doing

56 Saskia Van Viegen

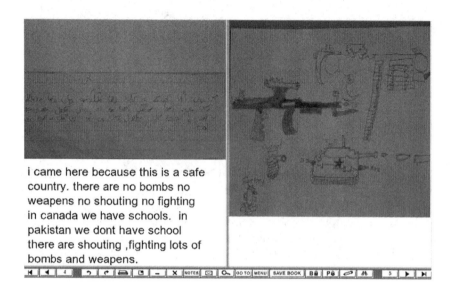

FIGURE 3.1 Image of Asad's story about his migration journey

beyond what we considered to be traditional approaches to language and literacy teaching. We engaged with the Grade 3 curriculum expectations for learning about communities, and began a class inquiry focused on understanding urban and rural spaces.

We took an emergent approach to curriculum planning and teaching, using pedagogical documentation, a kind of "visible listening" (Rinaldi, 2004), to gather artifacts, and to observe and reflect on the children's development and growing interests. Following this approach, we noted that the children were interested in the environment in which their school and their homes were situated. All of them lived in a cluster of high-rise apartment buildings surrounded by very little green space; however, the apartment buildings bordered a natural ravine, and the children grew curious about the ravine after the teacher planned a walk along some of its paths. Very rapidly, our inquiry context moved from the classroom out into the ravine. The teacher organized more walks and lessons in the ravine; he constructed a circle of logs to create an outdoor classroom there, and we conducted a clean-up in one section of the ravine where garbage dumping from the nearby apartment buildings was rampant. Slowly, we began conversations about environmental issues, including the consequences of urban development, plastic pollution, and global warming. We fostered awareness and understanding of eco-justice and environmental conservation, and soon the ravine became an extension of our classroom. As the weather grew warmer, the teacher and students turned their attention to cleaning up the school grounds. Fareeha (9 years old) explained this interest:

Our community, it's special, everyone, they cooperate and is really grateful to each other and they work together to make a difference. We want more people to come here and we want them to see how communities can change by everyone working together.

Finally, the teacher and students decided to create a school garden, and we made a short digital film to document our work (Stille, 2013).

The purpose of this chapter is to explore what a materialist analysis might do for understanding the garden project, and for the kinds of pedagogic futures imaginable for teaching and learning with children with complex migration journeys. Given that the number of displaced persons in the world is currently higher than at any time in human history, the chapter sheds light on ontoethical issues and directions for language and literacy teaching that are responsive to these circumstances. Recounted here as a written narrative illustrated with key quotes and images from the project, including digital photographs and still images from the short documentary film, I articulate the affective forces and intensities that passed between bodied- and earth-others as well as objects and technologies. As Toohey (2018) writes while describing new materiality, such approaches tend not to be the traditional focus of research on language teaching and learning. Thinking about language, learners, and learning in dynamic and indeterminable ways and about assembled forces of the material and immaterial comprises an altogether different way of understanding and doing pedagogy.

Thinking Beyond Language

Through the connection we make with the earth in our garden, the children are able to relate to concepts in a way that goes beyond language.

(Mr. Kendrick, teacher)

Initially constructed in and through a sociocultural perspective, like that which has tended to dominate critical applied linguistics and education research in the past few decades, our project viewed language as the primary activity through which meaning was constructed and represented, mediating access to the social and material world. The teacher and I also relied on language as the means through which to transform how learners were positioned in the sociocultural context of Canadian schools. Whereas learners are often seen from a deficit-oriented lens as struggling to catch up with their English-speaking peers and as being in need of remediation, our focus was to understand how these positions and identifications might be transformed through empowering social interactions, relationships, and activities.

However, thinking now with a new materialist perspective, it is evident that a sociocultural analysis tells only part of the story of our work, leaving out powerful exchanges and insights that emerged from engaging the agencies and affective intensities of non-bodied others that comprised the project – both the natural and organic objects (garden, plants, and ravine), and the technological objects (garden tools, camera, and computers).

As I revisit this project now, I experiment with letting go of language and social interaction as the primary tools for observing, documenting, and generating understanding about our work. In the context of creating the garden and the film, we were always working in activity, in movement among, and in relation to, the human and non-human, technologies, and bio-life. For instance, while picking up and carrying garbage in the ravine, sitting in a circle with the children among the trees in the sun, gently protecting the roots of small plants when transplanting them, or drinking tea brewed from the herbs we cultivated, it is obvious to me now, in light of my reading of Springgay and Truman (2018), that the procedures for and logic of gathering data and extracting meanings were inadequate. Not only do traditional qualitative methods rely on interpretation and representation, they also privilege the human in an anthropocentric perspective that tends to separate or overlook the material. And so in the present analysis, theoretically and methodologically, I endeavour to move beyond language as interpretation and representation; to address what Sedgwick calls "aspects of experience and reality that do not present themselves … in verbal form alongside others that do" (Sedgwick, 2003, p. 6). Whereas the fields of applied linguistics and language teaching and learning have tended to focus on discourses, on the social interactions in which they are produced, and on the interlocutors who produce them, Sedgwick's insights point to the permeable and shifting relations between words and things, and between linguistic and nonlinguistic phenomena. She writes that separating words and things privileges language and creates an unnecessary dualism. Thus inspired, in an effort to think beyond language in our language teaching and research, this chapter turns toward Braidotti's (2013) posthuman subjectivity and a relational ontology of *becoming* that comprises affective forces between and among objects rather than what objects are in and of themselves. Furthermore, these objects – the bodied and the non-bodied – are understood to be constituted by both material and incorporeal dimensions, as matter and energy together (Massumi, 2002).

Posthuman Subjectivity and Affective Intensities

> This is me and my mom talking about what we missed in our farm. We had a big farm in our country.
>
> *(Harshani)*

> The flowers, the smell. The fresh vegetables we get from our garden, the whole we miss.
>
> *(Harshani's mother)*

> The garden at school is like memories, you can learn it again … we miss our trees and our garden, the flowers, the smell.
>
> *(Harshani)*

Braidotti's (2013) articulation of a posthuman theory of subjectivity emphasizes the unity of all matter and recognizes a "relational self" that functions not only in culture and in technologically mediated environments, but also in nature (p. 60). Thinking about the school garden project with posthumanism offers an entry point to think about the mutual relations of humans, technologies, animals, and the earth; their entanglement in assemblages that generate affective intensities and potential for *becoming* differently. These affective intensities rise and fall in the incorporeal encounters of bodies, objects, animals, and earth within assemblages that have a perpetual capacity to affect and be affected.

Affect has been characterized through various philosophical perspectives, ontological assumptions, and vocabularies (Gregg & Seigworth, 2010) describing it as invigorating force and form. For instance, Ahmed (2010) defines affect as "what sticks, or what sustains or preserves the connection between ideas, values, and objects" (p. 230). Attending to affect from a posthumanist lens invites understanding beyond dualities of "subject and object," and beyond interpretation or labelling. Unlike emotion, which Massumi (2002) describes as a subjective sociolinguistic interpretation or "fixing" of the quality of an experience, affect does not presuppose social construction of internal states of arousal. Similarly, Sedgwick (2003) writes the following:

> Affects can be, and are, attached to things, people, ideas, sensations, relations, activities, ambitions, institutions, and any number of other things, including other affects. Thus, one can be excited by anger, disgusted by shame, or surprised by joy. This freedom of affects also gives

them a structural potential not enjoyed by the drive system: in contrast to the instrumentality of drives and their direct orientation toward an aim different from themselves, the affects can be autotelic.

(p. 19)

Rather than focusing attention on the objects of affect, she argues for thinking about *what affects do*. To understand this idea, it is helpful to consider how Grosz (2008) conceptualizes affect by writing about bodies experiencing art. Grosz (2008) writes that the meaning of art arises from the intensities and sensations that art inspires, beyond intention and aesthetic. From this perspective, art materializes sensations: "sensation is neither in the world nor in the subject but is the relation of unfolding of the one for the other ... created at their interface" (p. 72). With these ideas, I have begun to think about socio-material assemblages of bodies, space, earth, and objects in terms of a relational ontology and an ethic that recognizes them as having affective intensities.

Creating and Documenting the Garden

I had a garden in Afghanistan. My grandfather worked with me in the garden.

(Abdulazim, 9 years old)

The setting for the project was a Grade 3 class in a large elementary school in a central Canadian city. The school population comprised 2,000 students from kindergarten to Grade 5. Ninety-five percent of the students' families reported speaking a language other than English at home. The majority of families had arrived in Canada within the past five years, mainly from Afghanistan, Pakistan, Iraq, India, Kuwait, Turkey, and Sri Lanka.

To begin the inquiry, the children conducted broad research about communities, selecting and reading fiction and non-fiction books from the school library about communities, community resources, and land use. To connect with the children's previous experiences, we used Google Earth to view images of urban and rural communities around the world, especially the countries where the children and their families were from. The children also conducted research about the school community and immediate neighbourhood where they now lived. They interviewed each other to gather perspectives about the community, writing their own interview questions such as "Where were you born?" and "What do you like about our community?" The children recorded responses on a graphic organizer and used a digital video camera to document some of the interviews. We used these

Becoming in the Garden: Bodies, Affect, and Earth 61

interviews as an opportunity to teach the students about cameras and how to use them (Figure 3.2).

The camera facilitated children's changing forms of participation in the classroom and in curriculum learning activities. Reviewing many of the hours of raw digital video footage recorded by the students, the teacher, and/or me during our inquiry process, we noticed the children engaging different roles, interactions, and processes. Still images from the video data illustrate these changing forms of participation. To illustrate, Figure 3.3 shows an image from a recording of a rap song and hip-hop style dance performance the children wrote and performed in the garden.

FIGURE 3.2 Students conducting and recording interviews on film

FIGURE 3.3 Student rap and dance performance in the garden

As the image shows, the children used the affordances of the camera to showcase their creativity and to command an audience. During the course of the project, they began initiating, creating, and sharing more and more informal creative works to record and be recorded.

During the interviews, the children compared their school community with other communities where they had lived, reflecting on their experiences in their home countries. As we discussed these reflections, the children noted that they lacked access to nature in their new community, whereas many of their families had come from rural areas and had a great deal of experience in farming and agriculture. Because the children and their families now lived in a cluster of high-rise apartment buildings, they had few opportunities to draw upon these experiences in their new Canadian homes. The children created dual-language PowerPoint presentations to summarize and articulate their community's needs, and we connected these ideas to our experiences in the ravine. The teacher and children wanted to address the community needs they had identified to grow, plant, and work with natural materials, and thus the idea for the garden was born.

We recognized that parents might welcome the opportunity to work alongside their children in the garden and invited them to participate as volunteers. Most of the parents had never volunteered at the school, as cultural and linguistic differences had seemed to present a barrier to their involvement. In the garden, however, expertise resided with the parents. Their environmental knowledge and previous agricultural experience were necessary contributions to our work. Several parents returned day after day to work alongside their children in the garden (see Figure 3.4).

FIGURE 3.4 Parents and students working together in the garden

One of the mothers was a member of a local women's group, and she volunteered her group to care for the garden during the summer, when school was out. The presence of parents created connections between home and school, and provided an opening for parents to contribute to their children's learning. However, beyond pedagogic aims, perhaps the work engaged parents' desire to be in a garden again too.

Because of school board and union policies, we were not allowed to use any engine-powered or electrical machinery to till the garden. We had to do all the gardening work by hand. The day after we discussed this problem with the children, several came to school prepared with dishwashing gloves and cooking spoons to protect their hands, to dig and to weed. The day after that, even more children brought tools raided from their kitchens. Although the teacher and I also brought donated gardening gloves, shovels, and hand trowels, many children chose to use their tools brought from home (see Figure 3.5).

On the surface, creating the school garden had very little to do with language and literacy learning. However, it soon became apparent that the work in the garden constituted a "pedagogical border crossing" (Gallagher, 2007), a site for doing learning and generating knowledge differently. The

FIGURE 3.5 Students working in the garden wearing kitchen gloves and using sand shovels from home

first sign that we were crossing a border was that we had to seek permission to create the garden. Mr. Kendrick and I were apprehensive that the school administrators would reject the idea, but we were delighted when they gave consent for us to work in one of the school courtyards. The courtyards were overgrown with a tangle of weeds, over a metre in height. Bordered by hallways and classrooms with large windows that brought natural light into the school, the courtyards generated affective intensities when one passed by the windows – the wild, untouched, and littered space opened up opportunities for activity, potential, and intensities to unfold.

What do you like about gardening?

(Abdul, 9 years old)

I like to dig because it's messy and fun.

(Hasra, 10 years old)

Most of the kids they are not doing outdoor work, they are busy with homework and video games, normally they are not doing any physical things. Gardening is good for physical things; it's good learning. If you don't learn anything about agriculture, you don't understand how farmers are making food for you, how hard it is. So, this is real learning. They [the children] know how people are making food for them. When you get food on your table you want to take it; now [they] realize what people are doing for them, and that they should be grateful for that.

(One of the volunteer fathers)

We were reminded of our transgression into new territory every time we worked in the garden. At the outset, we worked cautiously under the gaze of other teachers, students, and administrators who paused as they walked by to watch our progress. As soon as the weeds were gone, we started tracking dirt into the school, clumps of mud stuck on the bottom of shoes that made a path from the outside to the classroom door. When we started to cultivate the garden, we made a noisy racket carrying shovels and rakes through the hallways. But in the end, the children's voices and laughter, their parents' firm but indulgent admonitions, the teachers' orders and instructions combined to create a spectacle. Other teachers brought their classes to help, and administrators brought visitors to tour the garden. Mr. Kendrick documented the work through his own observations, fieldnotes, and digital photographs, and shared his learning at a professional development presentation for other teachers in the school district. Notably, much of the work to prepare the garden site took place in May, the same month when Grade 3 students were supposed to be preparing for the province-wide standardized literacy exam. During exam week, Mr. Kendrick planned each day so that the students spent three hours in the morning preparing to sit the test, and three hours every afternoon in the garden. What was supposed to be a stressful time for the students turned into a great deal of fun. As the garden project unfolded, new learning assemblages formed that included parents, administrators, visitors, outside spaces, soil, gardening tools, dirty hands, and documentary recording equipment. These generated affective intensities, which reshaped what constituted learning activities and spaces in this environment.

> I really want to do the stuff that my heart wants me to do, get the kids outside and get their hands dirty. I've been able to get the kids outside, it's what I really want to do.
>
> *(Mr. Kendrick, teacher)*

> I am working with my mom in my garden plot. My mom is adding soil and I am fluffing and mixing it.
>
> *(Atif, 11 years old)*

The students documented the creation of the garden using digital film and photography, and we used iMovie software to produce the documentary film from this footage. Students took turns filming our work in the garden, and each student selected their favourite clip to include in the film. The clips were edited for length, and then drawing on the use of photo-voice as a method for prompting reflection (Mitchell, 2008) we invited the students to write captions or narrate voice-overs for the clips that they chose. The images below (see Figures 3.6a–d) show screenshots of some of the clips students selected; their voice-overs have been transcribed and some are included in this chapter.

Reflections

Telling people about the school garden generally produces a positive response. People tend to be delighted to hear a story about children doing this kind of activity in school. However, in a double(d) reading that is both "critique and complicity" (Lather, 2012), we might see the unseen stories and sacrifices that underwrote the garden and its needs in the first place, materializing as it does the social inequities and ecological crises manifest in this school and community, namely the forced migration and displacement of people from rural war-affected communities, the colonization of

FIGURES 3.6A–D Screenshots of video clips chosen by students to showcase their work in the garden

indigenous lands, and the consequences of development, capitalist marketization, and global warming.

The assemblages in the garden project therefore encompassed an expanded group of human and material participants, including local manifestations or appearances of *hyperobjects* (Morton, 2013), massive things like protracted war, global warming and/or the biosphere that are both collections or systems of other objects, and objects in their own right. Morton (2013) suggests object-oriented thinking can help us to reflect on our place on Earth, our existence, our society. Listening and bearing witness to the children's experiences, and reflecting on our own experiences, we connected understanding and critique of social and educational injustices to a relational ontology, and reflected on the negotiated and collective nature of knowledge production, across the human and non-human.

The normative, institutionalized construction of literacy often points to its transformative potential. However, Berlant's (2006) concept of "cruel optimism" challenges the belief in normative promises that are bound to disappoint. She writes of cruel optimism as

> [the] relation of attachment to compromised conditions of possibility. What is cruel about these attachments, and not merely inconvenient or tragic, is that subjects who have x in their lives might not well endure the loss of their object or sense of desire ... because whatever the content of the attachment, the continuity of the form of it provides

something of the subject's sense of what it means to keep on living on and to look forward to being in the world.

(p. 21)

Such cruel optimism might apply to how educators operate with a theory of change that expects that, if we offer language and literacy support, students' lives will improve. However, transforming social and educational inequities is a structural, rather than an individual problem. Meeting students' needs cannot be separated from broader struggles against social inequality. For instance, the students' experiences highlighted how

> the ways in which wealth, nationality, ethnicity, gender, class, age, location and so on mediate our relationships with the planet ... [that] the scale and impact of ecological damage is always unequal, unethical and unjust; indigenous colonialised peoples, women, children, and the other-than-human species we share this planet with are in it more than those entrenched in dominant western white masculine cultures.
>
> *(Malone, 2019)*

Toward the end of the project, Mr. Kendrick shared his reflections, pointing out the contradictions inherent in the garden project:

> What people are seeing is bare earth, they're ripping everything out and they are so proud of their industry. I want my students to recognize that this is a double-edged thing that we are doing. Although everyone says, "Oh this is a wonderful thing that you are doing," it isn't totally. This is the equivalent of, if you take what we're doing on a micro scale and you scale it up it's like forestry, like clear cutting.[3]

Mr. Kendrick's insights don't sit well with a neat, coherent narrative about the garden. A representational, interpretive, or narrative view of the garden tells a cheerful, easy story. However, unseen stories and sacrifices underwrote the garden and its very need in the first place. Materializing global inequities manifest in this school and community, the garden was about far more than beautifying an unused space on the school grounds. Identifying pedagogical pivot points, what the children (and we) took from the project cannot easily be narrated or retold, as it was constituted by the assemblage of objects, bodies, space, discourses, and practices that unfolded there. Moreover, the encounters within this assemblage produced differences as the ethics of cultivating land were questioned. Mr. Kendrick explained to me that by reclaiming the courtyard from the weeds, we were also taking the land away from the insects, birds, and small animals that called the unruly courtyard home. He was not focused only on the benefits of the garden for the children and their families, but considered too how the garden affected other living and inorganic things in the assemblage, thereby adopting a perspective on the garden project that appears to me now as converging with an anthropocentric gaze.

At first, Mr. Kendrick's comments came as a surprise to me, revealing my own entrenched commitment to dominant narratives of resolution. Pearce (2010) points out the desire for such coherent narratives, asking:

> Why, that is, should any of us wish to write or read a story that does not move its characters – and us – forward in some way? Why should we commit ourselves to a roller coaster of quest, test and suffering if there is not some reward, reprieve, or, at least, catharsis at the end?
>
> *(p. 151)*

The story of the garden project would not be quite right without accounting for the complexities that it provokes. Attempting to disregard this would mean appropriating the story of what took place; it would presume a coherence that could not exist. Identifying the contradictions in our work, Mr. Kendrick named the disjunctures. As Ahmed (2013) writes, "To obscure or to take cover by looking on the bright side is to avoid what might threaten the world as it is" (p. 43). Quoting Audre Lorde, Ahmed (2013) articulates a critique of happiness: "Let us seek 'joy' rather than real food and clean air and a saner future on a liveable earth! As if happiness alone can protect" (p. 43). These ideas are at the core of a feminist ethics and consciousness, which Ahmed describes as consciousness of the violence and power that are concealed under the languages of civility. She writes, "And if it can cause disturbance simply to notice something, you realize that the world you thought you were in is not the world you are in" (p. 43).

Schools are not neutral, but instead are constituted by particular structures, practices, and relations which organize students' experiences and activities and index what counts as powerful knowledge. Our creation of the garden drew attention not only to what had been gained in relation to this project, but also to what has been lost and sacrificed in educational practice that disregards the assets and resources that students bring with them to school. Indigenous communities whose land has been colonized, families displaced from rural, agricultural lifestyles who are forced to migrate to urban centres have few opportunities to teach their children what they know about environmental sustainability and local ecologies. Without access to land, families can struggle to pass on their knowledge and experience in food production, as one of the volunteer fathers pointed out it in a thought-provoking comment presented above. Considering the ecological circumstances of our present time, these families can make an important contribution to knowledge creation and production about environmental issues, for their own children and others.

Concluding Thoughts

> I always used to think that it's hopeless because I'm just a child, and whenever somebody, a child, has an idea, adults don't really listen to it. They just ignore that person, that child, and that child can really help make a difference. So, I thought to myself I'm going to stand up for myself and make a difference.
>
> *(Somayah, 9 years old)*

> This is the stuff that's at the core of the life and the planet. I don't think we should be creating a world where people can read and can have all the food that they need and other people don't; where those who can are going to grab what they're able to grab and to hell with everybody else.
>
> *(Mr. Kendrick)*

The garden created a dynamic experience of curriculum, through a pedagogy that was social and textual, but also material and s*ense-ational*. Reflecting on our work through a materialist perspective, a relational ontology takes no subject as fixed or a priori. Instead, decentred school subjects functioned as part of the material assemblage of school-based learning, artifacts of binary knowledge traditions that are maintained through curriculum policies and expectations (Smythe et al., 2017). In the project, we began to rearrange this assemblage by disrupting traditional approaches to language and literacy teaching and learning. I return to the assemblages emerging during work on the garden and the affective intensities they generated to consider what lines of flight (Deleuze & Guattari, 1987) opened up during the course of our collaboration, engendering transformations brought about by encounters and engagements with the complexity of our environment and human migration.

As I write this chapter, I am aware of the inadequacy of words in describing the curiosity, labour, and transformation in the garden; the moments and experiences that the work generated. Although the images attempt to illustrate the human-material encounters in the garden, the images do not capture the affective intensities and forces generated. This inadequacy is similarly reflected by the challenges of producing knowledge about bodied and non-bodied subjects – how to articulate the dynamic, uncertain qualities of experience and subjectivity without creating understandings that are frozen in time or collapsed into one-dimensional representations.

The garden was constituted not only by physical form, but also by forces and intensities that arose between the children, plants, earth, and tools – as well as the parents, teacher and I – working together in the space. Affective intensities materialized at the interface of creation, through clearing, sowing, watering, weeding, harvesting, and creating a documentary film; facilitating change and transformation that we could see, hear, smell, and feel. These processes happened both in particular moments and over time, and materialized in encounters as well as through relation, movement and becoming. The changes were visible in the very growth of seeds into seedlings, and seedlings into plants, flowers, and vegetables, materializing a becoming that Grosz (2001) describes as "the other's transition from being the other of the one to its own becoming, to reconstituting another relation, in different terms" (p. 27). Knowledge was generated at the liminal edges of these transitions, in the forces and intensities at work and becoming.

Notes

1 Pseudonyms are used for research participants.
2 This excerpt and those that follow are from transcriptions of voiceovers in videos that the children made about the garden project.
3 Clear cutting refers to the wholesale removal of all trees from a landscape.

References

Ahmed, S. (2010). *The promise of happiness*. Durham, NC: Duke University Press.
Ahmed, S. (2013). *The cultural politics of emotion*. London: Routledge.
Berlant, L. (2006). Cruel optimism. *Differences*, 17(3), 20–36. doi:10.1215/10407391-2006-009.
Braidotti, R. (2013). *The posthuman*. Hoboken, NJ: Polity.
Deleuze, G., & Guattari, F. (1987). *A thousand plateaus: Capitalism and schizophrenia*. Minneapolis: University of Minnesota Press.
Gallagher, K. (2007). *Theatre of urban: Youth and schooling in dangerous times*. Toronto, ON: University of Toronto Press.
González, N., Moll, L., & Amanti, C. (Eds.). (2005). *Funds of knowledge: Theorizing practices in households, communities and classrooms*. Mahwah, NJ: Erlbaum.
Gregg, M., & Seigworth, G. J. (Eds.). (2010). *The affect theory reader*. Durham, NC: Duke University Press.
Grosz, E. A. (2001). *Architecture from the outside: Essays on virtual and real space*. Cambridge, MA: MIT Press.
Grosz, E. A. (2008). *Chaos, territory, art: Deleuze and the framing of the earth*. New York: Columbia University Press.
Lather, P. (2012). *Getting lost: Feminist efforts toward a double (d) science*. Albany: State University of New York Press.
Malone, K. (2019). *Walking-with children on blasted landscapes*. Paper presented at the meeting of the American Educational Research Association, Toronto, ON,

April 5–9. Retrieved August 14, 2019, from https://childrenintheanthropocene. com/2019/05/14/walking-with-children-on-blasted-landscapes/.

Marshall, E., & Toohey, K. (2010). Representing family: Community funds of knowledge, bilingualism, and multimodality. *Harvard Educational Review*, 80(2), 221–242. Retrieved August 9, 2019, from www.hepg.org/her-home/issues/harva rd-educational-review-volume-80-issue-2.

Massumi, B. (2002). *Parables for the virtual: Movement, affect, sensation*. Durham, NC: Duke University Press.

Mitchell, C. (2008). Getting the picture and changing the picture: Visual methodologies and educational research in South Africa. *South African Journal of Education*, 28(3), 365–383. Retrieved August 14, 2019, from www.scielo.org.za/scielo. php?script=sci_issuetoc&pid=0256-010020080003&lng=en&nrm=iso.

Morton, T. (2013). *Hyperobjects: Philosophy and ecology after the end of the world*. Minneapolis: University of Minnesota Press.

Pearce, L. (2010). Beyond redemption? Mobilizing affect in feminist reading. In M. Liljestrom & S. Paasonen (Eds.), *Working with affect in feminist readings: Disturbing differences* (pp. 151–164). London: Routledge.

Rinaldi, C. (2004). *In dialogue with Reggio Emilia: Listening, researching and learning*. New York: Routledge.

Sedgwick, E. K. (2003). *Touching feeling: Affect, pedagogy, performativity*. Durham, NC: Duke University Press.

Smythe, S., Hill, C., MacDonald, M., Dagenais, D., Sinclair, N., & Toohey, K. (2017). *Disrupting boundaries in education and research*. Cambridge: Cambridge University Press.

Springgay, S., & Truman, S. E. (2018). On the need for methods beyond proceduralism: Speculative middles, (in)tensions, and response-ability in research. *Qualitative Inquiry*, 24(3), 203–214. doi:10.1177/1077800417704464.

Stille, S. (2013). "Sometimes children can be smarter than grown-ups": Re/constructing identities with plurilingual students in English-medium classrooms. Unpublished doctoral dissertation, University of Toronto.

Toohey, K. (2018). *Learning English at school: Identity, socio-material relations and classroom practice*. Bristol: Multilingual Matters.

Toohey, K., Dagenais, D., Fodor, A., Hof, L., Nuñez, O., Singh, A., & Schulze, L. (2015). "That sounds so cooool": Entanglements of children, digital tools, and literacy practices. *TESOL Quarterly*, 49(3), 461–485. doi:10.1002/tesq.236.

4

LEKTA AND LITERACY IN EARLY CHILDHOOD EDUCATION

Entwinements of Idealism and Materialism

Liselott Mariett Olsson

FIGURE 4.1 Albert's "old" name
"A is wrinkled, wears glasses, and has not many teeth left. L is an old man with grey hair and moustache. B rides in a wheelchair and waves. E has got too many lines because he doesn't remember how many he is supposed to have … [*Albert takes a pause and laughs a lot*] He has got a bad memory and forgets things all the time! R is riding a skateboard. Old folks can do that as well – they are also supposed to have fun!"

Introduction: Too Many Lines on an Old E?

How are we to understand this name with too many lines on an old E? Within many practices and theories this gesture of putting too many lines on a letter is explained as the child not yet being intellectually mature enough to understand the representative logic of language. The child is said to be lacking in meta-linguistic competency and is therefore considered not yet capable of understanding language as a homogenous system of abstract and universal representations to be used in communication and in transmission of information. This image of the child and of language could be said to be reductive, in that it will not acknowledge that an E with too many lines is a correct linguistic expression of knowing how to read and write the abstract and universal E. Such reductionism often leads to children being exposed to all sorts of domesticating gestures within a "system of semiotic capitalism" as Guattari (2011) puts it, expressed in neglect of children's sense-making as well as in neglect of corporeal and extra-linguistic expressions (Deleuze & Guattari, 2004; Guattari, 2011; Olsson, Dahlberg, & Theorell, 2016; de Freitas & Curinga, 2015; Toohey, 2018; MacLure, 2013, 2016; MacLure, 2012).

Literacy in Early Childhood Education

This image of the child, of language and its consequences for pedagogical-didactical work is, however, not a given and has been continuously transformed throughout the history of early childhood education practice and research. An overview of the field of literacy shows that, initially, the youngest children in preschool were studied predominantly in terms of their linguistic development and in relation to different language disorders (Lancaster, 2003; Elkind, 1983; Olson & Gayan, 2001; Björklund, 2008). Apart from a few contributions (Söderberg, 1988; Clay, 1966), research clearly focused on children aged five to six, that is, children approaching school age. The development of the literacy field – with the study of younger children eventually admitted and included – has been marked by a continuous contest between two positions, famously titled the "Literacy Wars." These "wars" have played out at an ontological level in a debate between *realism* and *idealism*, at an epistemological level between individual psychology and social constructivism, and at a practical level between "phonics" and "whole language" approaches to language, reading, and writing (Roy, 2005). For instance, within the "phonics" approach, language is, from an ontological realist and epistemological individual psychology perspective, seen as a closed system with a given set of organizing rules that need to be imitated. From this perspective, pedagogical-didactical practice focuses on individual mastery of techniques and decoding of the linguistic rule system. The "whole language" approach, on the other hand, rejects this instrumental view and considers language to be a historically, culturally, and socially constructed system from an ontological idealist and epistemological social constructivist perspective. Here pedagogical-didactical practice focuses on the construction of meaning, always closely connected to and dependent upon the context. In recent years, the field has moved, to a larger extent but not without struggle, from a realist, individual psychology and phonics approach, to encompassing mainly the perspective of idealism, social constructivism, and the whole language approach. This is expressed, for instance, in the "emergent literacy" tradition, whereby young children's capacity to learn to read and write is re-evaluated, as well as by the "early childhood literacy" movement, in which it is argued that it is important to see young children's literacy for what it is here and now, and to pay attention to how the context is conditioning and influencing children's active learning and conquering of literacy. "Literacy" is also talked about in broader terms as encompassing other and extra-linguistic expressions such as, for instance, body language, signs, symbols, and images (Gillen & Hall, 2003; Kress, 1997; Björklund, 2008; Wohlwend, 2008).

Recently, the field of early childhood education has gained new theoretical influences from new materialist perspectives. The steadily growing scholarship inspired by these perspectives extends over a large number of disciplines, but a common thread is the rejection of ontologically reductive and oppositional thinking and practice expressed in binaries, such as the ones actualized in the above-mentioned "Literacy Wars." The rethinking and reworking of ontological foundations of such binaries ultimately aims not only to create a different image of thought, but also to open up possibilities to experiment with different ways of existing in the world. The raison d'être and the modus operandi of these perspectives, then, reside in two conditions: "first, an ethical imperative to rethink the nature of being to refuse the devastating dividing practices of the dogmatic Cartesian image of thought and, second, a heightened curiosity and accompanying experimentation in the becoming of existence" (St. Pierre et al., 2016, p. 99). An important part of these perspectives is the focus on the *material* aspects of being and existence.

These ideas are also evident within recent research efforts in the field of early childhood education and literacy. Here, new materialist perspectives have been used to address the ontology and epistemology of science and scientists themselves, thus highlighting the need to bring in questions about the material aspects of the research process and to reconsider the role of language in research (Lenz Taguchi, 2013; MacLure, 2013; MacLure, 2016; de Freitas & Curinga, 2015; St Pierre et al., 2016). More specifically, and in relation to early childhood literacy, new materialist perspectives have been added to sociocultural readings and analyses of second-language learning

(Toohey, 2018), where attention is paid, not only to how humans relate to language, but also to the "material entanglements of things, discourses and humans" (Toohey, 2018, p. 3). New materialist perspectives have also treated children's play as part of a widened conceptualization of literacy by considering it as intra-actively capable of relating being and knowing in playful encounters between language and matter (Gutshall Rucker & Kuby, this volume; Rautio and Winston, 2015). These perspectives have also been used to theorize play with analogue and digital activities in early childhood makerspaces as literacies that are both sense-making and sensory (Wohlwend et al., 2017), and they have been used to highlight material aspects of children's non-linguistic sound-making in relation to place in early childhood literacy (Gallagher et al., 2018).[1]

One could, then, understand these efforts as navigating the old distinction between realism and idealism in a new way. Through evoking new materialist perspectives, the distinction made between idealism and realism in the field of early childhood literacy has given place to a new ontological figuration whereby the coupled figure of *idealism – realism* has been replaced by *idealism – materialism* (St. Pierre et al., 2016). However, even though it is clear that this new configuration within the field is necessary – not least in relation to the above-mentioned neglect of children's corporeal and extra-linguistic expressions – language is tricky business, especially when we consider its ontological status and modus, namely how to place language in relation to the ontological traditions of idealism and materialism. Language is, of course, in the most fundamental way, material: it is "in and of the body" (MacLure, 2013, p. 663), but it is also ideal since it has the capacity to represent, to signify and to express: it is also a "cultural and symbolic resource" (MacLure, 2013, p. 664). Herein lies a tension: on the one hand, language seems to be *overestimated* – as the sole and ideal stratum capable of constituting the ground for harbouring and explaining all other strata. On the other hand, it seems to be *underestimated* – as it also contains un-representational elements such as non-sense words, that are not purely material, but that constitute the "rebel becomings" of language itself (MacLure, 2016). It seems, then, that questions of the status and modus of idealism and materialism in relation to language remain to be posed.

Delicate Navigating

One particularly important question evoked in the current situation is whether the focus on *materialism* – despite non-dualistic ambitions – risks neglecting its ontological companion *idealism* and what consequences this might have for pedagogical-didactical work with language, reading, and writing in early childhood education. In her latest book *The Incorporeal: Ontology, Ethics and the Limits of Materialism* (2017), feminist philosopher

Elizabeth Grosz evokes the first part of this question through stating the need for "a more complex, more wide-ranging understanding not only of materiality but of the framing conditions of materiality that cannot themselves be material" (p. 5). In other words, what Grosz insists upon is the avoidance of any kind of reductive materialism. In relation to early childhood literacy and education, this seems of utmost importance in order to avoid falling into yet another dualism, this time between idealism and materialism. As will be stated in this chapter, children seem to activate not only material but also ideal aspects of language. Children not only express themselves bodily and extra-linguistically, they *also* let language express, make sense, signify, and represent. They *also* use language as an ideational cultural and symbolic resource. Moreover – and as seen in the introductory vignette with Albert's "old name" – through "play" and "non-sensical" experimentation with words and letters, children seem particularly interested in exploring the "rebel becomings" (MacLure, 2016) of language itself.

As Grosz (2017) states below, the distinction between idealism and materialism can be traced throughout the history of Western philosophy. It is one of the most frequently addressed ontological questions that, recently, through the rise of materialist perspectives, truly has become *the* question: "Today just about everyone is a materialist … it is almost impossible to find an explicit and credible contemporary advocate of idealism. Idealism at best lurks unknowingly within avowedly materialist texts" (p. 17). Even though Grosz (2017) recognizes the importance of and shares the endeavours of materialist perspectives, she calls for another relationship between idealism and materialism, and she asks questions about what might have become a reductive materialist perspective:

> How for example, do materialists consider concepts, thoughts, ideas? … How do materialists understand meaning or sense in terms beyond their materiality as sonorous or written trace? How can sense, in both its senses, as meaning and as orientation, be possible without some direction in matter itself?
>
> *(p. 17)*

These questions are of importance, not only at an ontological level, but also (and without necessarily constituting these as classical epistemological questions), in terms of the consequences they might have for early childhood education and literacy. If accepting that the fundamental idea of education is to give the new generation space and time to study and transform culture, values, and knowledge (and that this inevitably entails the creation of sense of/in the world through language in one form or another), Grosz's (2017) statement that "the increasing emphasis on an ever more open materiality must address what this entails for ideality – for ideas, concepts, for space and time, for language and its capacities to represent, signify and express" (p. 262) makes it necessary to acknowledge how children make sense in – and of – language both materially *and* ideally.

It is of utmost importance to navigate delicately here. Of course (as the history of the field of early childhood literacy tells us), it is exactly the material aspects of language that are often omitted from consideration in accounts of language learning and language using (de Freitas & Curinga, 2015; MacLure, 2013; MacLure et al., 2012; Toohey, 2018). Still, at this very moment, we might benefit from trying to *also* explore the richness of language as an ideational resource – a task that demands yet more delicate navigating. In the above-mentioned book, Grosz (2017) proceeds with such navigating through evoking the need for an "entwinement between idealism and materialism" (p. 13) and through a close reading of the Stoics and their notion of *Lekta* ("sayables"). This seems to be a promising entry point for further questions about the status and modus of sense and materiality in language in education, as the Stoic notion of *Lekta* "address[es] not only what is part of language, meaning or sense but also parts of the world, whose sense they render articulable in language" (Grosz, 2017, p. 38). This intriguing statement points towards the need for a different conceptualization, not only of ontological notions of materialism and idealism, but also of materiality and sense in language within educational practice and theory. It is this that will be further explored in what follows.

The Stoics

Stoicism emerged in Ancient Greece in the fourth century BCE as one of several philosophical schools, with philosophers such as Zeno of Citium (*c.* 334 – *c.* 262 BCE), Cleanthes of Assos (*c.* 330 – *c.* 230 BCE), Chrisyppus (*c.* 279 – *c.* 206 BCE), and later within Roman Stoicism, with philosophers such as Epictetus (*c.* 55 – *c.* 135 CE) and Marcus Aurelius (121–180 CE). According to Grosz (2017), even though very few writings remain and we cannot be sure that the various interpretations are reflective of this philosophical school, there is still something of great value and interest in the Stoic worldview. The Stoics presented us with a view of the relationship between idealism and materialism that is different from the dualistic one, which was put forward by later philosophers such as René Descartes (1596–1650), Immanuel Kant (1724–1804), and Friedrich Hegel (1770–1831). The Stoic view is one that, throughout history, has inspired philosophers who chose a non-dualistic path into this problematic, such as Baruch de Spinoza (1632–1677), Friedrich Nietzsche (1844–1900), Henri Bergson (1859–1941), Michel Foucault (1926–1984), Gilles Deleuze (1925–1995), Jacques Derrida (1930–2004), and Luce Irigaray (1930). All these scholars' attempts at non-dualism are helpful in creating an *amalgamated figure* [2] of materialism and idealism.

As Grosz (2017) suggests, the Stoics could be considered "the first thoroughgoing materialists" (p. 23). Their whole universe is composed of bodies that affect each other, and they resist, according to Grosz (2017), any kind of abstract universalization – that is, any kind of idealist and generalist classifications – to the point that, for the Stoics, "Universals are errors in reasoning" (p. 27). The Stoics' philosophy is more about living well than about rational reflection, and should, so to speak, be grounded on the Earth: the philosopher's real task is to develop knowledge about how to live well. The Stoic universe is composed of bodies, and these are not separated from ideas – to the point that for the Stoics "ideas are themselves bodies" (Grosz, 2017, p. 25).[3] However, the Stoic view is, as Grosz (2017) states, "a peculiar materialism" (p. 23), whereby not only material bodies, but also the very conditions of their existence – the framing – are highlighted. Grosz (2017) claims that any non-reductive materialism "requires a frame, a non-material localization, a becoming-space and time, that cannot exist in the same way and with the same form as the objects or things that they frame" (p. 28). She further adds that "[e]very materialism, whether this is acknowledged openly or not, requires an incorporeal frame" (p. 28). It is exactly the *incorporeal* within the Stoic worldview that is the condition for the existence of material bodies. There are four incorporeals in the Stoic universe: *void, space, time*, and *Lekta* and they are "the modes of presentation of objects, the conditions under which things exist, extend themselves, live in time and come to produce effects or sense" (Grosz, 2017, p. 32).

Lekta: The Ongoing Possibility of Sense

Lekta – sayables – are of particular interest to our discussion here, as they concern "conditions for the possible and actual existence of bodies to come to mean something, without these transformations being in any way corporeal themselves" (Grosz, 2017, p. 32).[4] *Lekta* have a particular status and modus, because despite the fact that they can be articulated in speech and are often considered to have a psychological character they should be understood as subsisting "outside human consciousness and independent of reflection and awareness" (Grosz, 2017, p. 38). *Lekta*, then, "can more consistently be regarded as a sense that adheres to bodies and their mixtures that minds are capable of comprehending and words are capable of articulating … they are the ongoing possibility of sense" (Grosz, 2017, p. 38). Perhaps, then, this could be understood as that which children activate in their "play" and "non-sensical" use of language: the ongoing possibility of sense. When children write too many lines on an old E, when they exchange the first letter in a name, when they rhyme and sing, when they invent alphabets never seen before, it is possible that they articulate (in often confusing ways to us adults) the sense that adheres to the material bodies (organic and inorganic) in any given situation.

That *Lekta* are sayables implies that they "articulate states of affairs, that is, what happens to a body" (Grosz, 2017, p. 38). Although sayables, a bit paradoxically[5], but importantly, do not entirely belong to language and linguistic propositions either, they are rather "an extradimension of the proposition, the sayable of an utterance, not the material of its saying" (Grosz, 2017, p. 42). Language must, then, be understood as tending towards materiality and ideality in two different ways:

> Language becomes oriented in two directions incapable of reconciliation, material and incorporeal. Language, as utterance, is material, and every statement it makes possible is material. Written traces, articulated breath, neurological connections, sign languages, computer screens are all material means by which language expresses. ... What language (rather than refers to, denotes, or designates, which is itself material) *expresses* is incorporeal, a process, an event, a change of state, a modification, something that adheres to or floats on the surface without penetrating the identity and the continuity of the body, a "thin film at the limit of things and words" (*LS* 31). This almost imperceptible layer is the condition of language and its capacity to represent what happens or what could happen.
>
> *(Grosz, 2017, p. 39, emphasis in the original)*

Production of Sense, Problems, and Solutions

The above-cited rich quote needs unpacking. It seems clearer now that language is of both material and ideal character: it is – in the act of expressing – in and of the (material) body, but it is also capable of inventing and stating (ideal) propositions that express the sense of events. Furthermore, that which is expressed by language must be added to the designation, denotation, and signification of the material. Grosz (2017) refers above to Deleuze and his way of describing the expressed of language as a "thin film at the limit of things and words" (p. 39). This thin film is further described as the necessary addition of sense to designation, denotation, and signification, as these are all used to claim the truth or falsity of a proposition, and none of them is capable of keeping events open-ended and in process.[6] Therefore, the introduction of sense is a way of escaping such claims, as sense in this context is considered to be continuously *produced*: "It is thus pleasing that there resounds today the news that sense is never a principle or an origin, but that it is produced" (Deleuze, 2004, p. 83). This is also where this notion of sense becomes extra interesting for education, as it also connects to the status and modus of problems and solutions and questions and answers. In *The Logic of Sense*, Deleuze (2004) presents a somewhat "reversed formula" for the relationship between problems, questions, solutions, and answers – whereby solutions and answers get their "deserved truth" in a proportional relation to the sense-production at stake in the very act of constructing a problem and formulating a question. For education, and especially early childhood education, this reversed formula makes it possible to pay attention to, analyse, and value young children's constructions of problems and formulations of questions in relation to the sense-production at stake rather than judging children's solutions and answers as true or false in relation to already-set sense and pre-established relations between problems, solutions, questions, and answers (which is really what school and preschool far too often is all about…). For instance, and as seen in the introductory vignette, rather than understanding too many lines on an E as an incorrect and "untrue" solution, it must be taken into account that here we are dealing with an "old E." We are dealing with an old E that forgets things all the time – including how many lines it is supposed to have, as Albert says. Albert's solution of how to write an E is not erroneous or "untrue," but stands in a proportional relation to the sense he produces of how to write an old name and an old E.

Lekta in Early Childhood Education

Elsewhere, we have described at length how the perspectives presented above might be used in early childhood education, both at a general pedagogical-didactical level (Olsson, 2009) and, more specifically, in relation to children's creation of sense in language, reading, and writing (Olsson, 2010, 2012, 2013; Olsson & Theorell, 2014; Olsson et al., 2016). We have shown how young children engage and seem interested in creating and constructing problems and questions in a proportional relationship to the sense that is produced – rather than reproducing given answers and solutions. We have shown how this is expressed in the way in which children "play" with language through reinventing it over and over again. We have reported on Deleuze's writings on the relation of sense and nonsense, whereby sense is always and continuously produced through nonsense, and we have connected this to children's above-mentioned play with language. Our research contrasts with the historical ontological configuration in the field of early childhood literacy. Realist, individual psychology and phonics approaches to literacy, but also idealist, social constructivist and whole language approaches often consider language as a set-up of mediating representations that children need to learn before entering and mastering language, reading, and writing. Our research shows that, when bringing in theoretical tools that are capable of delicately navigating between realist and idealist conceptions of language, interesting things happen. This is how we can get hold of how very young children already work with mediating representations, although in different ways from the fixed representations of adults. Children, if not "tamed" into "severe" and "closed" practices and representations, seem to be able to work with the *production* of mediating representations, rather than the *acquisition* of already set ones. Our studies have added to the field of early childhood literacy the idea that language is inherently creative and pragmatic, and that acquisition needs to be complemented by the notion of a continuous production of sense. For instance, the example illustrated in the introduction to this chapter (see Figure 4.1) when Albert puts too many lines on the letter E, has been analysed with a focus on how sense is produced in a proportional relation to how Albert constructs the problem of an "old name."

Our analysis described how Albert, with this old name – rather than being intellectually immature and incapable of understanding the representative logic of language – *chose* to put too many lines with intention, and, moreover, with a great deal of humour: an old E obviously forgets things all the time, including how many lines it has. This was analysed as an example of how sense is continuously produced and especially produced from nonsense, giving not an erroneous solution, but a solution that stands in a proportional relation to the sense of an *old* name.

Albert wrote this name within the research project *The Magic of Language* (funded by the Swedish Research Council from 2010 to 2012) where children, teachers, and researchers engaged in a study of how to read and write names over a period of one year in a class of 25 five-year-olds. The study entailed a long period of observations, where teachers and researchers discovered that alphabetical signs were most frequently produced when the children wrote their own names, or the names of their friends and families. However, teachers and researchers also discovered that not all the children participated in this activity, and that the children who did not participate said they did not know how to read and write. A choice was made – departing from what was considered as children's more unconventional writings of names – to invite the writing and reading of names "never seen before." This created an "explosion" of name-making – angry names, quarrelling and emotively transforming names, and also allowed us to study how the mouth transforms in accordance with what one says (as expressed in Figures 4.5 and 4.6 below). Here children carefully observed each other's mouths as they were speaking and made drawings of each other's mouths. During this project children, encouraged by teachers and researchers, engaged in a process whereby many different linguistic signs and material events could unfold.

In the final analysis of the project, we concluded that Albert and his friends seemed to be neither over- nor underestimating language, and that they "hang language up in Life, as part of Life" (Olsson, 2012, p. 105).

FIGURE 4.2 Märta
"I get so angry so I am on fire. It is fire up there at each letter."

Events that for them were important – such as losing one's teeth, conflicts between friends, activities they liked and disliked – were continuously brought into the reading and writing of names.

From the point of view of the "entwinement between idealism and materialism" (Grosz, 2017) evoked here, it might be possible, then, to add something to the analysis performed earlier focusing on children's sense-production and constructions of the problem of reading and writing names. From the point of view of the theoretical inspirations in this chapter, it may be suggested that what is at stake in children's reading and writing of names is an activation of *both* ideal *and* material aspects of language and events in the continuous production of sense. It is as if the children, with their reading and writing of names, evoke and produce sense, not in the material events as *they are*, and not in ideal language as *it is*, but through seizing the opportunity that is opened in this situation where neither bodies and what happens to them, nor names and letters, are already defined. It is as if they are seizing, or rather, as if they become caught up in an incorporeal dimension – *Lekta* – that surrounds both events and language, whereby sense is continuously produced, and whereby both words/letters and things/bodies *transform*. Here, alphabetical letters, words, and names become inhabited and *transformed* by material bodies, things, and events, which in turn become possible to represent and *transform* through alphabetical letters, words, and names. It becomes possible to collectively study and transform the sense that inheres in important events for children through the simultaneous study and transformation of the sense that subsists in language. Through "hang[ing] up [letters] in Life" (Olsson, 2012), the children seem

Lekta and Literacy in Early Childhood Education 83

FIGURE 4.3 Presley
"Sometimes there's a real quarrel and not only a little mischief, it depends on who is part of it. If somebody hits too hard there's quarrel. P is running after R, they both want to so that's just a little mischief. S is cheating, he is fighting, you must not fight with two people at the same time because you will not see if your friend is alright."

FIGURE 4.4 Hannah
"I have written hard because I am angry. And red because it gets red when you are angry. And you also forget to do all the letters. But the angry has passed now so I have written green Hannah twice and I have drawn some hearts as well."

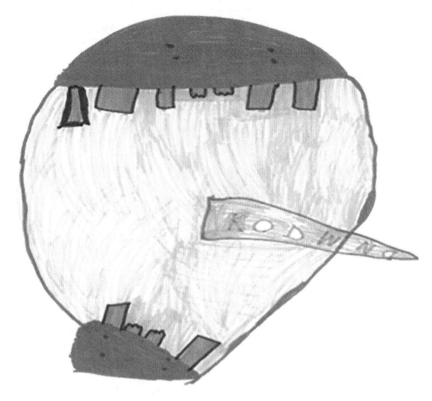

FIGURE 4.5 Denise
"I've made a "friends-mouth". It says nice things and asks if the friend wants to play" [observe the lost teeth].

caught up in intense sense-production whereby the sense of bodies, things, events, alphabetical letters, words, and names is expressed, linked, and transformed.

> Language, both material and incorporeal ... enables the sense that inheres in events to be the object of conscious and collective contemplation and engagement, linking human minds to the world, but also the world to the possibility and actuality of events that may in turn transform bodies.
>
> *(Grosz, 2017, p. 43)*

Entwinements of Idealism and Materialism

With the awareness that we always run the risk of putting our theoretical aspirations *onto* children (Olsson et al., 2016; MacLure, 2016), it still seems

Lekta and Literacy in Early Childhood Education 85

FIGURE 4.6 Denise
"This is a shouting mouth, you see the yucky thing in the throat. It looks angry and uses a bad language. He hasn't lost any teeth yet."

important to highlight at least the possibility of addressing questions of language and literacy in early childhood education through the perspective of an "entwinement of idealism and materialism" (Grosz, 2017). It would be unfortunate if the field of early childhood literacy took a leap into yet another dualism – this time between idealism and materialism. What might get lost in such a reiterated move is, not only ontological complexity, but also attention to how children creatively and in a subtle way make sense of and in language and events – both ideally and materially – through the very "thin film at the limit of things and words" (Grosz, 2017, quoting Deleuze). If we follow the theoretical resources deployed in this chapter, it is through this thin film that *Lekta* and the very production of sense occurs – and it is here that the most fundamental question of education becomes actualized: how to give time and space to the new generation so that they can study, but also *transform* culture, knowledge, and values (Masschelein & Simons, 2013). Throughout this chapter, realist, idealist, and materialist conceptions of language and how these may play out in early childhood literacy have been evoked. It seems now that we need to continue to refine our theoretical and practical tools for working with language and literacy in early

86 Liselott Mariett Olsson

FIGURE 4.7 Kelly
"K says: but what about L and E [observe that in the balloon there is an attempt to construct this sentence in Swedish: 'men E och L då?'] E and L have nothing to do so they think about what they want to do [observe the corresponding images in the balloons where E and L are illustrated with a puzzle in between them]. E thinks that it wants to do a puzzle [observe the happy mouth on E also in the balloon]. But L doesn't like to do puzzles so it's not going to do that" [observe the sad mouth on the L also in the balloon].

childhood education. Education and these tools must become much more finely tuned. Possibly, the Stoic notion of *Lekta* that "address[es] not only what is part of language, meaning or sense but also parts of the world, whose sense they render articulable in language" (Grosz, 2017, p. 38) can be of help here. Grosz's (2017) statement remains intriguing, and this chapter has not come remotely close to clarifying it in any complete way. However, some practical and theoretical resources have been presented that might be fruitful to consider in future work within early childhood literacy. Such work might want to pay particular attention to the fact that *Lekta* does not only belong to written language, meaning, or sense, as it is "an extra-sense of the world that must be added to materiality to enable it to be spoken" (Grosz, 2017, p. 40). We might, then, need to take into account other expressions – aesthetical, ethical, and political (Olsson, forthcoming). We might also need to resist all kinds of permanent "doing away" with any of the ontological directions – idealism, materialism, *or* realism – that are and have been of importance, not only in the history of philosophy, but also in the field of early childhood education and literacy, as well as in a local and global political context. In a time when both the materiality and the sense of and in education seem reduced to "abstract formalism" (Løvlie, 2007) and when what is "real" is continuously contested – not the least within populist and historical revisionist movements and forces – it seems important not to forget that "ideality and materiality are not two substances but two ways in which the *real* is distributed" as Grosz (2017) points out (p. 251).

Acknowledgements

The research presented in this chapter was conducted in close cooperation with a number of important people: children, teachers, and head-teachers in preschools, my artistic adviser Ebba Theorell, and last but not least Professor Gunilla Dahlberg, with whom I analysed and articulated the historical ontological figuration of realism-idealism in the field of early childhood literacy. Some of the text in this chapter (see the sections on Literacy in Early Childhood Education and *Lekta* in Early Childhood Education) was originally written in close cooperation with Professor Dahlberg as part of our application for funding from the Swedish Scientific Research Council. However, that text has been altered and adapted to the context of this chapter, but it is still important to acknowledge this cooperation.

Notes

1 See Eriksson & Sand (2017) for an account of how voice – through place-based theories and methodologies from the field of artistic research – might be theoretically conceptualized and didactically practised with toddlers in public spaces. See also Bylund-Martin (2017) for an account of bilingualism through the use of a material-semiotic perspective inspired by French philosopher Gilles Deleuze and French psychotherapist Félix Guattari. See too Masny & Cole's (2009) introduction of "multiple literacies theories," largely inspired by the same philosophers.
2 I particularly enjoy Elizabeth Grosz's (2017) statement that "Deleuze can neither be classified as a materialist nor as an idealist" (p. 9). I believe that it would be a mistake to attempt such a classification since it would undermine the entire project: to reformulate *exactly* this relationship between materialism and idealism in contrast to how it has been formulated throughout the history of Western philosophy. *Amalgamated figure* is my temporary and incomplete term for this inseparable woven-togetherness that indicates not a relationship between two separate substances, but rather the ontology of the relationship itself (see Olsson, forthcoming).
3 I am painfully aware that this account of the Stoics' philosophy is utterly incomplete. I mention nothing here about active-passive bodies, cause-effects or *pneuma* – the original material and active force – nor the ethical aspects of the Stoics' philosophy, that Grosz (2017) uses in her attempt to develop an *ontoethics*. For the present task, I cannot – due to frames of time and focus – go into these. I have tried to account for

as much as required with respect to the context of the task. In an upcoming book, this account of the Stoics will be developed (see Olsson, forthcoming).
4 In this account of *Lekta* I am staying particularly close to Grosz's account of it. It is necessary for me to do so, as I am not an educated philosopher, and I therefore need the support of a large number of quotations in order to be able to give as correct an account as possible, while also connecting this to my own discipline of pedagogy (for more accounts on the relation between philosophy and pedagogy, see Houssaye, 2002 and Olsson, forthcoming).
5 The paradox is of importance in *The Logic of Sense* (Deleuze, 2004) both in reference to the Stoics and to Lewis Carroll's works.
6 Elsewhere I have showed this often works in scientific studies and methods, whereby these functions often imply that we *comment* upon events (designation), *interpret* (denotation or manifestation), and/or *critically reflect* (signification) upon events (Olsson, 2009).

References

Björklund, E. (2008). Att erövra litteracitet: Små barns kommunikativa möten med berättande, bilder, text och tecken i förskolan. Unpublished doctoral dissertation. University of Gothenburg.

Bylund-Martin, A. (2017). Towards a minor bilingualism: Exploring variations of language and literacy in early childhood education. Unpublished doctoral dissertation. Linköping University.

Clay, M. (1966). Emergent reading behaviour. Unpublished doctoral dissertation. Auckland University.

de Freitas, E., & Curinga, M. X. (2015). New materialist approaches to the study of language and identity: Assembling the posthuman subject. *Curriculum Inquiry*, 45 (3), 249–265. doi:10.1080/03626784.2015.1031059.

Deleuze, G. (2004). *The logic of sense*. New York: Continuum.

Deleuze, G., & Guattari, F. (2004). *A thousand plateaus: Capitalism and schizophrenia*. New York: Continuum.

Elkind, D. (1983). *Barn och unga i Piagets psykologi*. Stockholm: Natur och Kultur.

Eriksson, C., & Sand, M. (2017). Placing voice meetings through vocal strolls: Toddlers in resonance with public space. *SoundEffects*, 7(2), 64–78. doi:10.7146/se.v7i2.102927.

Gallagher, M., Hackett, A., Procter, L., & Scott, F. (2018). Vibrations in place: Sound and language in early childhood literacy practices. *Educational Studies*, 54 (4), 465–482. doi:10.1080/00131946.2018.1476353.

Gillen, J., & Hall, N. (2003). The emergence of early childhood literacy. In J. Marsh, J. Larson, & N. Hall (Eds.), *The SAGE handbook of early childhood literacy* (pp. 3–17). London: Sage Publications.

Grosz, E. (2017). *The incorporeal: Ontology, ethics and the limits of materialism*. New York: Columbia University Press.

Guattari, F. (2011). *The machinic unconscious: Essays in schizoanalysis*. (T. Adkins, Trans.) Los Angeles, CA: Semiotext(e).

Gutshall Rucker, T. & Kuby, C. (2020). Making and unmaking literacy desirings: Pedagogical matters of concern from writers' studio. In K. Toohey, S. Smythe, D. Dagenais, & M. Forte (Co-eds.), *Transforming language and literacy education*. London: Routledge.

Houssaye, J. (2002). (Ed.). *Premiers pédagogues: de l'Antiquité à la Renaissance*. Paris: ESF éditeur.
Kress, G. (1997). *Before writing: Rethinking the paths to literacy*. London: Routledge.
Lancaster, L. (2003). Moving into literacy. How it all begins. In J. Marsh, J. Larson & N. Hall (Eds.), *The SAGE handbook of early childhood literacy* (pp. 313–328). London: Sage Publications.
Lenz Taguchi, H. (2013). Images of thinking in feminist materialisms: Ontological divergences and the production of researcher subjectivities. *International Journal of Qualitative Studies in Education*, 26(6), 706–716. doi:10.1080/09518398.2013.788759.
Løvlie, L. (2007). The pedagogy of place. *Nordisk Pedagogik*, 27(1), 32–36. Retrieved May 16, 2019, from www.idunn.no/np/2007/01/the_pedagogy_ofplace?languageId=2.
MacLure, M. (2013). Researching without representation? Language and materiality in post-qualitative methodology. *International Journal of Qualitative Studies in Education* 26(6), 658–667. doi:10.1080/09518398.2013.788755.
MacLure, M. (2016). The refrain of the a-grammatical child: Finding another language in/for qualitative research. *Cultural Studies ←→ Critical Methodologies*, 16(2), 99–110. doi:10.1177/1532708616639333.
MacLure, M., Jones, L., Holmes, R., & MacRae, C. (2012). Becoming a problem: Behaviour and reputation in the early years classroom. *British Educational Research Journal*, 38(3), 447–471. doi:10.1080/01411926.2011.552709.
Masschelein, J., & Simons, M. (2013). *In defence of the school: A public issue*. Leuven: Culture and Society Publishers.
Masny, D., & Cole, D. R. (2009). *Multiple literacies theory*. Rotterdam: SensePublishers.
Olsson, L. M. (2009). *Movement and experimentation in young children's learning: Deleuze and Guattari in early childhood education*. London: Routledge.
Olsson, L. M. (2010). Using material molecular politics in early childhood education. In G. S. Cannella & L. Diaz Soto (Eds.), *Childhoods: A handbook* (pp. 345–354). New York: Peter Lang.
Olsson, L. M. (2012). Eventicizing curriculum: Learning to read and write through becoming a citizen of the world. *Journal of Curriculum Theorizing*, 28(1), 88–107. Retrieved May 16, 2019, from http://journal.jctonline.org/index.php/jct/article/view/173/08olsson.pdf.
Olsson, L. M. (2013). Taking children's questions seriously: The need for creative thought. *Global Studies of Childhood*, 4(2), 230–253. doi:10.2304/gsch.2013.3.3.230.
Olsson, L. M. (forthcoming). *Becoming-pedagogue: Aesthetics, ethics and politics in early childhood education*. London: Routledge.
Olson, R. K., & Gayan, J. (2001). Brains, genes, and environment in reading development. In S. B. Neuman & D. K. Dickinson (Eds.), *Handbook of early literacy research* (pp. 81–94). New York: Guilford Press.
Olsson, L. M., & Theorell, E. (2014). Affective/effective reading and writing through real virtualities in digitized society. In M. N. Bloch, B. Swadener, & G. S. Cannella (Eds.), *Reconceptualizing early childhood care and education: Critical questions, new imaginaries and social activism: A reader* (pp. 215–234). Oxford: Peter Lang.
Olsson, L. M., Dahlberg, G., & Theorell, E. (2016). Displacing identity – placing aesthetics: Early childhood literacy in a globalized world. *Discourse: Studies in the Cultural Politics of Education*, 37(5), 717–738. doi:10.1080/01596306.2015.1075711.

Rautio, P., & Winston, J. (2015). Things and children in play: Improvisation with language and matter. *Discourse: Studies in the Cultural Politics of Education*, 36 (1), 15–26. doi:10.1080/01596306.2013.830806.

Roy, K. (2005). On sense and nonsense: Looking beyond the literacy wars. *Journal of Philosophy of Education*, 39(1), 99–111. doi:10.1111/j.0309-8249.2005.00422.x.

St. Pierre A. E., Jackson, Y. A., & Mazzei, A. L. (2016). New empiricisms and new materialisms: Conditions for new inquiry. *Cultural Studies ⟷ Critical Methodologies*, 16(2), 99–110. doi:10.1177/1532708616638694.

Söderberg, R. (1988). *Barnets tidiga språkutveckling*. Lund: Liber.

Toohey, K. (2018). *Learning English at School: Identity, Socio-Material Relations and Classroom Practice* (2nd ed.). Bristol: Multilingual Matters.

Wohlwend, K. (2008). Play as a literacy of possibilities: Expanding meanings in practices, materials, and spaces. *Language Arts*, 86(2), 127–136. Retrieved May 16, 2019, from www.ncte.org/journals/la/issues/v86-2.

Wohlwend, K. E., Peppler, K. A., Keune, A., & Thompson, N. (2017). Making sense and nonsense: Comparing mediated discourse and agential realist approaches to materiality in a preschool makerspace. *Journal of Early Childhood Literacy*, 17(3), 444–462. doi:10.1177/1468798417712066.

5
RETHINKING CAUSALITY THROUGH CHILDREN'S LITERACIES

Jacqueline Barreiro

In this chapter, I share a literacy-related story from a rural school in the Ecuadorian Andes. The story takes place in Highland School,[1] in a first-grade classroom where six-year-old Mauricito has a singular encounter with the letter "s." This is a story that, in its writing, entangles theory and memory. In the story, I bring together the concepts of affect and intra-action to trouble traditional conceptions of causality in literacy research and pedagogy that takes causality to be the relationship between *distinct* sequential events (Barad, 2007) that are constructed as causes and effects. Educators and researchers have long searched for the causes of children's and adults' struggles with literacy. Often this work relies on a linear view of cause-effect that leads to literacy "remedies" or preventions (Heath, 2010), which do not always result in expected improvements (e.g. Neuman, 2017). For example, an understanding of the causal relationship between low socio-economic status (SES) and academic achievement (Berkowitz et al., 2017) has led some educators and schools to pressurize and even to assign responsibility or blame to families from low SES backgrounds for not adequately preparing or supporting their children throughout schooling (Heath, 2010). However, the particular literacy experiences of children from low SES backgrounds in Highland School that are at the heart of this story lead me to wonder how a different understanding of causality might disrupt narratives of lack, deficit, and underperformance expectations.

Drawing upon Barad (2007), I propose *causal relationality* as a more complex but productive mode of thinking and doing literacy. Barad rethinks causality, not as a chain of events between distinct elements where one is taken to "be the cause of the effect left on the other" (Barad, 2007, p. 175), but rather as the intimate or intra-active continuous (re)configuring of the world. Central to Barad's causal relationality is "intra-action" which "*signifies the mutual constitution of entangled agencies*" (Barad, 2007, p. 33, emphasis in the original). This is distinct from *interaction*, which assumes distinct a priori boundaries and properties between agencies (Barad, 2007). In intra-action, subjects and objects, such as literacy, texts, bodies, and time are not separate ontological units acting one upon the other, as in a linear understanding of cause-effect relations, but rather these agencies are entangled and emerge together to produce events.

Another concept grounded in a relational causal structure is that of affect. Following Spinoza, Deleuze (1988) describes affect as the capacity of bodies to affect and be affected, and also as the passage of affect from one body to another. This understanding of affect also becomes vital in reconfiguring causality. Affect refers to those intensities and forces that bodies undergo as they encounter each other, and also to the passage or flow of those forces (Seigworth and Gregg, 2010). These forces, running through bodies, have their own rhythms; they can be forceful, gentle, subtle, and mostly imperceptible. According to Spinoza's (1949) concepts of affect that I draw upon in this chapter, affect is pre-conscious. It happens. The capacity of bodies of all sorts (Deleuze, 1988) to affect and be affected is vital to a theory of posthumanism, becoming, and change. Bodies are in continuous connection as capacities to affect and be affected, and, in so doing, take up or lay down rhythms (Deleuze, 1988). This also means that bodies are never a finished affair but are always in the process of becoming in affective flows.

Understanding affect as the capacity of bodies to affect and be affected helps us to rethink causality "in terms of intra-activity" (Barad, 2007, p. 393), because in order for bodies to exchange affect, they have to connect. In this sense, in Barad's relational causality, cause *and* effect emerge simultaneously in the intimate affective relationality of intra-activity. In other words, due to the intra-active work of affect, it is not possible to affect a body without simultaneously being affected by that body, and so on with all other bodies ad infinitum (Spinoza, 1949). If, for example, we think of pencils, we know that the child-pencil phenomenon is not the same as the child-iPad phenomenon. Different children and different iPads, pencils, emerge from each event, perhaps slowly and imperceptibly, but changing nevertheless. The pencil affects the child differently than does the iPad, because the histories and relations of the pencil and the iPad are different. They are enrolled in different assemblages. This can be understood as "*the mutual constitution of entangled agencies*" (Barad, 2007, p. 33, emphasis in the original), namely intra-action. It is in this way that the world or worldings emerge, including those of literacy practices.

In this chapter, I interweave the concepts of affect, intra-action, and causality through *storytelling with theory*. Storytelling with theory is the name I chose for an inquiry approach that emerged when writing stories about my educational practice as teacher and principal and my readings of posthumanist theory engaged with one another through embodied memory (Barad, 2007). Embodied memory does not faithfully represent the past in the present, but allows the continuous "openness of the narrative to future retellings" (Barad, as interviewed in Juelskjær & Schwennesen, 2012, p. 11). Remembering, for Braidotti (2013), is a creative reworking of both imagination and chronologically previous experiences. In accounting for the affective impact of remembering, the focus of loyalty, according to Braidotti (2013), shifts from replication to what a text can do, has done, and how it has had an impact on one and on others through the affective forces it engages. In this sense, memory is a relational event that enfolds the past, present, and future. Thus, a story is not simply the retelling of a past event, but also an opening to the future. The story I tell in this chapter resonated with me and called out to me (MacLure, 2013) in a way that led me to think literacy differently through theory.

In order to sharpen the focus of this literacy event, recounted below though the lens of storytelling with theory, it is important to situate the literacy practices of the families living in rural areas in the high Andes of Ecuador and the public schooling available to their children. Although this community has access to education, it might be making very little difference to the lives of the children. We must thus ask what counts as education, and what it means to participate in education. Below, I describe the Highland community in terms of its literacy rhythms and causal relations.

Literacy Rhythms in Children's Families

The children who attended Highland School came from families identifying themselves as *mestizos*,[2] whose main language of communication is Spanish, although it is a variation of Spanish with Quichua[3] influences. In most households, a grandparent still speaks this Indigenous language, and while some of the children understand some Quichua or know a few words, they have been made to feel ashamed to use it. This speaks to the ongoing work of colonialism that is part of the assemblages of these children and their parents' daily lives from which they emerge as outsiders, and thus are "seen to fall short of the standards of the dominant group" (de Finney et al., 2011, p. 362). The variety of Spanish that these children speak, their Quichua-derived last names, and their shared physical traits, all place them in a colonial category of mestizo. Although this group does not constitute a numerical minority in Ecuador, mestizos have been "minoritized" (de Finney et al., 2011) and are commonly regarded as less intelligent and less capable than the mainstream population. Localized in a lower socio-economical class (McLaren, 2009), mestizo communities have been consistently abused and oppressed by landowners and others who hold more powerful positions on the racial-social scale. Historically, the type and quality of education available to children in mestizo communities has ensured that social inequities are perpetuated (OECD, 2018; Torrecilla & Carrasco, 2011).

Families sent their children to Highland School because they understand the value of a formal education, and parents have typically suffered from a lack of educational resources and experiences in their own lives. Although Ecuador has made steady increases in its funding and investment in education, for example, by building 65 modern *Unidades Educativas del Milenio* (millennial elementary and secondary schools) between 2009 and 2017 (Redaccion Plan V, 2017),[4] the country's public education system, especially in rural areas, has remained dramatically underfunded since its inception. The uninviting tin roof, cement floor, and dirt patio are, sadly, still the norm for many elementary schools in rural communities. Besides the inadequate infrastructure, rural schools also lack learning materials, internet access and, more significantly, books.[5]

Access to secondary school in Ecuador is still only available in larger urban centres; consequently, most parents in rural mestizo communities have not completed high school. This means that children have had few models of extended engagement with complex texts and opportunities for practice that are associated with fluent school literacy skills (Ewing, 2018; Kalman & Street, 2013). Maintaining and enhancing their literacy skills was hard work for the Highland School community and others like it. It is a 2.5-kilometre walk from the Pan-American Highway, and another 30-minute bus ride to town, in order to get to a library with limited and dated resources. Few printed texts make their way into homes. In a similar socioeconomic context, Kalman's (2004) study on the access to written culture in a group of women from the Mixquic, a rural and agriculture-based community in Mexico, identified that, among the print materials available in the 49 households involved in his study, the most common reading material in 98 percent of homes were saint cards.[6] Kalman (2004) also found that 77 percent of families kept and consulted the free elementary school textbooks provided by the government. These findings are very similar among rural agriculture-based communities in Latin America (Kalman & Street, 2013), and resonate with the practices of the Highland School community where the story of this chapter takes place. Thus, families have little opportunity to engage with reading and writing activities (understood in the traditional definition of foundational and discrete sets of literacy skills), flowing from a racialized class system that has diminished access to the "social conditions necessary for literacy learning" (Kalman & Street, 2013, p. 7), including to the materialities of literacy such as printed texts, libraries, post offices, newsstands, the internet, and digital devices.

Although there are many other forms of learning underway in the community, engagement with printed texts is not typically part of family life, which in turn influences the way children are prepared for and supported through schooling (Heath, 1982; Prendergast & MacPhee, 2018), as well as how these children are positioned as "less than" in mainstream schooling practices. The children, like Mauricito, who is described later on in this chapter, came from families subscribing to the philosophy captured in the well-known Spanish saying *"la letra con sangre entra"* (or translated verbatim, "the letter enters with blood"). Thus, many children came to school with ideas of how difficult it is to read and write, and how hard it is to learn. There are colonial overtones that come with this belief, especially when we remember that the first encounter in *c.* 1532 between the Inca and the written word was a Bible. History tells us that a priest presents the Inca Atahualpa, the Emperor, with a Bible, which he refuses to accept and finally throws to the ground, providing the justification for his capture, and later, his death. Although there are differences in the ways this story is narrated, historians usually stress that this defiant act was used to justify the Spaniards' violent massacre of the Incas. For about three centuries afterwards, literacy instruction was provided to the Indigenous population by Catholic priests as an act of charity, rather than as a right to education, and, as such, it became closely attached to the Catholic faith. In this way, literacy education is equated with control and discipline, with the force of Western colonialism, and with violence. Children coming to school carry the weight of this history of literacy education, whether unconsciously or not. This makes it all the more difficult for them and their families to take learning risks as they become readers and writers.

The educational inequalities experienced by the children and families in Highland School are becoming more entrenched. This is part of a global trend. On average, across Organisation for Economic Co-operation and Development countries in the 21st century, schooling is not contributing to social mobility as it did in the second half of the 20th century (OECD, 2018). Nevertheless, it is worth noting that inequality is not only rooted in education processes, but that it is also driven by class, race, and political aspects, and that capitalist and neoliberal policies play major roles (Alvaredo et al., 2018). According to OECD's (2018) report on social mobility, "[i]n an 'average OECD country' it would take around four to five generations for children from the bottom earnings decile to attain the level of mean earnings" (p. 14). And this kind of mobility would take even longer for countries with developing economies.

Returning to my inquiry into causal relationality at Highland School, I now build upon emerging research that proposes thinking literacies beyond engagement with text and human agencies; the "unbounded ways of doing literacy," such as those presented by Kuby and Gutshall Rucker (2016, p.

xxi). With these authors, I want to imagine what literacies education could look like if relational causality were accounted for in pedagogy and educational research in the constitution of literacy events. My hope is that doing so would release a force to disrupt centuries-old narratives of educational detachment, lack, and underperformance of certain marginalized and rural populations. It would also open up worlds of possibilities for students in these communities by exploring strengths, developing potentialities, and even reaching dreams.

As we read the next story through a lens of relational causality, I would like to invite readers to be open to the indeterminate: literacies beyond literacy, interventions beyond intervening.

Stories with Theory: Affect, Intra-action, and Relational Causality in Literacy Pedagogies

Some afternoons, when the sun shines softly, my wife Valentina and I like to stroll around the neighbourhood. We usually walk the few steps down from the entrance gate of the building where we live to the sidewalk and interlace our arms side by side, and after a few awkward strides, we soon fall into a rhythmic and synchronic pace.

On these walks, we recall and (re)construct many of the stories of the 10 years we spent teaching at Highland School; Valentina as an elementary school teacher, and I as a high school teacher and principal. The rhythm of our walking permeates our bodies and our thoughts, and our memories interlace as we weave together snippets of life at school. Deleuze (1988) reminds us that it is through these rhythms of "speed and slowness that one slips in among things, that one connects with something else" (p. 123).

"S" Is for SSSSS ... Not "C": Mauricito's Story

One evening, at dinner, Valentina told me that in the morning, during class, Mauricito, one of our young students, had been writing about a story he had just heard from a classmate in the *diario compartido* (shared diary). This is an activity during which one student shares a personal experience with the group; the others ask clarifying questions to help to shape the narrative, and then the students write their story. Mauricito had abruptly stopped writing, got up from his chair, and asked Valentina for the folder containing his work. Every so often, Valentina would take out the students' folders and review students' work with them, discussing their writing and choosing with them what to put into their portfolios. But, she said, this was not one of those times. Mauricito's story was not finished, and the six-year-old boy looked a bit anxious. He shifted the weight of his body from one foot to the other and rubbed his hands together. She wondered what was going on, so she asked him, "What do you need your folder for?" "I need to correct my name," he said.

Valentina sensed that something was affecting Mauricito. Maybe it was something in the sharing of the story? They walked together to the cupboard, and Valentina handed him the folder, which he took and rushed back to his table, flipping through the pages while murmuring something to himself. Since the students were used to reviewing their work routinely with the teacher to discuss their progress, Mauricito was familiar with his own work. So, what was troubling him so much? Valentina wondered. She walked quietly towards him, not wanting to disturb him, and heard him say: "I knew it, I knew it, I knew it." Then he got up and walked directly towards the shelf where writing supplies lay until becoming entangled in a literacy event. Mauricito picked up a pencil and an eraser, and he hurried back to the table. One by one, he took each of his papers from the folder and patiently erased the letter "c" in his name and replace it with an "s." Customarily, the name Mauricio and its diminutive Mauricito is spelled with "c," not "s." So, changing "c" for "s" seemed rather odd to Valentina since he had been writing his name "correctly" since he was five years old.

After the erasing event was over, Mauricito, the table, and the floor around them were covered in eraser dust and chippings, his papers were all wrinkled, but he had a big smile on his face and the look of satisfaction of a job well done. He patiently put the papers back in the folder and returned it to Valentina, who saw this as the opportunity to ask him what had happened. "You see," he said, "When I say my name – Maurissssito – I hear *sssss* and not the /k/ /k/ /k/ of the letter 'c,', so I knew I had been writing my name wrong." "I just had to correct it," he explained. And then, with great solemnity, he declared, "It's important, it's my name."

In Latin American Spanish, the letter "c" has an /s/ sound when followed by the vowels "e" or "i," but a /k/ sound when followed by the vowels "a," "o," or "u." When Mauricito first "learned" to write his name, he could do it by heart, but the relationship between symbol and sound that characterizes standard written Spanish had not been part of his literacy becomings.

Kuby and Gutshall Rucker (2016) use the idea of *literacy desirings* to express the "intra-actions, movements, and surprises that students and materials produce *while* creating rather than their end products" (p. 5, emphasis in the original). For them, literacy desiring, as a construct of adjective and gerund, allows them to express the active and process-oriented aspect of a literacy event. The intra-action of the erasing and rewriting event in the story where Mauricito becomes Maurisito (with an "s") makes his literacy desirings more visible, entangled, affective. The written language is materialized and a source of pride for him, not merely a representation of his accomplishment, but a new becoming-with-literacy. Although Maurisito moves from a conventional spelling to an unconventional spelling of his name, which Ferreiro (1991) would refer to as "the logic of the error" or an overgeneralization of a spelling rule, in this entanglement of affective intensities among child-eraser-pencil-sound of the letter "s," Maurisito emerges anew as his literacy becoming now involves taking learning risks, and, at the same time, does not imply any "bleeding." It is also important to note the understanding of children's literacy becomings that Valentina demonstrates, given that she does not interfere with Maurisito's efforts but instead supports and respects his literacy desirings. Of course, in time, he became aware that the letter "c" also has a soft sound which accounts for the /s/ sound in his name.

In this story, when we account for the relational causality of the phenomenon, we find an array of components (intra-acting forces) that produce new affects and that disrupt the rhythms that sediment low expectations for children as literacy learners. All these pedagogical components combine in a surprising way so that it is no longer possible to identify one without simultaneously bringing others to the fore. At Highland School, love, care, generative pedagogies including place- and project-based learning (Smith & Sobel, 2010), high expectations, emphasis on communication and listening, balanced nutrition, educationally designed buildings and spaces, direct contact with the natural environment, inclusivity, diversity, mutual respect as a guiding principle, educational materials, reading and writing resources, preventive healthcare, community outreach, histories, caring teachers, and students, and so many other components intra-actively reconfigure, in their iterative performance, the real and the possible (Barad, 2007, p. 393) for these children. Nonetheless, let me clarify a point here. While our interventions as educators matter, and all the components mentioned above matter, in literacy becomings, relational causality is not about adding more causes to an effect. The affective flows of the unexpected and difference produced in the intra-actions of pedagogical components modify, transform, and interrupt rhythms among/of bodies in schools. Affective flows are about being open to the newness and the indeterminacy of learning events in the entanglement of these pedagogical intra-actions and not about guiding students through "rationally designed change" (Leander & Boldt, 2012, p. 32).

Maurisito's story is not unique but is typical of many at Highland School. It became clear to Valentina and to me that a positive school climate can mitigate the impact of a lower SES background (Berkowitz et al., 2017). At Highland School, we were determined to interrupt rhythms of deficiency and lack. We were also aware that, in order to make a difference, we needed to provide, create, and nurture a whole range of experiences, practices, events, and encounters that went beyond good literacy and numeracy teaching. Thus, for us, the question was not *what* happens in literacy assemblages, but *how* they happen.

Nothing Is Ever Just Literacy

As Manning says in an interview with Bruner and Massumi (Massumi, 2015), understanding that the human is only one part of the ecology of the event helps us to relocate the human as a becoming through encounters in events, or as we have discussed above, as effects and causes in affective intra-active phenomena. Many of the components that partake in this process of becoming might be over-coded, determined/ing (e.g. socioeconomic class, parents' educational experiences with literacy, inadequate nutritional practices, etc.). But the potential that is latent in affective flows, "the mutual constitution of entangled agencies" (Barad, 2007, p. 33), opens up to a different ethics and politics of education assemblages. In this case, this possibility lies in our response-ability (Haraway, 2016) as educators in how we understand and intervene through affect in pedagogical change. Affect works at the level of the pre-individual, and it also works at the level of the pre-experience. Attending to causal relationality in an event brings forward a focus on the potential of the emergent event *before* it becomes an experience. It means accounting for the causes and not just for the effects (Deleuze, 1988, pp. 19–20).

Therefore, going back to Maurisito's story, the observable part of the event is his desire to change the writing of his name. If we do not account for the affects created in the school by the material-discursive intra-actions (the relational causality) which he was a part of and that position him in a place where he can carry out the action, we would understand this effect as only a personal, cognitive achievement. However, accounting for the relational causality of his literacy becomings means that we consider the way different bodies intra-act with one another as they affect and are affected by each other. Maurisito's literacy becomings cannot be separated from the well-balanced nutrition he received at school, just as they cannot be detached from the wooden blocks that stimulated his imagination and desires, or the books and fellow students that engaged him with their stories, nor from the gentle but consequential interventions of his teacher, Valentina, listening, noticing, asking, following along. Thus, Maurisito's literacy becomings are not just in encounters with text, pencil, and paper, or to the occasional time spent at the computer in school, but to a much broader range of affective intra-actions his body and other bodies engaged in at school, undergoing intensities and flows of affective forces that shape, reshape, and change the rhythm of a body slipping into literacy practices.

Storytelling with theories of literacy, affect, and intra-action brings to the fore the need to rework the traditional understanding of causality. There are differences that matter in literacy assemblages when causality is theorized as a linear view of cause-effect, or when it is theorized as a relational phenomenon. How we theorize about causality changes the assemblage, and thus that which is produced. It matters for us as educators, it matters for our students, and it matters for our understanding of literacies. Causal relationality draws our attention to a "whole array of very complex material practices" (Barad, in Dolphijn & Van der Tuin, 2012, p. 56) that contribute to any literacy event but are not accounted for in a linear understanding of causality where we might then be pulled to look for single sources upon which to project blame or solutions. When material practices are left out of our accounts of literacy events, the entangled agency of humans and materiality tends to be overlooked, which makes it very hard to understand *how* literacy and learning happens.

For Manning, the real political question of the possibility of change is *how* an experience comes into formation because the process of formation, before it is formed as an experience, is really where "the force of the potential for change occurs" (Massumi, 2015, p. 150). Thus, a relational causal account of affective pedagogies of change unsettles discourses of language and literacy as linear processes that require certain prerequisites such as early exposure to rich written-language contexts. This also disrupts narratives of educational development that are desiring a different, more ready, more savvy, more resourced child than the child who arrives at school, and the well-worn education practices of "not-enough" that produce the status quo of rural, racialized, minoritized children.

And this is where Massumi's (2015) understanding of affect as "the margin of manoeuvrability" (p. 3) is useful for thinking about relational causality in literacies. As educators, the point of thinking with affect in relational causal fields in schools is that it pushes us to think about our engagement and implication in those relations. It also means being open to the pedagogical changes they could unfold. In re-membering and writing Highland School, here in Canada, so far from the Ecuadorian Andes, theory and memory entangle once more and *Maurissssito* rushes in, the feel and sound and touch and resonance of his name-pencil-voice unfolding a different literacy or maybe not a literacy at all.

Notes

1 The real name of the school has been changed to preserve its anonymity. This school no longer exists.
2 Mestizo is a complex and contested term used by most Ecuadorians to define themselves. At one level, it represents the European-Spanish and Indigenous mixed heritage of Ecuadorians. From this perspective, some observers describe certain groups as "white-*mestizos*" (see, for example, Muñoz, 2014). Others understand mestizos as non-Indigenous peoples (see, for example, Roitman, 2008). Conversely, Indigenous peoples who have adopted Hispanic customs may identify as mestizos and not as members of an Indigenous group. Although Indigenous cultural practices and identities are complex and diverse, in this sense the term *mestizaje* is commonly understood to refer to the acculturation of Indigenous

peoples (Roitman, 2008). The families and children depicted in this chapter would be considered mestizos in the latter understanding.
3 Quichua or Kichwa is the Ecuadorian variety of Quechua, an Indigenous language spoken in several South American Andean countries. You can find more information about this variety in *Languages of the World: Quichua* at www.peoplesoftheworld.org/text?people=Quichua.
4 Millennial schools boast modern educational infrastructures that accommodate between 570 and 1,140 students.
5 While I have mentioned several educational issues that shape literacy experiences for people in the area, these do not form an exhaustive list. For example, I have not discussed teacher training, retention, pay, or other curricular policies, as these would require a nuanced exploration, which is out of the scope of this chapter.
6 Saint cards are Catholic religious cards bearing a picture of a saint and a short message.

References

Alvaredo, F., Chancel, L., Piketty, T., Saez, E., & Zucman, G. (Eds.) (2018). *World inequality report 2018*. Cambridge, MA: Belknap Press of Harvard University Press. Retrieved August 9, 2019, from https://wir2018.wid.world/files/download/wir2018-full-report-english.pdf.

Barad, K. (2007). *Meeting the universe halfway: Quantum physics and the entanglement of matter and meaning*. Durham, NC: Duke University Press.

Barad, K. (2012). Interview with Karen Barad. In R. Dolphijn & I. van der Tuin (Eds.), *New Materialism: Interviews & cartographies* (pp. 48–70). Ann Arbor: University of Michigan Library, Open Humanities Press.

Berkowitz, R., Moore, H., Astor, R. A., & Benbenishty, R. (2017). A research synthesis of the associations between socioeconomic background, inequality, school climate, and academic achievement. *Review of Educational Research*, 87(2), 425–469. doi:10.3102/0034654316669821.

Braidotti, R. (2013). *The posthuman*. Malden, MA: Polity Press.

De Finney, S., Dean, M., Loiselle, E., & Saraceno, J. (2011). All children are equal, but some are more equal than others: Minoritization, structural inequities, and social justice praxis in residential care. *International Journal of Child, Youth & Family Studies*, 2(3/4), 361–384. doi:doi:10.18357/ijcyfs23/420117756.

Deleuze, G. (1988). *Spinoza: Practical philosophy*. San Francisco, CA: City Lights Books.

Deleuze, G., & Guattari, F. (2014/1987). *A thousand plateaus: Capitalism and schizophrenia*. (B. Massumi, Trans.) Minneapolis: University of Minnesota Press.

Dolphijn, R., & van der Tuin, I. (Eds.), *New materialism: Interviews & cartographies*. Ann Arbor: University of Michigan Library, Open Humanities Press.

Ewing, R. (2018). Exploding some of the myths about learning to read: A review of research on the role of phonics. *NSW Teachers Federation*, 23–33. Retrieved August 8, 2019, from www.alea.edu.au/documents/item/1869.

Ferreiro, E. (1991). La construcción de la escritura en el niño. *Lectura y Vida* 12(3), 5–14. Retrieved August 9, 2019, from www.lecturayvida.fahce.unlp.edu.ar/numeros/a12n3/12_03_Ferreiro.pdf.

Haraway, D. J. (2016). *Staying with the trouble: Making kin in the Chthulucene*. Durham, NC: Duke University Press.

Heath, S. B. (1982). What no bedtime story means: Narrative skills at home and school. *Language in Society*, 11(1), 49–76. Retrieved August 9, 2019, from www.jstor.org/stable/4167291.

Heath, S. B. (2010). Family literacy or community learning? Some critical questions on perspective. In K. Dunsmore & D. Fisher (Eds.), *Bringing literacy home* (pp. 15–41). Newark, DE: International Literacy Association.

Juelskjær, M., & Schwennesen, N. (2012). Intra-active entanglements. An interview with Karen Barad. *Kvinder, Koen Og Forskning*, 21(1–2), 10–23. Retrieved August 8, 2019, from https://doi.org/10.7146/kkf.v0i1-2.28068.

Kalman, J. (2004). *Saber lo que es la letra: Una experiencia de lectoescritura con mujeres Mixquic*. Mexico: Siglo XXI Editores. Retrieved August 9, 2019, from http://unesdoc.unesco.org/images/0014/001494/149457so.pdf.

Kalman, J., & Street, B. V. (2013). Introduction. *Literacy and numeracy in Latin America: Local perspectives and beyond* (pp. 1–16). New York: Routledge.

Kuby, C. R., & Gutshall Rucker, T. (2016). *Go be a writer! Expanding the curricular boundaries of literacy learning with children*. New York: Teachers College Press.

Leander, K., & Boldt, G. (2012). Rereading "A pedagogy of multiliteracies": Bodies, texts, and emergence. *Journal of Literacy Research*, 45(1), 22–46. doi:10.1177/1086296x12468587.

MacLure, M. (2013). The wonder of data. *Cultural Studies ⟷ Critical Methodologies*, 13(4), 228–232. doi:10.1177/1532708613487863.

Massumi, B. (2015). *Politics of affect*. Malden, MA: Polity Press.

McLaren, P. (2009). Critical pedagogy: A look at the major concepts. In A. Darder, M. Baltodano, & R. Torres (Eds.), *The critical pedagogy reader* (2nd ed.) (pp. 61–83). New York: Routledge.

Muñoz, M. F. (2014). Multiculturalidad ecuatoriana e historia nacional. *Barataria. Revista Castellano-Manchega de Ciencias Sociales*, 17, 215–227. doi:http://dx.doi.org/10.20932/barataria.v0i17.66.

Neuman, S. B. (2017). The information book flood: Is additional exposure enough to support early literacy development? *The Elementary School Journal*, 118(1), 1–27. Retrieved August 8, 2019, from https://doi.org/10.1086/692913.

Organisation of Economic Co-operation and Development (OECD) (2018). *A broken social elevator? How to promote social mobility*. Paris: OECD Publishing. Retrieved August 8, 2019, from https://doi.org/10.1787/9789264301085-en.

Prendergast, S., & MacPhee, D. (2018). Parental contributors to children's persistence and school readiness. *Early Childhood Research Quarterly*, 45, 31–44. Retrieved August 9, 2019, from https://doi.org/10.1016/j.ecresq.2018.05.005.

Redaccion Plan V. (2017). Lo bueno, lo malo y lo feo de las Escuelas del Milenio. *Plan* V. Retrieved August 9, 2019, from www.planv.com.ec/historias/sociedad/lo-bueno-lo-malo-y-lo-feo-escuelas-del-milenio.

Roitman, K. (2008). Hybridity, Mestizaje, and Montubios in Ecuador. Queen Elizabeth House, University of Oxford, Working Paper Series Number, 165. Retrieved August 9, 2019, from www.qeh.ox.ac.uk/sites/www.odid.ox.ac.uk/files/www3_docs/qehwps165.pdf.

Seigworth, G. J., & Gregg, M. (2010). An inventory of shimmers. In M. Gregg & G. J. Seigworth (Eds.), *The affect theory reader* (pp. 1–25). Durham, NC: Duke University Press.

Smith, G. A., & Sobel, D. (2010). *Place- and community-based education in schools*. New York: Routledge.

Spinoza, B. (1949). *Ethics*. New York: Hafner Publishing Company.
St. Pierre, E. A. (2018). Post qualitative inquiry in an ontology of immanence. *Qualitative Inquiry*, 1–14. doi:10778000418772634.
Torrecilla, F. J. M., & Carrasco, M. R. (2011). ¿La escuela o la cuna? Evidencias sobre su aportación al rendimiento de los estudiantes de América Latina. Estudio multinivel sobre la estimación de los efectos escolares. *Profesorado. Revista de Curriculum y Formación de Profesorado*, 15(3), 27–50. Retrieved August 8, 2019, from www.redalyc.org/articulo.oa?id=56722230003.
Waddington, R. (2003). *The Quichua people*. The Peoples of the World Foundation. Retrieved August 8, 2019, from www.peoplesoftheworld.org/text?people=Quichua.

6
A RHIZOMATIC CASE ANALYSIS OF INSTRUCTIONAL COACHING AS BECOMING

Brandon Sherman, Mari Haneda and Annela Teemant

Introduction

Instructional coaching has become recognized as having more impact on teacher professional development (PD) than traditional "one-and-done" teacher workshops, particularly in US K-12 settings (e.g. Aguilar, 2013; Knight, 2007). To date, much of the research on coaching has focused on establishing this impact (Kraft et al., 2018), often measured by gains/losses in students' achievement scores on standardized tests (e.g. Elish-Piper & L'Allier, 2011; Shidler, 2009). Other research has focused on the dynamics of coaching support and interaction (e.g. Coburn & Woulfin, 2012; Rainville & Jones, 2008). As valuable as this work has been, there remains a need to develop a greater theoretical understanding of instructional coaching as a force for change within the complex web of classrooms and schools, to say nothing of the lives of students and teachers. In this chapter, drawing on the work of Gilles Deleuze (1925–1995) and Félix Guattari (1930–1992), particularly *A Thousand Plateaus: Capitalism and Schizophrenia* (1987), we argue for an alternative conception of one-on-one instructional coaching, seeing it as a space of *becoming*, in which coach and teacher are free to explore and experiment with pedagogical ideas. The data we present are derived from analyses of episodes of coach-teacher conference conversations, drawn from a US-based PD programme (see Teemant, 2014).

The PD and instructional coaching explored here are built on critical sociocultural perspectives on education (Vossoughi & Gutiérrez, 2016). While this body of theory can be seen as establishing goals for transformative practices, we believe that concepts derived from rhizomatic thinking (Deleuze & Guattari, 1987) can also provide theoretical tools to understand the potentialities and processes of transformation involved in PD and coaching conversations.

Deleuze and Guattari (1987) describe traditional linear Western conceptualizations of knowing, such as linguistic sentence diagrams, as arborescent thinking (p. 5). Using the figuration of rhizomes, they propose an alternative way of thinking – rhizomatic thinking, or knowing as a process and a "present-becoming" (Deleuze & Parnet, 1987, p. 23). According to Deleuze and Guattari (1987),

> A rhizome has no beginning or end; it is always in the middle, in between things, interbeing, *intermezzo*. The tree is filiation, but the rhizome is alliance. The tree imposes the verb "to be", but the fabric of the rhizome is the conjunction "and … and …and." This conjunction carries enough force to shake and uproot the verb "to be".
> *(p. 25, emphasis in the original)*

While rhizomes have been referred to as a metaphor (e.g. Mackness et al., 2016), Deleuze and Guattari (1987) themselves seemed to be against this. Hagood (2004) treats the rhizome as a figuration. She notes similarities between figurations and metaphors but draws an important distinction in that figurations draw on the complexity of a phenomenon in order to aid in understanding it as becoming. This stands in contrast to metaphors, which are used to determine or define a phenomenon through description. We can consider the rhizome as a way of thinking.

Thinking rhizomatically means pursuing the interminable "*and*" through the multitudes of connections and encounters that stimulate new thinking and acting. This allows us to consider PD events, including the interactions that occur in coach-teacher conferences, as "assemblages," ecologies of complex and interrelated material and discursive elements that can produce surprising outcomes (e.g. Leander & Wells Rowe, 2006; Strom & Martin, 2017). Deleuze and Guattari held assemblages to be composed of "objects, bodies, expressions, qualities, and territories" (Livesey, 2010, p. 18). As shorthand for this, we have chosen the term "element," as has been used by Strom and Martin (2017), which is meant to convey agential parity between animate objects (which might otherwise be called actors) and inanimate, intangible, and/or discursive objects. Other terms that have been employed to this effect are components (Barad, 2007) and actants (Latour, 2017).

Any change in an element can have unexpected consequences for the entire assemblage and beyond. This fluidity is rooted in an ontology of becoming that underscores Deleuze and Guattari's work (Stagoll, 2010). A focus on becoming, as opposed to being, emphasizes a world that is evershifting, never-complete, always in motion. A state (being) can be nominalized or thingified, but a process (becoming) remains as a verb. Additionally, the concept of becoming helps us to shift from thinking of the world as consisting of isolated individuals and objects with inherent properties. Instead, heterogeneous elements come together in temporary and shifting alliances, or assemblages (Strom & Martin, 2017, p. 8). Thus, we understand instructional coaching not as an intervention, but rather as a space of becoming (Deleuze and Guattari, 1987, p. 272). This allows for the emergence of unexpected and powerful transformations, not only in teachers' practices and students' learning, but potentially in teacher and student identities and in classroom dynamics.

On this premise, in this chapter, we examine coaching interactions between Sabrina, an instructional coach, and Sharon, a fifth-grade teacher (pseudonyms have been used to preserve anonymity). Instead of focusing on a moment-by-moment analysis of fissures in an assemblage (Leander & Wells Rowe, 2006), drawing on key rhizomatic concepts, we examine coaching activities across events: how happenings in coaching conference (our focus) become extended and intertwined, and how progressively larger assemblages of Sharon's classroom and her students' school world occurred. In the next section, we define the key concepts that we use: *assemblage, rhizomatic lines,* and *territorialization*. Our aim is to show how rhizomatic ruptures or fissures that emerge in practice may open up new possibilities for the teacher and students.

Key Concepts

Assemblage

As a good entry point for thinking rhizomatically, we begin with the concept of "assemblage." Deleuze and Guattari used the French term *agencement*, usually translated as "arrangement," "putting together," or "laying out" (DeLanda, 2016). Agencement, as used by Deleuze and Guattari (1987), is commonly translated in English as assemblage, which is an approximation at best. For this reason, there are a number of points to bear in mind when thinking with this concept. First, what is emphasized is not the arrangement itself but the process of arranging, organizing, and fitting together. An assemblage is an ongoing process of becoming through arranging, organizing, or congealing heterogeneous elements. Second, it is not a set of predetermined parts that are subsequently pieced together to construct a preconceived structure, but rather a spontaneous relation of heterogeneous elements that envelop or "stake out" a territory (Deleuze & Guattari, 1987, p. 503). Third, it is not the product of an outside actor since it can shift and transform on its own through the dynamic interplay of various elements. Based on this understanding, we consider an assemblage to be an ensemble of elements, human and non-human, that "function collectively in a contextually unique manner to produce *something* (e.g. teaching practice, a situated identity)" (Strom & Martin, 2017, p. 7, emphasis in the original). Non-humans can take a variety of forms: concrete (a desk, a light), material (sounds, smells), discursive (ways of address, languages used), or abstract (ideas, protocols). Deleuze and Guattari (1987) note that assemblages are simultaneously semiotic and pragmatic, operating both in terms of enunciation and action, or "what is said and what is done" (p. 504).

Viewed from this perspective, a classroom can be considered as an assemblage "composed of humans, writing implements, writing surfaces, texts, desks, doors, as well as disciplinary forces whose power and agency are elicited through various routines (e.g., singing the national anthem) and references ('In algebra, we always do this...')" (Strom & Martin, 2017, p. 7). This allows teaching and learning to be understood as having been co-produced by classroom assemblages, with each element in the assemblage being recognized as an active agent in this joint production. Furthermore, assemblages can share elements with other assemblages, and occur within larger assemblages. For example, a classroom assemblage may consist of smaller assemblages, such as pair or group work, and at the same time act as a single element in the larger assemblage of the school. What is particularly relevant for this chapter is the emergent, indeterminate nature of an assemblage and the relational co-functioning of all the elements, both human and non-human, within it.

Territories and Lines

Rhizomes consist of a multiplicity of lines operating within a shifting territory, forming contours, connections, and breaks. By means of these lines, assemblages shift and reconfigure, potentially extending in any direction to form new assemblages. The dynamics of these changing assemblages (or a lack thereof) result from the interplay of two types of lines: molar, and molecular, the latter of which has the potential to become lines of flight (Deleuze & Guattari, 1987). In relation to teaching, rigid molar lines include curriculum standards, bell schedules, codes of conduct, and normative assumptions about what constitutes a good student; these "encapsulate the presently accepted norms, rules, social structures, and forms of communication" (Strom & Martin, 2017, p. 9). They are territorializing (or boundary enforcing) forces against which behaviour and conditions (e.g. classroom organization) can be constantly checked. On the other hand, supple molecular lines are micropolitical; they carry out the day-to-day work of the molar norm. In teaching, molecular actions may involve teachers implementing curriculum standards in their classrooms and observing various institutional norms, both academic and social. According to Strom and Martin (2017), "the individual thoughts, actions, and practices of teachers that feed into and reinforce the molar system are the molecular lines at work" (p. 9). However, molecular lines can also become lines of flight, lines that have the potential to transform a territory by bringing about new and unexpected arrangements and relationships both within and outside of it. As Boldt (2017) explains, in deterritorialization, "there is a breakdown of known patterns, expectations, norms, and authorities, and the production of new ... desires" (p. 183). In classroom practice, for example, this may happen when teachers respond contingently to students' unexpected answers, not following the expected learning path and potentially moving on to new, exciting engagement with students about the topic at issue. In and of themselves, lines of flight are neither good nor bad. They have potential for both creativity and destruction. The same can be said of territorialization and deterritiorialization, both of which can be beneficial or detrimental, often at the same time. It so happens that, in this chapter, we approach these concepts in relation to one teacher's application of Teemant's Six Standards Pedagogy. Here, it is the creative potential of lines of flight on which we focus.

The Six Standards Pedagogy

The Six Standards Pedagogy (Teemant, 2018), which is the basis of the coaching approach examined here, is informed by critical sociocultural theory (Lewis et al., 2007; Vossoughi & Gutierrez, 2016). The term "standards" is not used in the sense of a curriculum standard, but should be understood as a set of key pedagogical principles that guide practice. Five of the principles, derived from the "five standards for effective pedagogy" (Tharp et al., 2000), are grounded in sociocultural theories of learning and are formulated on the basis of cumulative research-based evidence for effective teaching practice for multilingual students. The five pedagogical principles include Joint Productive Activity, Language and Literacy Development, Contextualization, Challenging Activities, and Instructional Conversation (IC). Particularly important is the principle of IC (Goldenberg, 1992), in which a teacher and a small group of students collaborate in a purposeful dialogic discussion, because it enables the teacher to tailor her or his instruction to the zones of proximal development (Vygotsky, 1978) of the individual students involved – contextualizing learning in relation to students' lived experiences and interests (Contextualization).

Six Standards Pedagogy has an equity orientation, captured by the additional principle of Critical Stance (CS). CS is grounded in critical pedagogical thinking (Freire, 1970/2002; Lewison et al., 2014). Permeating and augmenting the other five principles, CS aims to cultivate critical thinking and critical consciousness (Freire, 1970/2002) among students. By enacting CS, teachers are expected to (a) engage students in identifying and reflecting on problematic issues in students' lives or in larger settings, and (b) help them take action to resolve them in an age-appropriate manner. For example, in the classrooms of past PD participating teachers, young children initiated a recycling initiative in school conservation awareness campaigns (Haneda et al., 2017), and an anti-bullying programme (Kopp, 2012). As with any other pedagogical concept, CS can become a molar line (i.e. a normalizing force). However, in calling for pedagogy that aids students in "interrogating conventional wisdom and practices" (Teemant et al., 2014, p. 140), CS has the potential to create lines of flight as well.

Following these same research-based pedagogical principles, Six Standard Instructional Coaching is designed to be dialogic in nature. The coach assists development within the teachers' zone of proximal development (Vygotsky, 1978) by helping them to understand, appropriate, and enact Six Standards Pedagogy (Haneda et al., 2019). In this way, the coaching process involves both sense-making, as teachers come to build their own understandings of the principles, and practical application, as coaches support teachers in applying and refining pedagogy based on the principles.

Research Methods

Context

The data used for this chapter were collected as part of a study of Six Standards Instructional Coaching, as carried out in an urban elementary school in the midwestern United States. Our focus is on coach-teacher conference interaction between Sharon and Sabrina. Sharon had 23 years of teaching experience and taught sixth graders. As with other PD participants, Sharon first learned about the six pedagogical principles through a five-day, 30-hour summer workshop, and then participated in seven cycles of one-on-one instructional coaching at intervals throughout one school year. Each cycle consisted of a pre-conference, a classroom observation, and a post-conference (conferences averaging about 30 minutes in length).[1] Sabrina had nine years of experience as an elementary English-Spanish bilingual teacher, and at the time of the study had been an instructional coach for over five years.

The demography of Sharon's sixth-grade classroom reflected the school, which was culturally diverse (75 percent Hispanic and 16 percent African American, with smaller populations of White, Asian, and multiracial students). The school served a poor neighbourhood with 95 percent of students receiving free/reduced lunch,[2] a proportion that surpassed both the national average (42 percent) and the state average (36.1 percent) (NCES, 2012). Owing to low performance scores, the school district had adopted a prescriptive curriculum that specified the what and why of teaching, resulting in a teaching environment that some teachers found constrictive (Haneda et al., 2017).

Data Collection and Analysis

Our primary sources of data were video and audio recordings of the Sabrina-Sharon coaching conferences, collected during the seven cycles of coaching. Other sources of data consulted were the coach's notes, audio recordings of three classroom events, and the exit interview with Sharon. Classroom observation data, collected by Sabrina, provided some insight into changes in Sharon's classroom over time. We, the authors, first viewed all the video-recorded conference interactions. Then, using Studiocode video analysis software, we extracted episodes related to CS and IC for analysis, as these pedagogical principles were our analytical focus in a larger study.

In this chapter, we follow the lead (if not the method) of Hofsess and Sonenberg (2013), who returned to data they had previously analyzed through conventional qualitative methods in order to "re-vision" it rhizomatically. We, too, have returned to CS-IC related segments of video-recorded data, but are viewing it anew through a rhizomatic lens. Though a number of scholars have drawn on rhizomatics to analyze empirical data (e.g. de Freitas, 2012; Leander & Wells Rowe, 2006), there is not, and likely could not be, an established protocol for doing so. Rather, it is the work of the authors (and, to some extent, of the readers) to engage with rhizomatic concepts and apply them to the work of analysis. Furthermore, while many of the cited examples of rhizomatic research focus on relatively short time scales, our analysis spans a school year, allowing us to consider how assemblages shift over time (see also Kuby, 2017). The following rhizomatic analysis aims to illuminate how the changes we observed in the instructional coaching assemblage had ramifications for the larger classroom assemblage and beyond.

Findings

The Coaching Assemblage

Recall that an assemblage is defined by the involvement of its elements in the production of *something*, in this case Sharon's becoming, along with the becoming of Sabrina, the classroom, the conferences, the students, and a multiplicity of others. From the assemblage of a coaching conference, its influences can be mapped into the larger assemblages of Sharon's classroom and, to some extent, of the school. The assemblage(s) represented by the conferences is at once singular and multiple, inasmuch as each conference can be seen as its own separate assemblage, and at the same time the seven cycles of conferences can be viewed as a single evolving assemblage. It is in relation to this latter frame that the following description is provided. Below, some of the elements constituting conferences, human, material, and intangible, are described in order to show the complexity and nuance that emerge when thinking about the conferences rhizomatically. Our goal is not to present an exhaustive list nor to trace direct causal relationships, but rather to call attention to the value of seeing the conferences as an assemblage.

Sabrina was an outsider, in that she was neither employed by the school district, nor was she from the area. As an external coaching consultant funded by a federal government's grant, Sabrina's official role was to support Sharon's learning. Instead of being authoritative, she took a more "responsive" approach by valuing a dialogue about Sharon's classroom and her pedagogical goals. To this end, she used a variety of interactional strategies such as posing questions and offering suggestions. Sharon was not a passive participant in this process. She offered her own interpretation of classroom events, her students, and her teaching; co-planned lessons and activities with Sabrina; evaluated the observed lessons; and responded to the suggestions Sabrina introduced, either agreeing with or pushing back against them.

In each conference, the two sat in a school office space (not always the same one), sometimes alone in the room, sometimes sharing it with others, as the business of the school day unfolded around them and occasionally intruded. In several instances, for example, loud announcements from the school's PA system put the conference on hold. The ringing of bells marked the regimented schedule of the day. Some conferences were conducted across a table, with documents and activity materials in sight and referenced, while in others Sabrina and Sharon sat across from each other in chairs with no intervening furniture or documents. Other intangible elements, such as the temperature, time of year, weather, and time of day, were occasionally referenced in conversation. A video camera and an audio recording device were used in each conference.

While varying in terms of the specific content under discussion, as noted earlier, each conference cycle involved a pre-conference, classroom observation, and a post-conference. The pre-conference generally focused on planning and preparing for the class to be observed. At times, Sharon's progress with regard to previously co-established pedagogical goals (e.g. the use of independent small group activities) would be discussed. The post-conference, following the classroom observation, focused on interpreting and co-evaluating the observed activities, as well as considering goals for the immediate and long-term future. In this way, the goals, as jointly negotiated products of coach and teacher, were enduring elements in the conference assemblage that kept being reshaped. These long- and short-term goals bridged the conferences across time and conference dialogue.

In both tangible and intangible ways, the key pedagogical principles of the Six Standards were important elements in the conference, often acting as molar lines. Materially, the principles were present in the form of official textual representations printed on sheets of paper that were referred to by both Sharon and Sabrina, helping them to shape and direct the course of conversation. Intangibly, they were present as abstract ideas and terminology, previously encountered by Sharon in the workshop and introduced into the coaching conversation so that Sharon could develop a deeper level of understanding to enact them in her classroom.

Taken together, these elements all functioned together to bring about changes in Sharon's professional practice over the course of the semester. Discussions in conferences, along with Sabrina's classroom observation notes, evidenced a consistent increase in Sharon's satisfaction with the results of her instruction in terms of student engagement, language use, and higher order thinking. What follows is a closer look at one example of changing dynamics rippling outward from the coaching conferences to the classroom and school.

Introducing Critical Stance

During the first few months, discussions between Sharon and Sabrina were largely concerned with practical classroom matters such as planning and the implementation of activities, particularly ICs. As a small group conversation during which teachers sit with three to five students, guiding dialogue between them through strategic questioning, ICs represent a contrast with the hierarchical teacher-centred whole-class instruction. Though she had already been implementing small group activities with her students to some extent, Sharon did not conduct an IC until her third conference cycle. It was in this cycle that Sabrina introduced CS into the conversation:

SABRINA: Here's the last [principle] that we want to think about ... It's that Critical Stance. Getting them to think about how to transform inequities ... So, the Critical Stance, I'm going to poke at you to think about how you want to do the Critical Stance with your kids, and what it will look like in your classroom. What do you think about that?
SHARON: I think it's a good one. I think it's easily done.

Two things are notable in this exchange. First, Sabrina frames CS in terms of thought rather than action (repeatedly using the words "think about"). Second, it should be noted that Sharon's immediate acceptance of the idea contrasted with the experience of other teachers, who had expressed resistance to CS. Some teachers, who were participating in coaching at the same time, could not initially see how to include CS, which called for the challenging of norms and conventions in their instruction (see, for example, Haneda et al., 2017). In contrast, CS, as Sharon understood it at this point, resonated with her pre-existing teaching practices and philosophy. Once explicitly introduced, CS seemed to become an important element in the conferences that followed. Conversations increasingly revolved around issues of power and equity, with Sharon saying, for example, of one of her lessons, "I wanted to take it one step further to go into civil rights: Why is it important for everyone to get a good education?" With the introduction of CS as an element in the conference assemblage, Sharon and Sabrina's discussion began to shift from practical pedagogical considerations noted earlier towards strategies to prompt students to identify and question inequity or problematic issues in their lived worlds. To take one example, in co-planning a lesson on the US civil rights movement, they discussed questioning strategies to encourage students to reflect on their own lives, and to question taken-for-granted assumptions:

SABRINA: I think what you're saying is you really want the kids to understand "how does this affect me?" In terms of civil rights, if civil rights had not happened, how would that affect you right now? Girls in the class, if you could not go to school, what would your life be like? ...
SHARON: That would be an interesting conversation. If you're a girl, you don't get to go to school, if you're African American or Latino you're not going either. How many kids in your class would get to go to school?

This exchange indicates a shift from a focus on instruction to a discussion of the lives of the students and their experiences, particularly where equity and justice were concerned. In this way, it was emblematic of a larger shift in the shape of the conference assemblage. Whereas Sabrina could previously function as an expert in terms of the pedagogy, on the topic of the students' lives Sharon became more of an authority. Furthermore, as Sharon conducted activities enacting CS in her classroom, she came back to the coaching conferences with issues raised by the students themselves. These issues included bullying in school, unfair lunchroom policies, and (to Sharon's distress) the existence of contract killers in the students' community. In this way, CS, once introduced to coaching conversations, became an important element in Sharon's classroom, and in turn affected the coaching conversations. We present one specific case to illustrate this dynamic, as the molar lines of state standardized testing became deterritorialized through Sharon's use of pedagogical principles, particularly those of IC and CS.

Interrogating and Deterritorializing ISTEP

Every spring, all third-grade to eighth-grade students in Sharon's school were required to take a standardized achievement test known as the Indiana Statewide Testing for Educational Progress (ISTEP) exam. Within the assemblages of the classroom and school, ISTEP was a major element, with students and teachers relating to it exclusively in terms of evaluation and satisfactory achievement scores. Sharon referred to it as "the elephant in the room," a ubiquitous presence that, while discussed, was rarely acknowledged in terms of its influence on the lived experience of the teachers and students (Sharon referred to it as an influence on the content of her curriculum, and also on her time). In the fourth cycle, Sharon described how ISTEP (and other school-wide activities, such as assemblies) disrupted her classroom time and made it difficult for her to maintain the consistent practices she felt were necessary to enable students to progress. In her description, ISTEP acted as a territorializing force, posing challenges for the new Six Standards practices to become established in the classroom.

Seen rhizomatically, coaching conferences worked against the territorializing force of ISTEP in several ways. First, in conference, Sabrina encouraged Sharon to set aside 45 minutes of "non-negotiable time" every day in order to consistently pursue her pedagogical goals rather than spending time preparing for the test, as required by the school. This non-negotiable time represents an active resistance to territorializing forces of ISTEP. Furthermore, as Sharon became more comfortable with the Six Standards Pedagogy, she drew on CS, which allowed lines of flight to arise as we describe in what follows.

Later in the school year, having already begun planning lessons around student experiences, Sharon and Sabrina explored the possibility of designing activities to address the role of ISTEP in the students' lives. At first, Sharon represented ISTEP as a force the students could react to, changing their own behaviours in ways that did not conflict with the unquestioned dominant position of the test in the classroom. She discussed how she wanted her students to reflect on how they could change themselves to better prepare for ISTEP through "their own sleep habits and having a pencil sharpened, and those kind of things." In response, Sabrina shifted their focus to interrogating ISTEP itself, suggesting, "You could get some interesting writing with what happens to ISTEP after it leaves the building. The whole idea of, where does it go? What do they think about it?"

Sharon then began to speculate how this might change the way the students related to the test, suggesting that she wanted her students to have "ownership" of ISTEP, "because they buy into it." In other words, she hoped to create an activity that could shift the students' relationship to ISTEP from acceptance (buy-in) to critique. Asked how this might affect her students, Sharon characterized it as reframing her students' perception of the test as "not this big scary thing someone's doing to me" but something over which they have ownership.

To this end, Sharon conducted ICs in which her students discussed and questioned ISTEP. After observing these ICs, Sabrina highlighted the surprise that emerged from this conversation:

SABRINA: Those kids, in the group yesterday, thought you loved ISTEP. They thought we loved ISTEP.
SHARON: They did. And they weren't going to tell us otherwise.
SABRINA: And that was very interesting, when they thought about it. You could see that moment of going, oh, she may not love ISTEP.
SHARON: Exactly. And what I thought was courageous of little Kimberly was, really, to share. It wasn't easy for her. I thought that took a lot of courage, because everybody else was like, it wasn't that hard. She was the first to say, well, some of it's hard. (And the rest said, oh yeah.) But I thought that took a little bit of courage, to say I have trouble with parts of it.

Through implementation of ICs and CS, Sharon was able to reposition herself in relation to ISTEP, becoming (in the regard of her students) not an enforcer of ISTEP but rather a person to consider separately from it, someone who might have her own reservations about the test. Additionally, the conversation opened up a space for students to name the difficulties they had with the test – another line of flight. The students began to see ISTEP not as an abstract authoritative force, but as a concrete element in the assemblages of their classroom and school. This represented a new perspective for the students to take with regard to ISTEP, with a newfound capacity to push back against it.

Towards the end of the school year, Sharon's students had written poems expressing their feelings about ISTEP (some overtly critical), and Sharon had displayed these in the hallway. She mentioned that other teachers had commented on the poems, saying "They're afraid I was getting into trouble, because it's about ISTEP," because the poems expressed negativity. In other words, her colleagues recognized ISTEP as a molar line in the school that was not to be questioned, and saw the students' critiques (such as they were) as a line of flight that might disrupt the status quo and thus incur territorializing attention from administration. In spite of her colleagues' concerns, Sharon expressed confidence that the display was appropriate and would not have negative repercussions.

Thus, deterritorialization occurred as students came to realize, through discussion, that Sharon was not an active agent of ISTEP, but in fact had her own feelings about it. Furthermore, the students' relationship to ISTEP changed in that they were able to interrogate it by questioning it in ICs (transforming a unidirectional relationship into a bidirectional one) and to express their feelings about it in a public setting through their poems. Finally, this public display quite probably influenced the larger assemblage of the school, as critiquing ISTEP was shown to be possible in terms of what students were both allowed and able to do. It can be argued that this emerged from the assemblage of Sabrina and Sharon's conferences, and specifically from changes brought about as Sharon and the students engage with the principle of CS in their lived world of the school.

Conclusion

By drawing on the key rhizomatic concepts, we examined how a discussion of the pedagogical principles of CS and IC in the coaching conversation led to a change in practice in Sharon's classroom. Sharon's enactment of CS permitted her students to voice their perceptions of Sharon as a test enforcer, thereby shifting the dynamics of the classroom assemblage. Contingently responding to students' voices, Sharon repositioned herself as an individual who struggled with ISTEP just like her students; this then led her students to express their feelings in poems that were displayed outside of the classroom in public spaces. Thus, currents that emerged during coaching sessions affected what happened in the larger assemblages of the classroom and the school. While our example from Sharon's classroom is limited in scope, we would like to suggest that coaching conversations have the potential to open up interstitial spaces to challenge institutional norms, which in turn may change not just isolated pedagogical practices, but the ecology of the classroom as a whole. Furthermore, though only hinted at here, change involves non-human, discursive, and intangible elements such as IC and CS. As shown in this chapter, ICs allow students to engage in an academic inquiry-oriented dialogue in which students can voice their opinions, which may lead to creative lines of flight, as shown in the example. The enactment of CS can be used to encourage students' critical thinking, helping them to identify ways in which they can act agentively against inequitable practices in their lives. These pedagogical principles can potentially become powerful elements that are capable of acting in and beyond assemblages to recast relationships between constituent elements, such as with the students and ISTEP.

The inherent aim of instructional coaching and associated professional development PD is often held to be that of bringing about positive change in teaching practice that benefit students. While any PD can become a territorializing force if it is implemented in a top-down manner, as we hope to have shown here, instructional coaching conversations embedded in a PD programme, such as Six Standards Pedagogy, has the potential to positively impact the classroom, the school, and even the students' lives in the larger world.

Notes

1 The structure of a coaching cycle noted here is used by other established coaching approaches (Costa & Garmston, 2002; Knight, 2007).
2 In the US context, to qualify for free/reduced lunch, a family must earn between 130 percent and 185 percent of the federally determined poverty line. For a family of four in 2007, the required annual income for free lunch would have been $37,000 or less (Government Publishing Office, 2006).

References

Aguilar, E. (2013). *The art of coaching: Effective strategies for school transformation*. Hoboken, NJ: John Wiley & Sons.
Barad, K. (2007). *Meeting the universe halfway: Quantum physics and the entanglement of matter and meaning*. Durham, NC: Duke University Press.
Boldt, G. M. (2017). Working with Deleuze and Guattari in early childhood research and education. In L. E. Cohen & S. Waite-Stupiansky (Eds.), *Theories of early childhood education: Developmental, behaviorist, and critical* (pp. 180–189). New York: Routledge.
Coburn, C. E., & Woulfin, S. L. (2012). Reading coaches and the relationship between policy and practice. *Reading Research Quarterly*, 47(1), 5–30. doi:10.1002/RRQ.008.
Cormier, D. (2008). Rhizomatic education: Community as curriculum. *Innovate: Journal of Online Education*, 4(5). Retrieved April 14, 2019, from www.learntechlib.org/p/104239/.
Costa, A. L., & Garmston, R. J. (2002). *Cognitive coaching: A foundation for renaissance schools* (2nd ed.). Norwood, MA: Christopher-Gordon.
Cuban, L. (1998). How schools change reforms: Redefining reform success and failure. *Teacher's College Record*, 99(3), 453–477.
de Freitas, E. (2012). The classroom as rhizome: New strategies for diagramming knotted interactions. *Qualitative Inquiry*, 18(7), 557–570. doi:10.1177/1077800412450155.
DeLanda, M. (2016). *Assemblage theory*. Edinburgh: Edinburgh University Press.
Deleuze, G., & Guattari, F. (1987). *A thousand plateaus: Capitalism and schizophrenia*. (B. Massumi, Trans.). Minneapolis: University of Minnesota Press.
Deleuze, G., & Parnet, C. (1987). *Dialogues*. (H. Tomlinson & B. Habberjam, Trans.). New York: Columbia University Press.
Elish-Piper, L., & L'Allier, S. K. (2011). Examining the relationship between literacy coaching and student reading gains in grades K–3. *The Elementary School Journal*, 112(1), 83–106. doi:10.1086/660685.
Freire, P. (1970/2002). *Pedagogy of the oppressed*. London: Bloomsbury.
Goldenberg, C. (1992). Instructional conversations: Promoting comprehension through discussion. *The Reading Teacher*, 46(4), 316–326.
Government Publishing Office (2006). Income eligibility guidelines. *Federal Register*, 71(50). Retrieved July 11, 2018, from www.gpo.gov/fdsys/pkg/FR-2006-03-15/pdf/06-2476.pdf.
Hagood, M. (2004). A rhizomatic cartography of adolescents, popular culture, and construction of self. In K. Leander & M. Sheehy (Eds.), *Spacializing literacy research and practice* (pp. 143–160). New York: Peter Lang.

Haneda, M., Sherman, B., & Teemant, A. (2019). Assisted performance through instructional coaching: A critical sociocultural perspective. In M. Haneda & Nassaji, H. (Eds.), *Perspectives on language as action: Essays in honor of Merryl Swain*. Bristol: Multilingual Matters.

Haneda, M., Teemant, A., & Sherman, B. (2017). Instructional coaching through dialogic interaction: Helping a teacher to become agentive in her practice. *Language and Education*, 31(1), 46–64. doi:10.1080/09500782.2016.1230127.

Hofsess, B. A., & Sonenberg, J. L. (2013). Enter: Ho/rhizoanalysis. *Cultural Studies ↔ Critical Methodologies*, 13(4), 299–308. doi:10.1177/1532708613487877.

Knight, J. (2007). *Instructional coaching: A partnership approach to improving instruction*. Thousand Oaks, CA: Corwin.

Kopp, B. (2012). IPS students start program to combat bullying. *WTHR*. Retrieved August 22, 2018, from www.wthr.com/article/ips-students-start-program-to-combat-bullying.

Kraft, M. A., Blazar, D., & Hogan, D. (2018). The effect of teacher coaching on instruction and achievement: A meta-analysis of the causal evidence. *Review of Educational Research*, 88(4), 547–588. doi:10.3102/0034654318759268.

Kuby, C. R. (2017). Rhizomes and intra-activity with materials: Ways of disrupting and reimagining early literacy research, teaching, and learning. In J. M. Iorio & W. Parnell (Eds.), *Meaning making in early childhood research: Pedagogies and the personal* (pp. 168–187). New York: Routledge.

Latour, B. (2017). *Facing Gaia. Eight lectures on the new climatic regime.* (Cathy Porter, Trans.). Medford, MA: Polity Press.

Leander, K., & Wells Rowe, D. (2006). Mapping literacy spaces in motion: A rhizomatic analysis of a classroom literacy performance. *Reading Research Quarterly*, 41(4), 428–460. doi:10.1598/RRQ.41.4.2.

Lewis, C., Enciso, P., & Moje, E. B. (Eds.). (2007). *Reframing sociocultural research on literacy: Identity, agency, and power*. Mahwah, NJ: Lawrence Erlbaum Associates.

Lewison, M., Leland, C., & Harste, J. C. (2014). Why do we need an instructional theory of critical literacy? M. Lewison, C. Leland and J.C. Harste (Eds.), In *Creating critical classrooms: Reading and writing with an edge* (pp. 1–23). New York: Routledge. doi:10.4324/9781315817842.

Livesey, G. (2010). Assemblage. In A. Parr (Ed.), *Deleuze dictionary* (revised ed.) (pp. 18–19). Edinburgh: Edinburgh University Press.

Lorraine, T. (2010). Lines of Flight. In A. Parr (Ed.), *Deleuze dictionary* (revised ed.) (pp. 147–148). Edinburgh: Edinburgh University Press.

Mackness, J., Bell, F., & Funes, M. (2016). The rhizome: A problematic metaphor for teaching and learning in a MOOC. *Australasian Journal of Educational Technology*, 32(1). doi:10.14742/ajet.2486.

National Center for Education Statistics (NCES) (2012). Number and percentage of public school students eligible for free or reduced-price lunch, by state: Selected years, 2000–01 through 2010–11. *Digest of Education Statistics*. Retrieved July 11, 2018, from https://nces.ed.gov/programs/digest/d12/tables/dt12_046.asp.

Parr, A. (2010). *Deleuze dictionary* (revised ed.). Edinburgh: Edinburgh University Press.

Rainville, K. N., & Jones, S. (2008). Situated identities: Power and positioning in the work of a literacy coach. *The Reading Teacher*, 61(6), 440–448. doi:10.1598/RT.61.6.1.

Semetsky, I. (2006). *Deleuze, education, and becoming*. Boston, MA: Sense.

Shidler, L. (2009). The impact of time spent coaching for teacher efficacy on student achievement. *Early Childhood Education Journal*, 36(5), 453–460. doi:10.1007/s10643-10008-0298-0294.

Stagoll, C. (2010). Becoming. In A. Parr (Ed.), *Deleuze dictionary* (revised ed.) (pp. 147–148). Edinburgh: Edinburgh University Press.

Strom, K. J. (2018). "That's not very Deleuzian": Thoughts on interrupting the exclusionary nature of "High Theory." *Educational Philosophy and Theory*, 50(1), 104–113. doi:10.1080/00131857.2017.1339340.

Strom, K. J., & Martin, A. D. (2017). *Becoming-teacher: A rhizomatic look at first-year teaching*. Rotterdam: Sense.

Teemant, A. (2014). A mixed methods investigation of instructional coaching for teachers of diverse learners. *Urban Education*, 49(5), 574–604. doi:10.1177/0042085913481362.

Teemant, A. (2018). Sociocultural theory as everyday practice: The challenge of K-12 teacher preparation for multilingual and multicultural learners. In J. P. Lantolf & M. E. Poehner (Eds.) with M. Swain (pp. 529–550), *The Routledge handbook of sociocultural theory and second language development*. New York: Routledge.

Teemant, A., Leland, C., & Berghoff, B. (2014). Development and validation of a measure of Critical Stance for instructional coaching. *Teaching and Teacher Education*, 39, 136–147. doi:10.1016/j.tate.2013.11.008.

Tharp, R., Estrada, P., Dalton, S., & Yamauchi, L. A. (2000). *Teaching transformed: Achieving excellence, fairness, inclusion, and harmony*. Boulder, CO: Westview.

Vossoughi, S., & Gutiérrez, K. (2016). Critical pedagogy and sociocultural theory. In I. Esmonde & A. Booker (Eds.), *Power and privilege in the learning sciences: Critical and sociocultural theories of learning* (pp. 138–161). Abingdon: Routledge.

Vygotsky, L. S. (1978). *Mind in society: The development of higher psychological processes*(M. Cole, V. John-Steiner, S. Scribner, & E. Souberman, Eds.). Cambridge, MA: Harvard University Press.

7

"THIS DOCUMENTARY ACTUALLY MAKES WELLAND LOOK GOOD"

Exploring Posthumanism in a High School Documentary Film Project

Amélie Lemieux and Jennifer Rowsell

Introduction

Our title derives from a remark made by a young woman as she watched the final documentary produced by media artist Vanessa Crosbie Ramsay about our research study and its central message. The study considered community engagement in Welland, Ontario, Canada, and how promising futures in the city might be seen. In this chapter, we focus on a six-week documentary film unit completed at a high school in Welland as one of five projects within a larger government agency-funded research study entitled Maker Literacies.[1] Fifteen Grade 11 students (10 who identified as girls and five identifying as boys) worked on the six-week documentary film project. These young people were poignantly aware of their town's deficit image within the broader landscape of Ontario, and they were particularly protective about their community. Pleased, even delighted, by the rendering of Welland in Vanessa's documentary, Beyonce[2] (a young woman) called out: "This documentary makes Welland look good!," thus encapsulating the spirit of this chapter's focus on how teenagers materialize their community through human and non-human engagements within documentary films. The posthumanist and new materialist dimensions of the chapter reside both in teenagers' non-human modes of expression coupled with the way in which they talked about their everyday lives in Welland as an entanglement of human and non-human forces (Pahl et al., 2020).

We conceptualize these students' maker processes through a posthuman approach to data analyses (Kuby, 2017), and, in our engagements with posthumanist theory, we draw on work by Kuby and Gutshall Rucker (2016) and Deleuze and Guattari (1980) to understand how these students thought and experimented with moving image techniques and technologies to create film narratives.

The chapter is divided into four sections in which we (1) consider how posthumanism framed our thinking about maker activities, and (2) think with posthumanism to look at interview transcripts. Our project team included two researchers (Amélie Lemieux and Jennifer Rowsell), a media artist (Vanessa Crosbie-Ramsay), and a high school teacher of English. Our aim was to offer students a unit of study to express, through documentary/film-making, their responses to the novel *Shattered* that contained difficult themes of homelessness, anxiety, depression, and Post-Traumatic Stress Disorder (PTSD).

During the first phase of the project students read *Shattered*, the story of a friendship between a war veteran, now homeless, and a teenager from an affluent background, who steadily learns about what it means to struggle with mental health, poverty, and a displaced existence. In the second phase, the English teacher and Vanessa elicited from students themes of anxiety and PTSD, and asked them to produce a short documentary that explored these issues more deeply. We found that bringing posthuman concepts to this work offered an entangled and complex view of how people and affective forces of anxiety and trauma "become-with" (Braidotti, 2018) the materiality of city streets, homes, and class differences. Posthumanism also helped us to think through experimentation (Deleuze & Guattari, 1994) and moments of becoming that unfolded as students played, improvised, and made with different modes (Rowsell & McQueen-Fuentes, 2017). This group of students had a particular dynamic, with the females in the group having stronger voices and a greater presence, while the few males in the class tended to gather at the back and work individually. Yet there was a cohesive feel to the group which had been in school together for some time. What we observed as the film-making process unfolded was a greater intensity to their work together and longer periods of silence with, paradoxically, periods of debate and arguing about visual effects, sonic decisions, and spatial orientations.

Engaging with Shattered

Shattered depicts the story of Ian, a 15-year-old who befriends a Canadian war veteran (Sarge) while volunteering at a local soup kitchen for homeless people. Ian experiences conflicting emotions as he listens to his new friend's stories of his past. As Sarge tells him about his time serving with the Canadian-led United Nations mission in Rwanda during the Genocide, he recalls painful memories that trigger PTSD episodes. Chosen by the English teacher, *Shattered* served as a catalyst for the documentary-film process given its focus on topics that were close to home for students who had observed homelessness in their own town. Based on their readings, we asked students to (1) familiarize themselves with the documentary genre (based on Vanessa's expertise in documentary film-making); and (2) produce a short documentary focusing on themes and with guidance from Vanessa, Amélie, and Jennifer. Students chose their topics of interest and concern – those that held personal and felt connections, and also those that captured their imagination.

During class hours, students were placed into groups of three or four and used iMovie on iPads to edit their documentaries. At the end of the project, we planned a final screening during which students presented their documentaries to an audience (their peers and us). Each film screening was followed by questions and answers moderated by the research team, and students were able to field questions, extend their ideas, and offer provocations.

Posthumanist Contributions to Our Thinking about Maker Approaches

There has been a growing movement to adopt posthuman perspectives in literacy research (Kuby & Gutshall-Rucker, 2016; Kuby & Rowsell, 2017; Nichols & Campano, 2017; Toohey, 2018). We build on this energy by applying posthumanist theories to a group of teenagers' efforts to produce short films. Shifting the traditional focus from human-oriented theories of learning (such as behaviourism, positivism, social constructivism) to posthuman theories, we hope to inhabit a "being/doing/knowing" approach (Kuby & Rowsell, 2017, p. 285) by excavating how humans become-with non-human subjects. In particular, we recognize thinking with materials as a form of making, whereby students think about their fleeting and affective relationships with "what might be" (Ringrose & Coleman, 2013, p. 125), that is, in this case, digital products (documentaries) that are materially shaped in real-time spaces. We cannot claim to be experts in posthuman or new materialist theories, but we recognize the value in maker education to account for assemblages of human-and-non-human becoming and intra-actions (Braidotti, 2018).

There is a natural coupling between maker/craft-based work and posthuman approaches to literacy. As a grassroots movement, maker approaches to literacy involve accessing technologies, resources, and materials to make texts and objects through experimentation and problem-solving. Maker approaches are considered grassroots explosions in do-it-yourself (DIY) and maker cultures (Peppler et al., 2016). The reported research adopts a maker approach, but rather than focusing on technologies and materials, we focus instead on concepts of craft knowledge and material engagements (Rowsell & Shillitoe, 2019), understood as the practices and processes of working with materials, as opposed to focusing exclusively on the forms of materials themselves (see also Ingold, 2013). Maker and multimodal approaches to literacy work are established ways of researching and analyzing the qualities of meaning-making (Rowsell et al., 2018). However, aspects of meaning-making can be fleeting and they get missed, or are at least eclipsed, when adopting an exclusively representational, production-oriented focus on the qualities of work across different modes. Posthumanism and the concept of agential realism (Barad, 2007) have considerably pushed our thinking about conducting multimodal fieldwork. Through posthumanism, we de-centre youth identities and view these identities as entangled or assembled with matter and materials that emerge in making, designing, and producing. Such an approach allows us to account for the ways that material humans work with other materials and foreground more embodied and affective engagements as well as ways that matter and materials animate agentive qualities. Different materials, such as the iMovie software on the iPad and the iPad hardware, produce affective flows and human and material desirings that make some things possible and constrain others; in this case, the iPads were consequential as we elaborate later in this chapter.

Karen Barad (2007) distinguishes interactions from *intra*-actions. Interaction references an ontology of separateness, such as individual elements, things-humans-subjects-objects. Intra-action, in contrast, is Barad's concept and refers to entangled human and non-human where individual separations dissolve. An agential cut happens when differences are made by our research apparatuses, discourses, and educational practices. In this way, meanings and subjectivities are made rather than found as pre-existing entities. Drawing on this distinction, we believe, as Barad (2007) argues, that what we witnessed during the research was a "mutual constitution of entangled agencies" (p. 33), whereby intra-activity emphasized the assemblages between human and non-human agents (students ⟵⟶ camera ⟵⟶ editing work). These entanglements point to the indeterminacy of matter across time (Smythe et al., 2017). Ontologically speaking, taking this stance as we analyzed film and interview data, we argue that humans and non-humans involved in the research *became* (Deleuze & Guattari, 1980) together in a dynamic process, whereby process and product took on an equally important and relational role. These relationships were observed in software ⟵⟶ matter ⟵⟶ editing tools ⟵⟶ humans (students, research team). Thinking with the concept of intra-action allowed us to foreground an emergent quality of the young people's film work. Hence, we drew on posthumanist theory to access and extenuate the dynamic and hybrid quality of each group's moving image compositional work.

We drew on such scholars as Doucet (2018), who used an affective, posthumanist approach to analyze a family photograph to delve into memory work and Indigenous storytelling. Doucet (2018) created an ontological narrative derived from a family picture of her aunt Hannah to consider (1) the people present in the picture (with descriptions and positions of subjects); (2) the context and setting of the picture, i.e. by whom it was taken, when, where, and for what purposes; (3) the aesthetic choices and technologies that made this picture possible; and (4) how the photograph is received and perceived in real-time situations. Doucet (2018) defines ontological narratives as being two-fold, with a first emphasis on how they are agential, and a second focus on how they unfold "subjectivities and narrative identities" (p. 18). Our approach was also to "think with" (Doucet, 2018; Mazzei, 2016), by adopting a mindset of decentring ourselves as human-researchers and the young people who were involved in this documentary/film-making project, and focusing instead on intra-actions in space ⟷ matter ⟷ time ⟷ affective flows.

Being relatively new to posthumanist and new materialist theories, we hesitated over operationalizing such terms and concepts. Nonetheless, we found the collaborative thinking with and thinking through of posthumanist theory generative and most certainly amplifying, animating and enlightening when conducting and analyzing maker and multimodal research. We attempted to decentre ourselves when we conducted research, especially as we analyzed data in co-writing this chapter. To decentre the human, we question humanist assumptions by accounting for aspects of production and the ways that materials and modalities design and production (Rowsell et al., 2018) offer potentialities, possibilities, and moments of becoming. To illustrate our method for analyzing humanist-decentred moments, we draw from a research moment with Liza. Liza, a student participant, wanted to try the green screen for her documentary on Romeo Dallaire.[3] After we set up the green screen in an empty classroom, Liza stood in front of it and experimented with poses. When we projected these poses on the iPad, she transformed into a different person – Liza with a tropical backdrop; Liza with skulls from Rwanda in the background; and Liza in close-up. Considering the capacity for the green screen to transform Liza into a more intimate, close-up, and personal space with just her face, or, placing her in an exoticized island setting entangled a human body ⟷ natural worlds ⟷ semiotic forces. The iPad took on a life of its own. It was a portal into different locales and spaces of becoming and with each one we saw Liza in different lights. Each person in the room (including Jennifer and Vanessa who were part of the process) took turns looking through the iPad at Liza in multiple ways until we all agreed on the shot that captured her biography on Dallaire. This human-decentring stance is not a direct application of posthumanist theory, but instead is a diffractive approach to data with bits of the more-than-humanness of the iPad and the green screen *becoming* with Liza. The green screen gave form to Liza as much as the iPad animated and materialized her.

Data Collection and Procedure for Analysis

Our research methods rest on ethnographic fieldnotes combined with multimodal analyses (Heath & Street, 2008; Thompson, 2014). At the end of the research project, we conducted one-on-one interviews with five students who were willing to speak with us. These conversations were recorded with an audiorecorder, and the transcriptions were outsourced and transcribed professionally. What emerged from those conversations were intensities (Massumi, 2007) and moments when documentaries (as product and as a making process) clearly impacted students' self-identification as makers and their engagements with materials. We detail these intensities below.

To engage with our corpus of interview data, we draw on Kuby's (2017) posthumanist method for presenting interview data in literacy research and we ponder the question she asks: "How do we talk to students and (re)present entanglements with humans/non-humans?" (p. 167). That is, we emphasize the "discursive relationships of becoming" (Kuby, 2017, p 167) that take place between interviewer ⟷ interviewee ⟷ topic ⟷ themes ⟷ situations, in no particular order even though writing prescribes such structured procedures. Some participants narrated complete monologues and so we included these verbatim and left the repetitions to show emphases on topics and content. Like Ehret (2018) and Kuby (2017), we tried to find ways of illustrating human and non-human interactions and throughout the research we thought about non-representational theories. We thus acknowledge, as a limitation, that our analysis entails coding-oriented ways of looking at data. Like Kuby (2017), as well as Toohey and Dagenais (2015), we mark intensities through different fonts and typeface styles, but they also indicate restrictions that do not often resonate with posthumanism because it is difficult to escape the representational discourses embedded in language constructs (Barad, 2003; St. Pierre & Jackson, 2014). These restrictions, affective intensities, and the ways in which discourses of language are entangled in our research methods, highlight the differences and distinctions we make as we do our analytic work.

Adjusting font and layout is not intuitive; rather it is pushed by writing conventions (Genette, 1987). In other words, it is a structured way of representing data within the scientific genre that is in an academic register. Like Kuby (2017), we found issue with using traditional, human-centric ways of sharing transcriptions and, in a similar fashion, we used different fonts to represent parts of the discourse: **this rhetorical convention highlights a theme, this one marks the interviewer/interviewee**, and this one illustrates emphases/intensities from the participants. These conventions focus on relational moments between materials ⟷ humans, as well as entanglements between human and non-human actors, or what Kuby (2017) defines as the "processes and doings" (p. 170). For screen captures of documentary footage, we experimented with a method of looking at the intra-activity of modes in the moving image work. We looked at how students included still images within their documentaries (a practice also identified in Toohey and Dagenais, 2015), how human representations (through images and sounds) found themselves as part of the documentaries, and how in some cases the documentaries did not incorporate the students and in fact decentred them. In one case, which we will explore later, sonic and visual representations of the late actor Cory Monteith played an integral role in all stages of the film-making process. As he was a celebrity who struggled with anxiety and depression, a group of students wanted to make him (or representations and becomings of him) central in their work from beginning to end, and he occupied those spaces in the student-made production.

Agential Cuts

In analyzing interview data from a posthuman lens, we identified moments within the multimodal work that young people completed. For example, Bella shared her concerns and the implications of her documentary for other teenage girls who struggle with eating disorders, anxiety, and depression:

BELLA: A lot of girls eat junk food and then are self-conscious about their weight and think everybody hates them, and then certain people know other people and then a few years later they're acting completely different 'cause they have anxiety and depression. So we tried to make it like when the viewers watch it they can even be like I've been in that situation. Or I know somebody who's been in that situation. So you can relate to it on a personal level.
AMÉLIE (LEMIEUX): Okay, so you guys were thinking about the audience when you were making?
BELLA: Yeah, we were thinking about that. That was part of the planning process too.

What emerged from the conversation between Bella and Amélie was an acute sense and emphasis on feelings of anxiety linked to fast food and considerations for the audience ("like when the viewers watch it ... so you can relate to it on a personal level"). Amélie wanted to know if the latter sentence was coincidental and therefore probed about audience – the notion of making for people with these people in mind – and wanted to know if, at all, the group thought beyond "making in the moment," with consideration for viewers other than themselves. Film-making presupposes thinking about others than the self, therefore also including entanglements such as film-makers⟵⟶materialities⟵⟶audience. Recalling the girls' project and their wishes in making, including the entanglement Timbits[4]⟵⟶anxiety, was a priority to communicate to future viewers what it felt like to be anxious about eating disorders.

Drawing on Barad's (2003) new materialism, we put to work the notion of *agential cuts* as defying Cartesian binaries of the mind/body, and therefore view the qualities of meaning-making as entanglements of human and non-human worlds. Barad's notion of agential cuts allows us to see the ways in which spaces, people, and objects are entangled, making moments across time and space messy (Rowsell et al., 2018). In this way, and within this larger assemblage, anxiety ⟷ Bella ⟷ other participants ⟷ depression ⟷ junk food ⟷ Timbits ⟷ interview is an agential cut. Through this agenial cut, anxiety and depression emerge as main concerns of the group's documentary. They all performed roles in the documentary as teachers (who offer help) and as students (who struggle with anxiety and depression), and the narrator provided statistics, symbols (Timbits, heavy women, body shaming), and figures/bodies that allude to body image. Incorporating Cory Monteith as a visual and conceptual anchor in the documentary, the group showed how people from all walks of life suffer from anxiety and depression, and the varied ways that the condition manifests itself. Rosie, one of the members of the group, insisted on including Monteith as a strong presence in the film and, given that he passed away due to addiction, she felt that he was a fitting icon. There were several smaller arguments between Bella and Rosie about including him, and after compromising, the entangled agencies of Monteith and a whole array of other elements could be felt in the music (his songs), and through a camera shot of his face.

When Bella talked through her process of narrowing down and negotiating a topic with her group, her decisions, choices, and beliefs during conversations connected strongly with embodied feelings. These embodied feelings relate to the ways that she experiences the world and her own materiality across time and space as well as how her modulations and intensities were experienced throughout the research process. We noticed Bella in particular because she is so open about her emotions, and we witnessed her ebbing and flowing during classroom conversations, group interactions, private conversations with us, and her behaviour during the project. However, in addition to a focus on Bella, our posthuman analysis needed to pay attention to discourses about anxiety, depression, addiction, body image, appearances, and gendered stereotypes that circulated in the press (and in youth's online discourses). In addition, we needed to consider the affect, emotions, and politics (whose voices were stronger, for example) in this intra-action, and how they were entangled with the students' reading and representation of *Shattered*.

For Bella's group, strong associations between eating Timbits and obesity, and between gyms and thinness became desired foci for their film, matters that connect with Bella's own "weight issues" and anxiety. Bella's group collaboration was a particularly fraught one at times because Bella and Rosie clashed about how they conceived of the content. This recognition of entanglements between human (Bella, Rosie, Geri) and non-human (Timbits, gym equipment, drawing of a heavy woman, etc.) elicits what we regard as an agential cut, or as Barad (2003) describes, it enacts "a *local* resolution *within* the phenomenon of the inherent ontological indeterminacy" (p. 815, emphasis in the original). There was a screen capture in their documentary that showed a materialization of the emotions that Bella described she had experienced growing up with anxiety and depression. Written in black ink on a girl's body, the words ("FAT," "disgusting," "gross," "pig," "ew," "thinner," "diet," "eat," "starve," etc.) spoke to inner human feelings that someone dealing with eating disorders may experience in addition to self-harm, visible in the form of cuts on one of the forearms. This picture echoed multiple material-discursive relationships: the girls' selection of this image and the impact of the image on the girls (and on us when we watched the short film); its design and the focus on material-discursive relationships; the physicality of the flesh, the cuts, the white bra the subject on the picture is wearing, two black lines on each side of the subject's waist where the flesh *should* have stopped if she was thinner. Literal cuts thus unfolded as follows: the group's decision to include the still image; the Google image search (we observed this and spoke with them about it), the process of embedding the picture in the documentary, the group (researchers and participants together) viewing of the documentary, and the process of reinterpretation that occurred in writing this chapter. The cuts do not end there – with chapter reviewers, chapter readers, and so on participating in agential cuts themselves as they engage with this chapter in different spaces, at different times, and involving other materialities.

A Refrain

There is another layer to Bella's documentary film-making story which concerns some of the tensions that she experienced with Rosie. The inclusion of Monteith in the documentary film was central to the girls' discussions about how they would design and film their piece. Following the interview transcript, we included a still (Figure 7.1) which originally showed the editing work and transition between images, from the girls' performance in a classroom setting to Monteith's profile (including a picture taken from Google Images that could not be included here due to copyright issues). In the following conversation, Bella expands on the struggles with her peers (interactions) and how the group trouble-shooted and tinkered with iMovie to make their project come to fruition:

Exploring Posthumanism in a Documentary Film Project   129

FIGURE 7.1 Intra-active becoming with Cory Monteith

BELLA: Drug overdose, yeah. So she said oh, I want to put him in our project and I said okay but we've got to figure out how to relate to him. We can't just throw him in there. She didn't listen to me, she threw a picture of him in there. Vanessa turned around and said you can't just throw a picture of him in there. And so we put a voice-over and then Rosie was completely not on board with the voiceover over his picture. She was like oh, there shouldn't be any sound behind him. Just him singing. The song we have is his song from Glee and it makes sense because it's called Stand by You I think. It's talking about I won't let anybody hurt you. I'll stand by you through the hard times, it doesn't matter. And that deals with anxiety and depression because you need someone to be there, standing with you when you have anxiety and depression to help you.

Bella's group spent several days debating how Monteith would be represented in the short film, and Vanessa, the media artist who worked with the students, felt that there had to be a purpose for him in the film narrative, as otherwise it would appear arbitrary to include him. After several heated discussions, the students kept a photo of him and one of his songs, *Stand by You*. The image above originally showed a transition between two scenes: (1) an interaction between a student struggling with anxiety and her teacher, and (2) Cory Monteith's picture with the song playing in the background (not shown here due to copyright issues).

There are flows of desiring in this description of multimodal production. On the one hand, there is Bella's desiring for an arc to the film's story, structure, and cohesion across the three-minute film where Monteith was a choice without direct and substantive connections with the film. On the other hand, there is Rosie's desiring to include him in the film. What is happening during these relational moments involves largely human material Bella ⟷ Rosie ⟷ Cory Monteith ⟷ Vanessa (media artist) ⟷ Jennifer (researcher) – and non-human words ⟷ images ⟷ sounds ⟷ colours ⟷ iPad ⟷ iMovie ⟷ microphone, etc. The group's discussions relate to Guattari's (1995) description of *refrains* as patterns of expectations and behaviour. Rosie's devotion to Monteith and Bella's argument about lyrics and sounds merged, flowed, and became together as a leitmotif in the short film. There had to be a compromise, and Rosie and Bella needed to agree on the Monteith visual and substantive anchor. In other words, this refrain – Monteith, his voice, *Glee* – became a space that tied desire with matter and materialization.

Posthuman Relationships and Collaborative Mindsets

We found that collaboration among students, researchers, and professionals took place at all stages, and that working in groups was generative in finding solutions and coming up with a finished product that pleased everyone. Hackett et al. (2015) made similar findings about incorporating cross-sector professionals into their multimodal fieldwork during the Community Arts Zone research project. They found that when young people collaborated with adults and professionals, generative learning happened, producing synergies in terms of perspectives and implications for multimodal meaning-making. In the excerpt below, Beyonce emphasizes how helpful it was to work with experts in the classroom in addition to her teacher, notably because she felt nervous about being included in a group as a newcomer to the school:

JENNIFER (ROWSELL): Can you just talk through how you felt about the project as a whole?

BEYONCE: At the beginning I was pretty nervous about it because it's a kind of experience for me especially me coming to a new school this year so I was really nervous because especially if we were going to make our own groups I felt like I was gonna be the lonely one but throughout you including Daniele, Amélie, and Vanessa were helping and at the end of it, it became really easy and I enjoyed it. So I'm really excited to present them now and watch everyone else's.

JENNIFER: and what were the bits that you really liked? And then I'm gonna ask you about the bits that you didn't like and [felt] iffy about and all of that.

BEYONCE: The parts that I really enjoyed was probably putting it together 'cause I've never done anything like that so it was a whole new experience for myself. So when we were putting it together and I finally saw it I was like I can't believe we actually did that. It was really shocking to me 'cause I didn't know I could do something like that. So I really enjoyed that part and I also enjoyed working with you yourself, Vanessa, and Daniele.

In this conversation with Jennifer, Beyonce stresses how surprised she was at her own capacities as a maker and at the skills she did not anticipate having. Making affords reflections, temporal changes, and realizations (for example, Beyonce looking back and being happy and surprised about her accomplishments, discovering "a whole new experience"). Her comments answered the questions put to her, but her recognition of her growing expertise seemed to surprise her. That is, while Jennifer's questions tended to enact agential cuts – a process through which the conversations could take certain discursive pathways – the paths these took were unpredictable, surprising, and indeterminate.

Guiding students in their making and film-making, we see ourselves as "doing/being/thinking" with teenagers: we were there with them, answering their questions and them answering ours, being in their documentaries, assisting with editing, pushing their thoughts in either new directions or ones they wanted to pursue. Throughout the interviews, we also found that the students, as makers, enjoyed helping each other along the way.

BELLA: Geri, she's an exchange student, I think she came last year. She didn't know how to use an iPad. She's never touched an iPad. And now she knows because we sat there and we said okay, Geri, this is how you do it. We taught her. And then me and Rosie learned to work together, and I feel it's an educational purpose because you learn how to make documentaries. You need to learn about the topic you're filming. You also learn I think personal life skills like how to work with people, how to teach people, how to listen to people because in a group you have to listen to each other and help each other, and like I said cooperate with one another. So I think it was a big learning process and I had tons of fun doing it. I'd do it again if I had to.

Bella emphasized in her response how this experience was educational, collaborative, and generative. These three dimensions shaped how Bella viewed her experience of making as a transformative practice, whereby she felt a sense of responsibility that came with designing film, editing with iPads, and showing friends who struggle with technology how to play with commands in order to make, produce, design, and edit. Not only was this process educational and transformative, according to Bella, but it was also "fun" and instructive ("I feel it's an educational purpose because you learn how to make documentaries. You need to learn about the topic you're filming"). A humane, collaborative, and community-building dimension is embedded in making documentaries, as Bella expressed, because working in groups and with people who come from outside the school generates learning about "personal life skills" in Bella's words, like teaching, listening, helping, and cooperating.

Future Research Considerations

We acknowledge that recent early childhood literacy research based on posthuman thought has only recently been taken up in English Language Arts (Hackett & Somerville, 2017; Kuby et al., 2017). In this chapter, we took up the challenge of thinking with posthumanism, which was a steep learning curve for us, but which provided us with a more textured picture of the flows and intensities in the making of documentaries. That is, we appreciated the ways in which posthumanist theories add complexity, layers, and texture. We committed to understanding the topologies of "co-ing," "inter-ing," and "intra-ing" not only with our participants, but also in our research praxis, especially during research presentations in which we made a commitment to focus more on the process than on the product. As such, in this chapter, we investigated the relationships between high school students' perspectives on their film-making practices, sensitive topics such as anxiety, eating disorders, homelessness, and PTSD, and the affective dimensions embedded in maker education at the high school level.

Posthumanism paves the way for more complex understandings of the self in relation to others, evolving environments, and contextual circumstances that are situated in time, and that are, in other words, "entanglements with the world" (Hackett & Somerville, 2017, p. 388). Magnifying these entanglements in educational research through posthumanism has the potential to bolster productive changes for literacy futures, in that they may:

1. Open possibilities for interpretive research on "e/affect" (Kuby et al., 2017, p. 365) in maker education;
2. Situate learning within flexible networks including conversations with the self and with others; and,
3. Help teachers and researchers alike in situating students' learning processes in "being/doing/knowing" (Kuby & Rowsell, 2017, p. 285) as it responds to maker mindsets.

In conclusion, we probed the shift from exploring multimodal productions as we have in the past to experimenting with a more non-representational account of what we witnessed over the six weeks of fieldwork. For instance, through a posthumanist approach to interview analyses (Kuby, 2017), we were able to locate discursive-material entanglements within interview data. Yet another example of the contribution of posthumanist theories to our analyses is our effort to pin down and locate how cuts and edits to documentaries were affectively driven during the process and the intricacies of this process as a group chose modes and matter to illustrate their ideas, beliefs, and interests.

In our efforts to think about maker approaches in ways that de-centre humans, we ventured into a maker project that gave teenagers the necessary space to design, plan, storyboard, and record their own direct views on human issues like depression, anxiety, PTSD, and homelessness. As we wrote and edited this chapter, we appreciated how central matter and materials were to these young people, and how modes and materials were the stuff that moved them. Being able to express how they feel about their community was so grounded in and imbricated with intra-actions between human and non-human forces that it was not a spoken or tangible element of the research, but instead something that we all felt and experienced – students, teachers, and researchers alike – as we sat at the final viewing to witness what the cuts made.

Notes

1. Maker Literacies is a government-funded research project on Maker Education led by Jennifer Rowsell. This research is supported by the Social Sciences and Humanities Research Council of Canada (grant number 435-2017-0097) and is associated with a European Grant led by Dr. Jackie Marsh entitled Maker Spaces in the Early Years: Enhancing Digital Literacy and Creativity *(MakEY)*.
2. The real names of all students have been changed to preserve their anonymity, and they chose their own pseudonyms.
3. Romeo Dallaire is a Lieutenant-General and Canadian war veteran who served as Force Commander for the United Nations Peacekeeping force during the 1993–1994 Rwandan genocide.
4. Timbits are small balls of doughnuts commercialized and sold by the fast food restaurant chain Tim Hortons.

Acknowledgements

The authors would like to acknowledge the suggestions made by the editors and reviewers, which were helpful in crafting this final version of the chapter.

References

Barad, K. (2003). Posthumanist performativity: Toward an understanding of how matter comes to matter. *Signs: Journal of Women in Culture and Society*, 28(3), 801–831. Retrieved August 8, 2019, from www.journals.uchicago.edu/doi/abs/10.1086/345321?journalCode=signs.

Barad, K. (2007). *Meeting the universe halfway: Quantum physics and the entanglement of matter and meaning*. Durham, NC: Duke University Press.

Braidotti, R. (2018). A theoretical framework for the critical posthumanities. *Theory, Culture, and Society*, 1(1), 1–31. doi:10.1177/0263276418771486.

Deleuze, G., & Guattari, F. (1980). *Mille plateaux: Capitalisme et schizophrénie* II. Paris, France: Éditions de Minuit.

Deleuze, G., & Guattari, F. (1994). *What is philosophy?* New York: Columbia University Press.

Doucet, A. (2018). Decolonizing family photographs: Ecological imaginaries and nonrepresentational ethnographies. *Journal of Contemporary Ethnography*, 47(6), 729–757. doi:10.1177/0891241617744859.

Ehret, C. (2018). Moments of teaching and learning in a children's hospital: Affects, textures, and temporalities. *Anthropology & Education Quarterly*, 49(1), 53–71. doi:10.1111/aeq.12232.

Genette, G. (1987). *Seuils*. Paris, France: Seuil.

Guattari, F. (1995). *Chaosmosis: An ethico-aesthetic paradigm*. Bloomington and Indianapolis: Indiana University Press.

Hackett, A., Pool, S., Rowsell, J., & Aghajan, B. (2015). Seen and unseen: Using video data in ethnographic fieldwork. *Qualitative Research Journal*, 15(4), 430–444. doi:10.1108/QRJ-06-2015-0037.

Hackett, A., & Somerville, M. (2017). Posthuman literacies: Young children moving in time, place and more-than-human worlds. *Journal of Early Childhood Literacy*, 17(3), 374–391. doi:10.1177/1468798417704031.

Heath, S. B., & Street, B. (2008). *On ethnography: Approaches to language and literacy research*. New York: Teachers College Press.

Ingold, T. (2013). *Making: Anthropology, archaeology, art and architecture*. London: Routledge.

Kuby, C. R. (2017). Poststructural and posthuman theories as literacy research methodologies: Tensions and possibilities. In R. Zaidi & J. Rowsell (Eds.), *Literacy lives in transcultural times* (pp. 157–174). New York: Routledge.

Kuby, C. R., & Gutshall Rucker, T. (2016). *Go be a writer! Expanding the curricular boundaries of literacy learning with young children*. New York: Routledge.

Kuby, C. R., Gutshall Rucker, T., & Darolia, L. H. (2017). Persistence(ing): Posthuman agency in a writers' studio. *Journal of Early Childhood Literacy*, 17(3), 353–373. doi:10.1177/1468798417712067.

Kuby, C. R., & Rowsell, J. (2017). Early literacy and the posthuman: Pedagogies and methodologies. *Journal of Early Childhood Literacy*, 17(3), 285–296. doi:10.1177/1468798417715720.

Massumi, B. (2007). *Parables for the virtual*. Durham, NC: Duke University Press.

Mazzei, L. A. (2016). Voice without a subject. *Cultural Studies ⟷ Critical Methodologies*, 16(2), 151–161. doi:10.1177/1532708616636893.

Nichols, T. P., & Campano, G. (2017). Post-humanism and literacy studies. *Language Arts*, 94(4), 245–251. Retrieved July 4, 2019, from www.ncte.org/journals/la/issues/v94-4.

Pahl, K. & Rowsell, J., with D. Collier, S. Pool, Z. Rasool, and T. Trzecak (2020). *Living Literacies: Rethinking literacy research and practice through the everyday.* Boston, MA: MIT Press.

Peppler, K., Halverson, E., & Kafai, Y. (Eds.) (2016). *Makeology: Makerspaces as learning environments.* New York: Routledge.

Ringrose, J., & Coleman, R. (2013). Looking and desiring machines: A feminist Deleuzian mapping of bodies and affects. In R. Coleman & J. Ringrose (Eds.), *Deleuze and research methodologies* (pp. 125–144). Edinburgh: Edinburgh University Press.

Rowsell, J., Lemieux, A., Swartz, L., Burkitt, J., & Turcotte, M. (2018). The stuff that heroes are made of: Elastic, sticky, messy literacies in children's transmedial cultures. *Language Arts,* 96(1), 7–20. Retrieved August 8, 2019, from www.ncte.org/library/NCTEFiles/Resources/Journals/LA/0961-sep2018/LA0961Sep18Stuff.pdf.

Rowsell, J., & McQueen-Fuentes, G. (2017). Moving parts in imagined spaces: Community arts zone's movement project. *Pedagogies: An International Journal,* 12(1), 74–89. doi:10.1080/1554480X.2017.1283995.

Rowsell, J., & Shillitoe, M. (2019). The craftivists: Pushing for affective, materially informed pedagogy. *The British Journal of Technology in Education,* 50(4), 1544–1559. doi:10.1111/bjet.12773.

Smythe, S., Hill, C., Dagenais, D., Sinclair, N., & Toohey, K. (2017). *Disrupting boundaries in education and research.* Cambridge: Cambridge University Press.

St. Pierre, E. A., & Jackson, A. Y. (2014). Qualitative data analysis after coding. *Qualitative Inquiry,* 20(6), 715–719. doi:10.1177/1077800414532435.

Thompson, J. (2014). On writing notes in the field: Interrogating positionality, emotion, participation and ethics. *McGill Journal of Education,* 49(1), 247–254. https://doi.org/10.7202/1025781ar.

Toohey, K. (2018). *Learning English at school: Identity, socio-material relations and classroom practice.* Bristol: Multilingual Matters.

Toohey, K., & Dagenais, D. (2015). Videomaking as sociomaterial assemblage. *Language and Education,* 29(4), 302–316. doi:10.1080/09500782.2015.1006643.

8

AFFECT THEORY AS A LENS ON TEACHER THINKING IN ADULT LANGUAGE CLASSROOMS

Monica Waterhouse

This chapter focuses on the usefulness of new materialist theorizing within the context of a three-year qualitative study with English and French second language teachers in government-funded programmes for adult newcomers in the Canadian provinces of Ontario and Quebec. Guo's (2015) pan-Canadian survey of such programmes shows that they "typically serve four purposes: English [or French in Quebec] language training, preparation for the labor market, preparation for the citizenship test, and integration into Canadian society" (p. 43). As guides to language and a new way of life, teachers in these programmes become important social actors in the Canadian context (Lussier, 2011). They accompany learners through their integration experience, the complexity of which is ignored in many language programmes that place heavy emphasis on preparation for and adaptation to the local job market (Guo, 2015).

Similarly, the affective/emotional dimensions of integration that play out in language classrooms tend to be marginalized in the mandated curricula which frame emotions narrowly as either affective barriers to language acquisition or as sociolinguistic competencies to be acquired by students (Waterhouse & Mortier-Faulkner, 2014). Yet research shows that second language teachers regularly engage in significant emotional labour as they respond not only to their students' emotions, but also reflect on their own in relation to classroom events (Benesch, 2012). Moreover, this kind of emotion work can be especially demanding in situations involving individuals who have experienced violence as in the case of refugee students in newcomer language classes (Horsman, 1999, p. 200). Thus, this current study considers the problem of how teachers pedagogically juggle teaching French or English, fostering their students' societal integration, and responding to the challenges presented by affectively charged classroom life.

In this chapter, I draw on questionnaire data that include the pedagogical responses of English and French second language teachers (ESL and FSL, respectively) with regard to affective/emotional situations that occur in classrooms. However, before I turn to the empirical study, I elucidate how I view materialism in relation to Deleuze-Guattarian affect theory and how it offers a useful lens on teachers' pedagogical thinking in adult newcomer language programmes.

Materialism and Deleuze-Guattarian Reframings

In 2005, after completing a Master's thesis in language teaching and learning, I volunteered as an ESL conversation group leader with adult students in the Canadian federal government's Language Instruction for Newcomers to Canada programme (LINC). This practical experience presented me with a new research problem, namely the problem of unexpected affectively charged events. My journal entry written after a conversation session on April 25, 2005 is a good example:

> We were reading *Canada's Food Guide*. One student told me she did not eat red meat, so, curious, I asked her why. Was she a vegetarian? Was it for health reasons? Her reply was matter-of-fact: She saw her husband murdered with a machete and since then she found she could not bear cooking red meat because of the blood. ... I was speechless.

This event was the impetus for my return to research as a doctoral student. My project focused on adult immigrant language classrooms as I sought some way to explain the unpredictability and contingency of affectively charged events that seemed to spontaneously arise despite best efforts to avoid them. I began reading the materialist philosophy of Deleuze and Guattari (1987) and it immediately engaged me; I found their conceptual repertoire and associated onto-epistemological assumptions to be extremely helpful for thinking about experiences in adult immigrant language programmes like LINC.

Situating (My) Research with/in Materialism

I was both pleased and surprised when I was invited to contribute a chapter about materialist pedagogies in adult language and literacies: pleased because the invitation signalled an acknowledgment of the importance of materialist theorizing in adult language learning contexts, an area in which materialist-oriented research is relatively rare. I was surprised because to date I have not explicitly characterized my research with adult immigrant second language learners, theoretically framed by Deleuze-Guattarian affect theory (Deleuze, 1980; Deleuze & Guattari, 1987), as situated within new materialist frameworks. Yet I increasingly find my work identified as materialist or posthumanist which speaks to the growing prevalence of these perspectives, in educational research generally, and in language education research more specifically, as a reaction against the perceived hubris of humanist inquiry traditions (Pennycook, 2018). However, I associate with the terms *materialist* and *posthumanist* cautiously recognizing that they index a broad spectrum of theories and theorists, each with their own onto-epistemological assumptions that are not always viewed as being commensurate with one another (Hein, 2016).[1]

That said, materialist or posthumanist language and literacy research, including my own, shares "the premise that humans never act in isolation, but rather in concert with changing networks of people, objects, histories, and institutions" (Nichols & Campano, 2017, p. 246). Similarly, Deleuze and Guattari's philosophy may be considered materialist in so far as they "do not deny that human subjects can initiate novel and creative action in the world. However, they refuse to mystify this creativity as something essentially human" (Bonta & Protevi, 2004, p. 5). In addition to the materialist decentring of special privilege accorded to the agentive human subject and the concomitant recognition of the doings of the material world, Deleuze and Guattari join the materialist project of epistemologically suturing Cartesian dualisms including the mind-body split and the rationality-emotion opposition. This refusal to separate cognition from affect becomes essential in the current materialist consideration of teaching thinking in response to affectively charged classroom events.

In short, the basic tenets of a materialist perspective also hold within Deleuze and Guattari's relational ontology: The world is continually produced as things (both human and non-human) undergo becoming. This transformation happens in unpredictable ways as a result of immanent relations *with* other things. A relational ontology is particularly evident in their concept of *affect*. I now turn to a conceptual presentation of how Deleuze-Guattarian affect theory reframes the notions of affect and teacher thinking through a materialist lens.

What Is Affect?

Deleuze and Guattari's concept of *assemblages* is useful for thinking about social-material "networks of people, objects, histories, and institutions" (Nichols & Campano, 2017, p. 246). Adult second language classrooms are such an assemblage, "an intermingling of bodies reacting to one another" (Deleuze and Guattari, 1987, p. 88). These embodied reactions are shaped by each body's capacity to *affect* and be affected. Importantly, Deleuze (1980), drawing on Spinoza's *Ethics*, insists that these capacities cannot be known in advance of said intermingling. In other words, a body's powers to affect can only be understood relationally.

This concept of affect breaks from received understandings of the term as essentially equivalent to emotion and makes a clear distinction between affect and emotion. However, Deleuze-Guattarian affect theory still acknowledges a close relationship between affect and emotions. While affects may actualize as emotions, they express the pre-conscious, visceral response to an encounter *before* that response is named as a specific emotion. Again, affect is the relational power of a body to affect and be affected through encounters with other bodies (Deleuze & Guattari, 1987).

> Affect may be understood as emotions that are collectively or intersubjectively manifested, experienced, and mobilized out of the 'private', individual realm and into shared, even public spaces [such as classrooms]. ... The relationality of affect and emotion offers a grammar to understand the collective and intersubjective dimensions of felt experience.
>
> *(Boler & Davis, 2018, p. 81)*

Thus, affect shifts the focus from what emotions *mean* for individuals to what emotions *do* in the context of classroom life unfolding between human and non-human bodies (Benesch, 2012). From a materialist stance, emotions are not the property of an individual – they are not something one *has*. They are the effect (enactment) of affective relations between teacher-bodies, student-bodies, text-bodies (like *Canada's Food Guide* in my journal entry above), and so forth. They are active forces within the socio-material assemblage in which teaching and learning take place.

Given how affects pervade the classroom assemblage, Benesch (2012) regards them as "tools for understanding moment-by-moment pedagogical decision-making, grounded in teachers' ... embodied reactions to classroom events" (p. 134). Her referencing of decision-making explicitly links the question of affect with teachers' pedagogical thinking. I now turn to a discussion of how Deleuze-Guattarian affect theory reframes the very notion of thinking.

What Is Thinking?

Teacher thinking is usually described in terms of teacher cognition in the research literature. Predominant models in the field of language teacher cognition are based on an individual's pedagogical knowledge, practical knowledge, principles, beliefs, instructional concerns, and contextual factors

(Borg, 2006). Golombek and Doran (2014) noted that Borg's influential definition of language teacher cognition does not account for "what teachers feel about what they think, know, believe, and do" (p. 103), and Borg (2006) himself predicted that this emotional or affective dimension of teacher cognition "is likely to become more prominent in continuing research as we seek to understand how cognitive and affective factors interact in shaping what teachers do" (p. 320). Indeed, a recently published collection entitled *Emotions in Second Language Teaching* (Martínez Agudo, 2018) suggests that the field is responding to calls for greater attention to the role of emotions in teacher cognition and decision-making. However, the chapter authors remain decidedly humanist in their theoretical orientations; their studies are informed by psychological, cognitive, sociological, sociopolitical, social constructivist, and sociocultural theories. In sharp contrast, Deleuze-Guattarian affect theory reconceptualizes an individual teacher's thinking as an affective, relational event that happens to her/him.

Materialism raises a strange question: What if thinking isn't something individuals do, but rather something that happens *to* them? This is Deleuze's provocative proposition that stems from his relational ontology. In this view, the origin of thought is not the human brain, at least not exclusively. The brain is one part of a larger assemblage of immaterial elements and material bodies each with their own relational, affective capacities (Deleuze & Guattari, 1987). Watkins (2006) argues that if we take seriously the notion that teacher thinking is "a result of the impact of bodies affecting other bodies" (p. 272) within an assemblage, then this has significant implications for understanding the pedagogical choices of teachers and is, consequently, pertinent to the current study of how ESL and FSL teachers respond to emotions that manifest in classrooms.

Deleuze (1968/1994) articulates the affective, relational nature of thinking this way: "Something in the world forces us to think. This something is an object not of recognition but of a fundamental *encounter*. ... It may be grasped in a range of affective tones: wonder, love, hatred, suffering" (p. 139). To further underscore how affect is primordial to thinking events, Colebrook (2002) offers the following example: "I watch a scene in a film and my heart races, my eye flinches and I begin to perspire. Before I even think or conceptualise there is an element of [embodied] response that is prior to any decision" (p. 38). She helpfully summarizes: "Thinking is not something 'we' do; thinking happens to us, from without. There is a *necessity* to thinking, for the event of thought lies beyond the autonomy of choice. Thinking happens" (p. 38).

At this point it should be apparent that relational, affective thinking has important consequences for what might conventionally be termed teacher *agency*. Eschewing the humanist subject who thinks and controls events, materialists view "language, cognition and agency not merely as distributed across different people but rather as distributed beyond human boundaries" (Pennycook, 2018, p. 43). The implication is that while second language teachers still do make decisions and engage in particular pedagogical practices, the agentive impetus for these must be understood as co-enacted or distributed across socio-material assemblages (Nichols & Campano, 2017). In sum, Deleuze-Guattarian affect theory challenges long-standing cognition-affect separations in the study of second language education and reinstates embodied affect as a mode of thinking and becoming with the world in second language classrooms.

Pedagogical Experimentations with Affective Thinking

The following sections put materialist reformulations of affect and teaching thinking to work in relation to an empirical study and focuses on qualitative data from the first phase of the three-year project. In this phase, an online questionnaire invited Quebec FSL and Ontario ESL teachers working with newcomers to pedagogically respond to affectively charged classroom vignettes. A total of 82 teacher-respondents completed and anonymously submitted questionnaires over a twelve-month period in 2017 (Quebec FSL teachers n = 9 and Ontario ESL teachers n = 73).

Vignettes as Affective Text-Bodies in Research Assemblages

Kuby (2016) rightly asserts that "researchers cannot use old tools for new theories if the tools paradigmatically do not align with the theories" (p. 127). Thus, the first hurdle I faced was establishing a data collection approach appropriate to a study conceptually framed by Deleuze-Guattarian affect theory. I was initially attracted to a vignette-based approach because of its well-established utility for addressing research questions that hinge on rarely occurring phenomena, sensitive topics, ethical issues, dilemmas, and context-dependent decision-making situations (Tierney, 2011). Certainly, these characteristics applied to my questions around how second language teachers respond to affectively charged events in their classrooms. However, from a materialist standpoint, I was also interested in how vignettes might help to account for the socio-material assemblage of bodies in moments when emotions actualized in classrooms. Thus, even as the vignettes were carefully constructed following conventional principles for vignette development (Tierney, 2011), I also sought to foreground various affective bodies: teacher-bodies, student-bodies, and non-human bodies that have their own powers to affect and be affected (e.g. song-texts, poem-texts, story-texts, food). In addition, I foregrounded various actualizations of affect as emotions across the vignettes: anger, hope, excitement, happiness, unhappiness, loneliness, homesickness, regret, sadness, surprise.

Ultimately, I crafted four vignettes that were written in a teacher's first-person voice to comprise the questionnaire. Given the scope of this chapter I have opted to limit my discussion to data associated with Vignette 1:

> Today I worked on oral fluency with my students by teaching them to sing a folk song. I love doing this particular song with my students because it exemplifies a message that I strongly believe in: Canada is a country of immigrants and a place where everyone belongs, including newcomers. So it was really unexpected when one of my students reacted very angrily to the song's message. He shouted out that he has stopped believing that Canada is his country too. I told him I hoped he believed the song's message because he and his classmates are starting to become Canadians. Then suddenly the bell rang, my students left, and there was really no resolution to the situation.

Following each vignette, respondents were asked to imagine that the teacher in the vignette was a colleague and to share their thoughts in response to this prompt: "What concrete pedagogical advice might you offer to this colleague in light of what happened?"

Finally, from a Deleuze-Guattarian affective perspective, the vignettes do not operate in a conventional way in data collection. They are not aimed at authentically simulating real classroom experiences, although their writing was inspired by actual classroom events. Instead, the vignettes themselves are understood as text-bodies with powers to affect, powers which could not be known in advance of their encounters with teacher-respondent-bodies, as both became caught up in the complexity of a research assemblage. Each encounter was a singular experimentation; each time a different assemblage was created, it functioned in its own way to produce teacher thinking and the teacher's response.

Rhizoanalytic Approach

Deleuze-Guattarian concepts also reconfigure our approach to analysis as rhizomatic (Masny, 2016). This has several important implications. First, in rhizoanalysis, data escape interpretation. Data within a research assemblage are disruptive, "a becoming-problem that de-territorializes the givens of data. … To palpate data and construct questions from data might open up avenues for discussion" (Masny, 2016, p. 667). Thus, vignette response data in this study do not directly describe what teachers think or explain why they think it, rather the data operating in a rhizomatic research assemblage form connections that in turn prompt ongoing inquiry.

Second, rhizoanalysis maintains the decentred subject. Recall the materialist assertion that thinking happens to teachers – thinking happens to researchers as well. This means that the analytic thinking and sense that emerges from any given research assemblage is also shifting as elements of the assemblage enter into different relations and transform. Elements may include, but are not limited to, data transcripts, images, audio recordings, researcher brain, research assistant brains, eyes, ears, books, theories, analytic software, computer screens, audio recordings, and office spaces. Echoing this fundamental aspect of rhizoanalysis, MacLure (2013) explains that in materialist research, data have a way of participating in their own selection:

> We are no longer autonomous agents, choosing and disposing. Rather, we are obliged to acknowledge that data have their ways of making themselves intelligible to us. This can be seen, or rather felt, on occasions when one becomes especially 'interested' in a piece of data.
>
> *(p. 660)*

MacLure continues: "On those occasions, agency feels distributed and undecidable, as if we have chosen something that has chosen us" (p. 661). MacLure's comments resonate as I reflect on the process that produced the rhizoanalytic data assemblages presented in the next section. As I read and reread the questionnaires and discussed them with research assistants, certain data fragments "grabbed" us, asserting their affective force and demanding to be shared, proliferated.

Third, difference is also essential to the relational ontology underpinning rhizoanalysis (Masny, 2016). Although sense emerges from a particular research assemblage in a particular way, it is understood that this is just one potential actualization and it could be different. Research assemblages continually transform, and thus any rhizoanalysis could be otherwise and is always necessarily provisional and unfinished. As Toohey (2018) reminds us, materialist research requires an acknowledgement "of the partiality of the documentation, the indeterminacy of causal relations and the impossibility of permanent knowledge" (p. 89). Therefore, the following rhizoanalysis is not offered as an attempt to accurately describe the pedagogical responses of second language teachers to affectively charged events, but rather serves as a provocation to think differently about the potential of affectively charged language pedagogies in classrooms for adult newcomers.

Rhizoanalysis

The assemblages presented below address specific disruptions or tensions emerging from the rhizoanalytic process, thereby producing new problems and questions at the intersection of materialist theory and language pedagogies. Tensions discussed include how teachers validate students' emotional responses while still maintaining a positive classroom climate; how teachers understand what constitutes positive and negative emotions in the classroom; and how teachers attempt to harness the pedagogical potential of emotions while at the same time acknowledging the unpredictability inherent to classroom life as a socio-material assemblage. This last tension becomes particularly relevant in terms of distributed agency and the enactments of text-bodies (i.e. teaching materials) selected by the teacher.

Assemblage: Rethinking Problems-to-Be-Solved as Productive Pedagogical Life

Without exception, the respondents asserted that the teacher in the vignette, their imaginary colleague, should engage in some kind of follow-up. One advised: "Use the student's strong expression of emotion as an indicator that this was an important issue and definitely [do] not ignore it."[2] At a minimum, respondents specified that a private one-on-one conversation with the student who had had the angry outburst was warranted in order to learn more about why he reacted the way he did. They found it important, as one teacher mentioned, to attempt to "identify the root of the student's frustration and anger." Respondents frequently subsumed the student's emotional reaction under the rubric of a stage of culture shock, deeming it "normal." For example, one respondent wrote, "The student's response may have been unexpected but is quite understandable. Newcomers are at very different stages of adaptation, and there is no predictable, linear pattern of enculturation." While this comment can be linked to culture shock as a process of adaptation newcomers typically experience, it also stood out from others for its explicit recognition of the *unpredictability* of such affective processes.

When ascribing meaning in a conventional way, the student's affective response becomes a problem-to-be-solved (i.e. culture shock) and teacher thinking then led to recommendations that the vignette-teacher refer the student to community services or support resources available in their institutions, for example, social workers, counsellors, or other psychological professionals. The affective outburst was also thought of as problematic in terms of managing the affective climate of the classroom. In her research, Horsman (1999) noted that teachers, especially those working with students who have been victims of violence (e.g. refugees), often find themselves navigating "a difficult balance between expressing and restraining emotions" (p. 200). This seemed evident in the teachers' responses to the vignette. On the one hand, they repeatedly emphasized the importance of validating students' realities, experiences, and feelings. On the other hand, some also sanctioned "acceptable" or "appropriate" responses in the classroom even in moments of anger. These two sides of the emotional management coin are exemplified in this respondent's comment: "Of course, it's a good idea to express understanding and sympathy to him but still [...]. Anyway, first of all, you should introduce rules for the classroom: no aggression, no shouting, etc."

This kind of ambivalent teacher thinking emerges from a complex affective assemblage involving both cognitive and affective ways of knowing, acting, and becoming in classrooms. Benesch (2017) might call this the *emotion labour* teachers experience when faced with incompatibilities between the *feeling rules* of their teaching context (i.e. the explicit and implicit expectations with respect to emotions), their own personal ethics, and their professional training. Moreover, responses to the vignette suggested that teacher thinking is influenced by predominant learning theories that place a positive classroom climate and a learner's personal positive mental state at the centre of effective language acquisition. One teacher thought that "Pre-empting culture clash is part of providing a positive affect in the classroom."

Deleuze-Guattarian affect theory problematizes such conventional thinking on several counts. First, it begs the question: To what degree does sanctioning emotions imply a denial of the complexity of emotions as forces shaping the classroom milieu and a refusal of the inevitability of embodied affective relations through which teacher- and student-bodies are continually transformed? Second, rather than categorizing emotions dichotomously as positive versus negative states of being, affect theory considers the potential of affects to produce becomings or to transform socio-material assemblages and the bodies that constitute them. Deleuze and Guattari (1987) recognize that the affects at play in certain relations have very destructive effects on bodies; however, other relations may enhance the power of bodies to act. Viewed this way, teachers are not necessarily obliged to avoid a "culture clash" or the actualization of affect as the emotion "anger," and besides, the unpredictable nature of affect makes this an impossibility in any case. In contrast, teachers are called to consider the productive potential of all kinds of affects within pedagogical spaces, even those that might actualize as anger or other so-called negative emotions.

This idea that affect, actualized as anger in Vignette 1, could become an active force seemed apparent in teacher thinking when respondents saw this not as a problem-to-be-solved or -managed, but as a pedagogical opening to inspire future lessons. One respondent encouraged the imaginary colleague to "delve into the complexities of life ... What the angry student has to say may be the teacher's inspiration for the next lesson plan." From a materialist perspective, this suggests how affective relations within assemblages – between text-bodies, teacher-bodies, student-bodies – actually produce pedagogy and curriculum in ways that are not necessarily anticipated. Many concrete recommendations emerged from the respondents' pedagogical thinking in relation to the vignette, recommendations which varied based on students' language proficiency levels and learning needs. For example, one respondent suggested that "depending on the level, the incident could also spark journal and essay writing exercises and classroom debates." Speaking activities, both whole class and small group discussion, were also commonly suggested as in the following response that I have opted to quote at length.

> 1 I would initiate a discussion next time I teach this class. I would ask class if anyone felt the same as the Angry Student (AS). Then I would ask AS why they had lost their faith in Canada. I would ask class if anyone had an instance of feeling they belong/do not belong and let them share their experiences. I would ask class of an opposite situation when they felt they did not belong in the countries of their origins. What makes people feel they belong and what makes them feel they do not. Next, to move to discussion how the situation can be changed and how people can work together to bridge this discontent.
> 2 If the class has students of different generations of a marked gap in age I would ask them about time, whether modern time and technology (culture, art, fashion, politics) make them feel they belong or not. I would continue to discuss the feelings that the song evokes (pride or else).
> 3 I would ask the students to share their favourite songs and discuss the feelings that the songs evoke (pride or else). The rest is imagination – weave it into curriculum.

This respondent's advice not only shows how a teacher might follow-up on the affectively charged event described in the vignette, it also shows the potential of affects to produce teacher-thinking and creative pedagogical responses. In particular, the last sentence – "The rest is imagination – weave it into curriculum" – struck me as profoundly materialist; imagination can be understood as novel thought that emerges from a socio-material classroom assemblage. Imagination then becomes an onto-epistemological basis for inventing new pedagogical realities. However, Deleuze and Guattari (1987) would remind us that these generative potentials can be, and often are, tempered by ever-present stabilizing forces at work in socio-material assemblages. In this particular case, these might include forces like mandatory curriculum documents or the *feeling rules* of the context (Benesch, 2017) that serve to tie pedagogical creativity back to that which already exists, thereby stifling pedagogical creativity.

A number of other respondents also seemed to think like affect theorists with a socio-material orientation. They underscored the complexity and unpredictability of how classroom pedagogy will function. One ESL teacher wrote, "That is life. The students bring baggage with them which you cannot control," and an FSL teacher echoed this materialist sentiment, writing,

"C'est une situation à prévoir,[3] une situation qui peut arriver à n'importe quel moment et qui peut être déclenchée par n'importe quelle séquence pédagogique" ("It's a predictable situation, a situation which can happen at any time and which can be triggered by any pedagogical sequence"). Perhaps more succinctly than I have done, these respondents evoke a fundamental principle of Deleuzian affect theory: "We never know in advance what a body can do" (Deleuze, 1980, para. 17). Not until the actualization in real time of a particular assemblage on a particular day can we know how a pedagogical event will unfold as a result of the immanent affective encounters between bodies in classrooms.

Accepting this affective principle requires relinquishing the idea that teachers are fully in control of what goes on in classrooms. Affect theory disrupts cherished beliefs that through careful planning and prediction *before* a pedagogical event, a teacher can pre-empt affectively charged events if they "establish the clear objectives of the lesson and set up the tone in advance (i. e. encourage objectivism and common goals/discourage subjective statements and strong emotional reactions)" to quote one of the respondents. Teachers' acknowledgement of the unpredictability introduced by the distributed agency of diverse forces at work in the classroom assemblage extends to the affective powers of text-bodies, a question explored in the next assemblage.

Assemblage: Rethinking Text Selection in Light of the Affective Powers of Teaching Materials

Like the respondents in the previous paragraph, it was interesting that several others expressed the pedagogical thought that affectively charged classroom events are to be expected and yet also have an unpredictable quality. Reflecting on their own experiences using song-texts in particular, one respondent commented, "Things like this can happen especially with this type of activity," while another disclosed, "I have had a student start to cry during just about all of the songs I've used in class – you can't predict what emotional triggers a song may have for each student." Despite the unpredictability of the affective actualizations of song-texts, these respondents seemed pedagogically committed to using them.

For others, Vignette 1 evoked contrasting pedagogical thoughts with one respondent going so far as to recommend avoiding song-texts altogether:

> I would never do songs in a classroom. Songs are interpretive and some require a high degree of fluency to figure out what the real meaning is behind the words. There are plenty of opportunities for misinterpretation when it comes to a song. So, as an activity, I'd stay away from this.

This response assumes that there is a *real* meaning to be discovered and does not allow for a socio-materialist understanding of reading as an affective event in which sense emerges from a reader-text-assemblage (Masny, 2016). Moreover, it would constrain students' "divergent personal responses" to reading song-texts (Tomlinson, 2018, p. 171).

In other cases, the pedagogical thinking articulated by respondents seemed to be premised on the humanist assumption that teachers can control pedagogical outcomes through careful planning and, in this case, careful text selection. One respondent advised, "Use other songs to achieve [the] same outcome." In a similar vein, another wrote, "I would suggest the song be changed. There are many good songs that have nothing to do with Canada or Canadian culture. The goal is to teach English." This assertion was remarkable not only for its refusal to adopt a socio-materialist appreciation of the agentive power of texts themselves, but also for its singular focus on English teaching as the goal of pedagogy. On the contrary, these programmes have a mandate not only to teach one of Canada's official languages, but also to facilitate newcomers' integration into Canadian society, including its cultural elements (Guo, 2015). Besides, the field of language education has accepted that language and culture are inseparable in language teaching and learning, and therefore circumventing cultural elements in text selection becomes questionable.

From a socio-materialist perspective, teaching materials are not passive objects that are used unproblematically by teachers to achieve fixed ends (i.e. learning objectives). More specifically, Deleuze-Guattarian affect theory enables an examination of how teaching materials may create unexpected effects through their affective capacities in classrooms. From song-texts for oral language practice to reading comprehension texts, such text-bodies contribute to the distributed agency in classroom assemblages that collectively produce pedagogical potentiality. Thus, a socio-materialist orientation necessarily reframes the role of teachers and teacher thinking in the selection of teaching materials.

Teaching materials and pedagogy are intimately intertwined in language teaching practice. Brian Tomlinson has written extensively over the past two decades about materials development for language learning in diverse contexts around the globe. He observes that teachers choose materials that they deem appropriate or relevant to their students' language proficiency, needs, interests, and cultural backgrounds (Tomlinson, 2018). Tomlinson makes a clear distinction between affective and cognitive decision-making in describing teachers' thinking when choosing teaching materials. He encourages teachers to avoid "uninformed emotive decisions" (p. 167) by making "positive, principled selections" (p. 166) which he argues will yield the most effective use of the materials selected. Tomlinson's separation of affect from cognition and his privileging of cognition in decision-making reflect a perspective that is antithetical to the Deleuze-Guattarian framing of teacher thinking that I am positing. Yet his affective-cognitive division is surprising in light of the significance he does accord to affect in the series of questions he proposes that teachers consider in order to select interesting texts that promote learner engagement. For example, he invites teachers to consider: "Does the text engage me cognitively and affectively? Is the text likely to engage most of the target learners cognitively and affectively?" (p. 171). I note the socio-materialist grammar of these questions which accords text-bodies the affective power to actively engage teacher- and learner-bodies.

Although not explicitly stated by Tomlinson (2018), it is implied that if the answer to each of his guiding questions is "yes" then the given text would be a promising choice for a teacher to use in the classroom. However, the questionnaire data presented in the current rhizoanalysis suggests that while some respondents embrace the pedagogical thought of introducing texts that may prompt affective responses from students, others quite purposefully avoid such texts. Tomlinson also asks teachers, "Is the text likely to stimulate divergent personal responses from the target learners?" (p. 171). This question yields yet another tension in the data between pedagogical thinking that welcomes heterogeneous student responses and thinking that seeks to contain difference by discouraging emotional responses or at least to limit these to emotional responses conventionally perceived as positive.

(Non)recommendations for Materialist Language Pedagogy

Materialist, affective theorizing has important implications for considering language teachers' pedagogical thinking when affectively charged events happen in newcomer language classrooms. It reframes the very act of thinking in teachers' pedagogical decision-making, not to mention the researchers' analytic thinking when studying teachers' pedagogical choices. A number of key problems emerged from the current rhizoanalytic experimentation with Deleuzian affect theory and teacher thinking in adult language classrooms. First, there is the challenge of understanding emotions/affects not as individual traits, but as agentive elements of the larger assemblage in which teaching and learning takes place. Second, there is the uncomfortable recognition that what happens in classrooms may be less the result of an individual teacher's decision-making and more the effect of a distributed agency (student-bodies, teacher-bodies, text-bodies, and so forth). Finally, there is an appreciation of the agentive power of texts used in classrooms and how this might influence teachers' selection of teaching materials for their students.

While the implications of this study are numerous, concrete pedagogical recommendations are few. Materialist "theories do not provide explanations or foolproof ideas about how schools and language learning can be improved, but they raise interesting questions and encourage us to think in new ways about students, classrooms and pedagogy" (Toohey, 2018, p. 174). Accordingly, this affect theory-informed research does not propose a new regime of strategies for language teachers or teacher educators to implement. What it does offer is a more complex take of life in newcomer language classrooms than has been possible through humanist-oriented applied linguistics frameworks (Pennycook, 2018). It helps teachers to reflect differently about apparently successful or unsuccessful pedagogical outcomes and how it is that classroom events come to be thought of in these terms. Rather than judging teachers' classroom choices against the constraining standards of best practices, materialist theory favours an ethical engagement with the pedagogical potential of classroom assemblages. It offers teachers a way of thinking about classroom life that is not premised solely on the choices they make or on a particular teaching strategy they use. Instead, teachers can account for the vast array of elements that create the classroom assemblage which in turn functions in a particular way. Ideally, this may enable teachers and students to live more satisfying classroom lives in their future pedagogical experimentations, but minimally it opens up possibilities by framing teacher thinking and teaching practice in a new light.

Notes

1 My take on "posthumanist materialism" to borrow Pennycook's term (2018, p. 9) leans exclusively on Deleuze and Guattari's conceptual repertoire. It may seem remiss to ignore the writings of Karen Barad, a central figure in new materialist work; however, I do so based on Hein's (2016) convincing argument that there are important distinctions between Deleuze and Barad at the level of ontology. His is a philosophy of immanence and difference, while hers is one of transcendence and identity. I have neither the space in this chapter nor, frankly, the philosophical background required to do justice to this argument here, but I recommend Hein's description of this essential ontological distinction that leads him to conclude that these two philosophies are ultimately incommensurable.
2 Each time a teacher-respondent is quoted, the quotation is drawn from a different respondent. Translations of French responses offered by FSL teachers are clearly indicated, while all other quotations are, by default, from ESL teacher-respondents.
3 I have read this FSL teacher-respondent's comment about "une situation à prévoir" (a situation that can be predicted) not as a call for teachers to somehow anticipate a situation in order to avoid or pre-empt it (as in the case of a respondent quoted earlier in the chapter), rather, I have taken it to mean that this is not an unusual situation; it is a common occurrence and is to be expected.

Acknowledgements

I gratefully acknowledge the Fonds de recherche du Québec – Société et culture whose support enabled the realization of this study. I also wish to express my gratitude to the anonymous teacher-respondents and to research assistants working on the project: Célia Santiago for her role in developing the questionnaire vignettes and Christina Driedger for her participation in the analytic research assemblage.

References

Benesch, S. (2012). *Considering emotions in critical English language teaching*. New York: Routledge.
Benesch, S. (2017). *Emotions and English language teaching: Exploring teachers' emotion labor*. New York: Routledge.
Boler, M., & Davis, E. (2018). The affective politics of the "post-truth" era: Feeling rules and networked subjectivity. *Emotion, Space and Society*, 27, 75–85. doi:1016/j.emospa.2018.03.002.
Bonta, M., & Protevi, J. (2004). *Deleuze and geophilosophy: A guide and glossary*. Edinburgh: Edinburgh University Press.
Borg, S. (2006). *Teacher cognition and language education: Research and practice*. London and New York: Bloomsbury.
Colebrook, C. (2002). *Gilles Deleuze*. New York: Routledge.
Deleuze, G. (1980). *Sur Spinoza*. (S. Duffy, Trans.) Cours Vincennes: Ontologie-Ethique. Retrieved August, 3, 2018, from www.webdeleuze.com/textes/190.
Deleuze, G. (1968/1994). *Difference and repetition*. (P. Patton, Trans.). New York: Columbia University Press.
Deleuze, G., & Guattari, F. (1980/1987). *A thousand plateaus: Capitalism and schizophrenia*. (B. Massumi, Trans.). Minneapolis: University of Minnesota Press.
Golombek, P., & Doran. M. (2014). Unifying cognition, emotion, and activity in language teacher professional development. *Teaching and Teacher Education*, 39, 102–111. doi:10.1016/j.tate.2014.01.002.
Guo, Y. (2015). Language policies and programs for adult immigrants in Canada: deconstructing discourses of immigration. *New Directions for Adult and Continuing Education*, 146, 41–51. doi:10.1002/ace.20130.
Hein, S. F. (2016). The new materialism in qualitative inquiry: How compatible are the philosophies of Barad and Deleuze? *Cultural Studies ⟷ Critical Methodologies*, 16(2), 132–140. doi:10.1177/1532708616634732.
Horsman, J. (1999). *Too scared to learn: Women, violence, and education*. Toronto, ON: McGilligan Books.
Kuby, C. R. (2016). Emotions as situated, embodied, and fissured: methodological implications of thinking with theories. In M. Zembylas, & P.A. Schutz (Eds.), *Methodological advances in research on emotion and education*. (pp.125–136). Switzerland: Springer International Publishing.
Lussier, D. (2011). Language education as the entry to intercultural communicative competence (ICC). *Canadian Issues. Diversity and Education for Liberation: Realities, Possibilities, and Problems*, Special Edition, Spring, 60–66.
MacLure, M. (2013). Researching without representation? Language and materiality in post-qualitative methodology. *International Journal of Qualitative Studies in Education*, 26(6), 658–667. doi:10.1080/09518398.2013.788755.
Martínez Agudo, J. D. M. (Ed.). (2018). *Emotions in second language teaching: Theory, research and teacher education*. Cham: Springer.

Masny, D. (2016). Problematizing qualitative research: Reading a data assemblage with rhizoanalysis. *Qualitative Inquiry*, 22(8), 666–675. doi:10.1177/1532708616636744.

Nichols, T. P., & Campano, G. (2017). Post-humanism and literacy studies. *Language Arts*, 94(4), 245–251. Retrieved May 4, 2019, from www.ncte.org/journals/la/issues/v94-4.

Pennycook, A. (2018). *Posthumanist applied linguistics*. New York: Routledge.

Tierney, R. D. (2011). *Vignettes as a complementary method in educational research*. Paper presented at the annual meeting of the American Educational Research Association, New Orleans, Louisiana.

Tomlinson, B. (2018). Emotional dilemmas faced by teachers in ELT materials selection and adaptation: implications for teacher education. In J. D. Martínez Agudo (Ed.), *Emotions in second language teaching: Theory, research and teacher education* (pp. 165–181). Cham: Springer.

Toohey, K. (2018). *Learning English at school: Identity, socio-material relations and classroom practice* (2nd ed.). Bristol and Blue Ridge Summit, PA: Multilingual Matters.

Waterhouse, M., & Mortier-Faulkner, G. (2014). *Conceptualizations of affect in Canadian adult immigrant second language education*. Paper presented at the annual conference of the Canadian Association of Applied Linguistics, Brock University, St. Catherine's, Ontario.

Watkins, M. (2006). Pedagogic affect/effect: Embodying a desire to learn. *Pedagogies: An International Journal*, 1(4), 269–282. doi:10.1080/15544800701341533.

9

THE PROBLEM AND POTENTIAL OF REPRESENTATION

Being and Becoming

Margaret MacDonald, Cher Hill and Nathalie Sinclair

> [T]hinking is about tracing lines of flight and zigzagging patterns that undo dominant representations.
> *(Braidotti, 2011, p. 2)*

> Make rhizomes, not roots, never plant! Don't sow, grow offshoots! Don't be one or multiple, be multiplicities! Run lines, never plot a point! Speed turns the point into a line! Be quick, even when standing still! Line of chance, line of hips, line of flight. Don't bring out the General in you!
> *(Deleuze & Guattari, 1987, p. 25)*

For Deleuze and Guattari (1987), language practices are entangled embodied acts and involve what they call territorialization and deterritorialization, in which connective forces assemble to reproduce "what is" *and* create lines of flight to produce something new (Colebrook, 2002). However, rather than seeing territorialization and deterritorialization as dichotomous, Deleuze and Guattari view them as the creation or pulling through of one from the other when thinking is rhizomatic. For them, rhizomatic movement is unpredictable, extends in all directions, and assumes diverse forms. As they note, "every rhizome contains lines of segmentarity according to which it is stratified, territorialized, organized, signified, attributed, etc. as well as lines of deterritorialization down which it constantly flees" (Deleuze & Guattari, 1987, p. 9).

Taking up this invitation to think rhizomatically, we wish to trouble fixed, static notions of reality and their corresponding representations, and champion smooth fluid spaces of thought. Dominant representational practices are territorialized as cognitive acts and are usually described, interpreted, and understood via written text. These serve to reify the same patterns and predictions and continue to polarize our thinking by creating hierarchical ways of being with language and standardized ways of communicating knowledge. Rather than imitate normative ways of arriving at pre-determined uniform outcomes, we suggest in this chapter that we look for the "yes/and" openings in our pedagogical ways of being to create multiplicities and recognize embodied lively emergent forms of engagement and disengagement. We recognize the advantages of seeing our practices experimentally and emergently so that they are responsive to deviations and openings. In this challenge, we wish to re-imagine ways to assemble, un-assemble, re-assemble and commune in both diverse and uniform ways. We propose teaching and learning that becomes playful and holistic, and both scripted and unscripted, performed and felt intuitively.

We enter this work from a posthuman point of view whereby we conceive of objects in their own right, not wholly dependent on the human social-construction of them (Colebrook, 2014); rather, we see objects as part of assemblages connecting things, knowledge, and knowledge-making practices ontologically to our (human) becoming. This work has been inspired in part by Braidotti's (2013) discussions of nomadic forms of thought and representation, and particularly her suggestion to take into account the ways that we (and objects) are becoming through and with the world. As she contends, "nomadic thought conceptualizes matter as self-organized and relational in its very structures. This means that each nomadic connection offers at least the possibility of an ethical relation of opening out toward an empowering connection to others" (p. 3). The act of seeing beyond the standard, stereotypical, judgemental, or deterministic ways is seen as a position of ethical relationality to others (people or objects).

We begin this chapter by examining the determinate qualities used in what we refer to as "traditional forms of representation" and look towards the possibilities in emergent, indeterminate, and fluid processes in which we come to see our worlds in new ways and represent those worlds nomadically. We do this through three examples from diverse discipline areas (which we acknowledge as delimiting and artificial but potentially generative) to highlight the problem and potential of representation. Our examples are drawn from primary school geometry (Nathalie), pedagogical documentation (Margaret), and forest cartography (Cher).

Primary School Geometry: The Triangle as an Object in Its Own Right

Primary school geometry is usually taught as botany. In other words, the goal is for children to be able to recognize and name shapes – simple, Euclidean shapes such as triangles, squares, and circles. This kind of activity usually involves showing children prototypical images of these shapes (for example, a triangle that is equilateral, sitting on one of its sides), either using posters on the classroom walls, picture books, or small plastic manipulatives. Children come to believe that the prototypical image of a triangle *is* the triangle. This kind of activity does not prepare children very well for their future mathematical experiences. However, it emerges easily from a representationalist view of mathematics learning in which the image represents the shape, the latter being some kind of Platonic entity that is too pure, too ideal, for human consumption. It also falls in line with most socio-constructivist theories as well, in which the meaning of triangle is grounded in social systems such as a language. A triangle is what we have agreed upon as a discursive artefact – a three-sided polygon.

Most theorizing in mathematics education over the past 20 years can be loosely described as being socio-constructivist. Social constructivist theories extend previous constructivist theories by stressing the ways in which social systems – rather than Platonic forms or God – shape, largely through language, the meanings of things, concepts, beliefs, and values. Social constructivist theories have been powerful in focusing attention on a range of issues such as the nature of mathematics (human created), the genesis of mathematical thinking (through communication), and the power dynamics at play in the mathematics classroom (through critical theory, positioning theory, and so on). One consequence of this attention to social systems as the grounding of meaning, however, has been a de-valuing of matter, which is seen as being passive or inert, as being subject to human agency. Recent posthumanist theories in philosophy and the social sciences have attempted to de-centre the human in theories of knowing and being (see, for example, Braidotti, 2013; Wolfe, 2009). These thinkers argue that, for the most part, the human-centric view of social constructivism has demoted non-human entities to playing subservient and predictable roles in human activity (including school mathematical activity), namely as entities that are entirely determined through human perception, action, and design.

One strand of posthumanism has emerged from studies of the intersection of the human and various kinds of machines (see, for example, Hayles, 1999). As Donna Haraway's "A Cyborg Manifesto" (1985) contends, we have long been posthuman in that we live in a world where the fixed boundaries of the human body have been made porous, so that they no longer strictly separate humans from animals and machines. Indeed, some posthumanists are primarily interested in how humans can be improved by these human/machine breeches. But others are more interested in how posthumanism might de-stabilize and help us to re-think what it means to be human, what it means to be, what it means to talk about identity, subjectivity, ethics, aesthetics, in a world where the distinction between human and non-human is blurred (see Snaza et al., 2014). These questions have been of particular interest to feminist scholars, who are eager to consider ontological, ethical, and epistemological questions about identity in new ways.

Posthumanism has, so far, had little interaction with theories of education, let alone mathematics education. Perhaps the first significant contribution, within the wider educational sphere, was Snaza et al. (2014). Within mathematics education, de Freitas and Sinclair (2014) wrote from a materialist perspective urging a re-thinking of the role of the body and the materiality of mathematical concepts, drawing significantly on the work of Karen Barad (2007, 2014). Since these ideas have already appeared in our joint work (Smythe et al., 2017), we explore here a slightly different strand of posthumanism that can be traced back to the writings of British mathematician, philosopher, and educator Alfred North Whitehead.

Whitehead's (1929, 1933) notion of the fallacy of misplaced concreteness, which is any form of perceptual or conceptual reductivism, describes well the problem of fixedness that we have been discussing thus far. To this point, Whitehead saw no essential or stable distinctions between human and non-human, and, therefore, no need to begin a philosophical programme based on that fundamental ontological split. He pursued a metaphysics that was non-anthropomorphic and non-anthropocentric. This approach takes any object in the world (a hammer, a human being, a whale, a rock, an ocean, an army, a triangle) as sharing a fundamental ontology, namely that an object exceeds what any other object (including a human) will ever know of it. As a human, I may know things about a rock – that is it hard, that it is heavy, that it can be engraved, and so on – but the rock will be known very differently by the window it has shattered from the way it will be understood by me. Of course, Whitehead does not then proceed to say that humans are the same as rocks. Indeed, they have many ontic differences that matter a lot in education. But for him, these are differences in degrees rather than differences in kind.

From this point of view, we would be encouraged to think of the triangle as an object in its own right and not wholly dependent on a human social-construction of it. Like any other object, the triangle is a thing that exceeds all of the qualities that children (or teachers, or rocks) can perceive. The triangle is really there, and is not just the sum of our perceptions and conceptions of it. When a child looks at it, she sees some of its qualities, but she can never know or sense the triangle as a whole. This is not to say that the triangle can think and feel like we, the authors, do. But between the triangle and the child, new relations can be created, perhaps by colouring its vertices, rotating it around, stretching one of its vertices to make it long and skinny. Or perhaps through other ways of feeling that do not fit neatly into the five gospel senses, but also the "non-sensuous perception" that Whitehead (1933/1967) wrote about that forms our experience, such as "our awareness of the immediate past", our sense of foreboding, our feeling "that we see by our eyes, and taste by our palates" (pp. 180–181). The child who says "I don't like it" when shown an "upside-down" triangle (see Sinclair, 2018) expresses this kind of feeling. Such feelings are selections that can attract or repulse, the same way that "a jellyfish advances and withdraws" (Whitehead, 1929/1978, p. 176), without conscious judgment or intention.

Mathematical objects can be seen as part of this ontological multiplicity as well – indeed, Whitehead saw no stable or essential distinctions between physical objects and mental or subjective acts. Imagine a triangle constructed on a screen, where the vertices of the triangle can be moved around without breaking the triangle apart (see Figure 9.1). Perhaps it looks upright and equilateral at first, when the sides are joined. But then, the vertex on top starts to move around, first transforming the triangle into something short and stout, and then into something extremely long and skinny. At a certain moment, the vertex lands *on* the opposite side. This triangle is less as a static figure and more in terms of the virtual motions generative of it. As de Freitas and Sinclair (2014) write:

> A triangle does not exist as a rigid figure, or as a sign perched in space, but rather it exists as a mobility or set of gestures. One might think of a geometric figure like the triangle as a provisional cutting-out, or articulation, of the indeterminate multiplicity of pre-figures.
>
> *(p. 205)*

Any particular triangle, as in the static images below, is but one actualization.

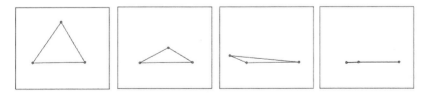

FIGURE 9.1 A triangle constructed on a screen where the vertices can be moved

What might happen when a teacher asks her students whether the collapsed shape is a triangle? Might it be taken as a triangle because it was a triangle? Because it still has three vertices (albeit now collinear, but with the potential to wriggle free)? Perhaps it is no longer a triangle, having lost its inside? And in the spirit of yes/and, perhaps it is both a triangle *and* not a triangle. In most classrooms, this indeterminate situation is safely ignored – the triangles in such classrooms are safely kept under control, in their place, monomaniacally represented.

However, perhaps it is in embracing chance encounters, singularities (extreme or limit cases – like the infinitely big or small), and ambiguities around mathematical concepts such as triangles, that we can seek a posthuman point of view, one that comes closer to the "power of imaging that is not oriented to the eye of recognition, the eye that views the world according to its own already organized desires" (Colebrook, 2014, p. 77). I can no longer recognize the line as a triangle – it doesn't fit my images or representations – but from the point of view of the ruler, sitting on the same piece of paper as the triangle, that triangle is indeed a line.

In this example contesting representation in mathematics, particularly in primary school geometry, we see Alfred North Whitehead's concept of the fallacy of misplaced concreteness as an important point of departure. Here, we see the limits of social constructivism, and instead entertain the possible through the notion that the thingness of a thing (or person) can never, as Whitehead asserts, be fully understood by another. In this there is great potential for interpretation of objects, people, and concepts beyond what anyone currently knows of them or may teach about them. In these ways, static and orthodox representations of triangles, or other archetypes, can be dangerous in their limits to wonder given that a learner can enter into new relations with these materials, objects, and concepts in ways that we (as teachers and researchers) often cannot imagine.

We shift now to other views of representation in education and look at the practice and potential of pedagogical documentation (PD) in our consideration of places where passage, movement, and transformation may have the potential to reveal our becoming.

Pedagogical Documentation: Incorporeal Transformations

In early childhood education, representation of children's learning has often taken the form of PD. Through these forms of close written notes and/or video documentation of and for learning, thought and voice and images are materialized to convey what happens during particular learning moments as part of project work, and, occasionally, in ordinary classroom moments, (see MacDonald, 2007). With PD, we seek to draw attention to the significance of children's learning and engagement by connecting these moments to the life of the child or children, and, more broadly, to what counts as *knowledge* or *knowledge making practices*.

In producing PDs for other teachers, children, and parents, we typically share where that learning journey may go and/or how it will be guided, deepened, or focused to the next level or stage. What is often omitted in this depiction is a discussion of what occurs tangentially, rhizomatically and playfully when learning involves not only the embodied, but also the incorporeal (Deleuze & Guattari, 1987), whereby knowledge and knowledge making are delightfully "unstable" and experimental, and cognition and logos are often simultaneously entangled with materials, both embodied and disembodied.

Here, most forms of representation (often including PD) cannot capture what really takes place or will take place, but instead capitulate to our desire to stabilize knowledge and separate it from knowledge making, random experimentation, and the power and *potentia* of the material encounter. In this section, we focus on three (but ultimately there are many more) challenges of representation in PD: (1) standardization of knowledge; (2) ontological oversights (and/or an emphasis on the rational logical) and a related challenge; and (3) the *im*possibility of conveying the incorporeal when representation becomes fixed.

In this discussion, we draw on projects involving children's explorations and emerging understandings of an environmentally sustainable building that has, as its heart, living systems for heat and waste exchange (see MacDonald, 2015). The building is engineered with geothermal mechanics to provide heat and cooling properties and a bioreactor for sewage treatment. This *living building* is also a childcare centre, and a place where children come to play, explore, and learn about relationships with each other, and with their teachers, and through these processes also develop a relationship to the building and the environment.

Standardization of Knowledge

In early childhood education (and in general throughout education), binaries exist between teacher and learner; tools (technology) and knowing; content to be learned and the learner (as subject). Learning is often conceptualized, in temporal ways, to occur sometime during or soon after the time of teaching. These truncations and boundaries create images of teaching and learning and development that both support and are the products of our static notions of linear time in space and linear (staged) notions of development. These images territorialize and act against playful encounters and memories pulled through time and unique assemblages of the human, non-human, and material that float across linear time to help us to imagine, think, and feel differently and rhizomatically.

In their explorations of the "living building," true to their agendas as teachers and researchers in the childcare centre, Margaret and her colleagues initially held a vision of sustainability that they looked towards as a way to teach the children. The group felt at times that they needed to know more about the building so that they could "teach" the children about it. Pedagogically, this is akin to having a learning goal and working with the children towards standard ways of knowing and understanding, but, ironically, it first involved the teachers setting their own learning goals to come to know the building. For example, as part of their Foundation curriculum document (MacDonald, 2015), they promoted and documented the children's group time discussion, their representational drawings of the building, and planned timely dissemination of facts (knowledge), which they intended would lead the children towards meaning making. This hierarchical approach to learning was supported by representational thinking and standardized to some degree through the pedagogical documentations produced by the teachers and researchers. The dilemma of this type of representation in the form of PD, when used retrospectively by the teacher, is that it fails to listen to or honour the "in between," the before, the afterwards, or the possibilities in becoming, and misses a mapping of learning and lines of flight that are powerful to the children.

FIGURE 9.2 Representational drawing of the bioreactor used in one of our pedagogical documentations

Although PD was created as a mechanism to open up space for discussion of learning and about lines of flight, it is often used (as in the case discussed here) retrospectively to share out a consolidation of knowledge. More rarely is it used "in process" as a contagion or provocation for learning (when the incomplete interpretation or "in-process" documentation is shared with the children as a means of opening up spaces for other ideas and igniting thinking and feeling). Finalizing documentation leads instead to an end (a product, a standard, a level), creating only the message and missing other vital moments in children's learning. For example, moments of inventiveness, experimentation, and in-dwelling with ideas through discussion and multiple perspectives, all of which contribute to intuitive feeling states. When this in-process action is missed, we run the risk of providing a wording with words and images that can be evocative but stops us from continuing growth, movement, and becoming and other embodied ways of knowing. Olsson (2012) points this out, when she says that "children, when allowed to, seem to enjoy a certain kind *of intense, undomesticated, and vital experimentation* rather than looking for any kind of permanent or stable knowledge" (p. 89, emphasis added). Children revel in process, and we know that the summative aspects of representation of knowledge can herald a fixedness or stasis that often overemphasizes product over process – when both should matter.

Ontological Oversights

The downspouts can't keep up with the rain and it puddles onto the playground. There is a "rain warning" in effect in Vancouver and the skies seem to have opened. Instead of staying indoors, the children get their outdoor muddy buddies on and explore the puddles, jump, splash, listen to the rain sounds, and, yes, also feel the rain. It's damp, cold and after a matter of minutes, it's impossible to be anything but soaking wet. In this action, these children are becoming west coasters. They are immersed in the day to day of our Fall experience and a part of the classroom environment that impacts their ontology and shapes them in a way that the "formal curriculum" (our building exploration) cannot. This becoming is, as Robertson Davies (1985) would say, "bred in the bone." Yet moments like this are seldom documented, and when they are, they aren't often connected to the material that creates them and performs on/with them.

The picture you see has no children in it because there were no cameras outside to document the children's experience. This photo was taken after the children had come inside. Somehow, and perhaps this is the beauty of these ordinary moments, they seem to be out of reach, exceeding, in Whitehead's terms, the camera gaze and the focus of learning. We might consider how pedagogically locked and committed we are to the notion that

FIGURE 9.3 Rainwarning as rainteacher

humans are the only teachers, and that materials are mere tools. Or, that humans are the only receivers of new learning: what does the window know about the rain as it works to wield little droplets that trickle down erratically towards the sill?

The Impossibility of Conveying Transformations

In the *Oxford English Dictionary*, the *incorporeal* is defined as not consisting of matter; having no material existence. Deleuze and Guattari (1987) refer to incorporeal transformations as transformations that occur through *order-words* in language whereby the attribute(s) of bodies (i.e. the body of a collective assemblage; a political body, or an institution) are passed on indirectly. This incorporeal transformation is more than a "speech act" in that it communicates or describes directly the sign and the signified but also has indirect (incorporeal) properties that move and stir emotive states. In this discussion of order words, they write:

> Language is not content to go from a first party to a second party, from one who has seen to one who has not, but necessarily goes from a second to a third party, neither of whom has seen. It is in this sense that language is the transmission of the word as order-word, not the communication of a sign as information. Language is a map, not a tracing.
> *(Deleuze & Guattari, 1987, p. 77)*

Institutional assessment of children is a prime example of order-words that flow through institutions, producing particular types of students and hierarchical ordering. Another example of the incorporeal transformations of school through the institutional assemblage would be the reputational salience that the institution holds around power and authority, structure and role differentiation, including the many binaries that exist (i.e. teachers and learners, curriculum and extra-curricular event, and so on). For children, incorporeal transformations may include the feeling of power and emotions in learning, and/or feelings of transgressions from learning.

When, as teachers, we capture an experience through PD or narration, we represent *our* experience of it and convey it to a third party (other teachers, the children, and parents). This documents what we see and feel through the order-words we value. Our selection, unless it adequately includes the children's voice, or "in-process" discussion, can only be hearsay, unless we find adequate ways to open up space for other incorporeal transformations that are sensed by the children. Importantly, these transformations are beyond words – not strictly "feeling words" that the child is conscious of and can reflect upon and articulate, but are emerging dispositions that are felt, such as an openness to wonder or an inquisitive stance towards the world.

In our discussion of the representational elements of PD, we point out the dangers of working from binaries between teachers, learners, tools (technology), and knowing, including the content to be learned and the learner as a subject. These binaries may have the dangerous pull of creating images of teaching and learning and development that are static and create staged notions of what one should and should not be at a particular time. In this section, we also note the power of incorporeal transformations that occur through order-words, namely attributes of bodies. Insofar as it relates to PD, this discussion of order-words and the incorporeal suggests that we may look towards more affective ways to describe learning, and seek poignant, perhaps obscure moments when learning stirs from within the child.

In our final example, we continue our journey into becoming and nomadic representation in our discussion of an incorporeal transformation of Mia with Peach the Tree.

Living Cartographies: Becoming Literate with/in the Forest

In schools, becoming literate often involves the reproduction of predetermined standardized texts that are typically organized (as well as hierarchically ordered) along disciplinary lines. Disrupting this representationalist view, we embrace more nomadic forms of literacy that encourage divergent, entangled, unbounded, and embodied becomings. We view the former practice as akin to what Deleuze and Guattari (1987) call tracing, and the latter practice as akin to what they refer to as mapping. They say,

> The map is open and connectable in all of its dimensions; it is detachable, reversible, susceptible to constant modification. ... A map has multiple entryways, as opposed to the tracing, which always comes back "to the same." The map has to do with performance, whereas the tracing always involves an alleged 'competence.'
>
> *(Deleuze & Guattari, 1987, pp. 12–13)*

Grounded within a relational ontology, the process of mapping involves the continuous creation of experimental readings and renderings through the folding of human and more-than-human bodies into one another to produce something new. Dominant perspectives of literacy view the student as an independent subject *inter*acting with texts, demonstrating their ability (or lack of ability) to mirror them. Within a relational ontology, however, human and more-than-human materials are viewed as open intra-active systems (Bennett, 2010; Ingold, 2011), that assemble to produce bodies of knowledge (as well as bodies of knowers) through *intra*-action (Barad, 2007). Within this perspective, representations are fluid, embodied, entangled, and co-constitutive.

In this example, we draw on Cher's work to support her children in becoming literate with/in a forest. As a teacher-educator new to nature-based pedagogies (see Hill & Piersol, 2018), Cher and her children regularly visit an urban forest called Mundy Park in order to learn in, from, and with the forest. During their visits, they document knowings through a series of photos, sketches, and conversations. The sedimenting of this documentation produces a living cartography in which they are becoming literate *with* the forest. Like an animated weather map in which conditions are contextualized and are constantly in motion, so too are readings and renderings of the forest. Unlike the standard map of Mundy Park involving a bird's eye view of the trails, lakes, and points of interest, their cartography is a situated material mapping that envelops multiple dimensionalities and is constantly evolving as bodies change and material entanglements re/configure. Whereas the standard map of the forest conveys an omnipotent static, human-centric perspective of it, their living cartography is rhizomatic, situated, and attends to the agential vitality of the material world, as well as to the intra-actions among bodies (Barad, 2007) as they make themselves intelligible to one another. Together, the fluid renderings produce complex, holistic, multidimensional, albeit partial and incomplete, mappings of bodily entanglements in/with the forest, and resist the foreclosure of knowledge. This process differs greatly from the disembodied, discrete literacies that Cher's children learn at school which involve reproductions of determinant texts. Literacy as mapping involves few a priori expectations about learning, which is co-constituted with various organic and inorganic bodies.

Within the forest, there are particular places that are predominant within the family's cartographic mapping. One such site is a tree that Cher's daughter (Tinks[1]) calls *Peach*, for reasons that can't or won't be articulated (see Figures 9.4a and b). The family visits Peach each time they go to the park, and the tree has become an epicentre of literacy with/in the forest in which readings and renderings are constantly evolving.

Intra-active representation

There are many ways in which trees can be known, such as according to family, genus, species, and the like. Ironically, Deleuze and Guattari (1987) call this type of linear thinking a "tree model" in which the world is organized into binaries and hierarchies. Cher and her family, however, endeavour to engage in rhizomatic thinking, and come to know *with* trees rather than about them. One day in the park, Cher invited the children to pick a tree, close their eyes and imagine what it feels like to be the tree. Her goal was for them to recognize some of the trees' vitalities they might normally overlook, and to connect them with the subtle energies (Flowers et al., 2014) within the forest. That is not to say that it is possible to ever fully come to know a tree, as trees have lives of their own beyond their entanglements with humans. As Bennett (2010) contends, objects possess an efficacy "in excess of the human meanings, signs, or purposes they express or serve" (p. 20). Much tree-ness however, is often overlooked in absence of a distinct human need or goal involving the tree (MacDonald et al., 2017), and it was Cher's intention for the family to engage with the tree with minimal pre-determined human objectives.

Although the tree was not in visual range, Tinks chose Peach. In becoming-with the tree, she described how she made shade, and how things grew on her, which of those things tickled, and then, Tinks spontaneously picked up a clipboard and drew a picture of Peach. This rendering did not appear to be mirroring the tree but rather a sensory driven creation – or perhaps, a re-experiencing, re-actualizing – of the tree~girl assemblage. The main features of the sketch included the bushy foliage at the top of the tree, which highlighted the production of shade, and the feeling of things growing on the trunk (see Figure 9.5). Building on the notion of the extended brain, which is comprised of the brain, body, and "outside" world (Cutler & MacKenzie, 2011), this reading of/with Peach can be viewed as an extended bodily literacy in which the tree and Tinks are in communication and are making themselves intelligible to one other. They are both embodied *and* disembodied and sensory *and* intellectual, and cannot necessarily be reduced to representations or conceptual knowledge.

FIGURES 9.4A Peach the Tree

Representation: Being and Becoming 167

FIGURES 9.4B Peach the Tree

Diffracted Representation

More than a month later, when Cher asked her kids to draw important places in Mundy Park as part of their cartographic process, Tinks immediately started drawing a "fairy tree" (see Figures 9.5 and 9.6). At first, Cher wasn't sure if she was responding to her request or was engaging in a separate activity, but when asked about her drawing, Tinks said, *"Peach is my tree because it has a fairy connection. Peach ... we name all the trees in fairyland. Someone named this tree Peach so they are basically sisters."* With the naming of Peach the Tree, Mundy Park became entangled within the drawing of the fairy tree.

This rendering, which can be read as a twinning of Peach the Tree, producing her fairyland counterpart, involves a diffraction (Barad, 2007; Hill, 2017) in which the texts of Mundy Park were read through the plot of a book series that Tinks was reading about two girls who visit fairyland (the Rainbow Magic series by Betsy Bozdech). Diffractive reading involves attending to correspondences and inviting interference among bodies to produce something new. In other renderings, the fairyland books and Mundy Park are read through the plot of an environmental film about protecting a watershed (*The Peel Project*), equating activists with fairies, and developers with goblins. Within this living cartography, fairies, goblins, activists, developers, trees, and girls all enter into the mangle, and boundaries of time and space are continuously reconfigured, producing new texts and various subjectivities. As Barad (2014) contends, "there is no absolute boundary between here-now and there-then" (p. 168). In Tinks' renderings, boundaries between fairyland, the *Peel Project* watershed, and the Mundy Park collapse, and she is constituted as a protector of the forest, in the same way that the girls in the book protect fairyland from goblins, and the activists protect the watershed from developers. These nomadic renderings of Peach do not stand for truth or knowledge, but rather signal an ontology of being and knowing with the forest as Peach and Tinks and other bodies make themselves intelligible to one another. Engaging in a living cartography with/in the forest involved a multisensory attentiveness to cues within the environment and responsive participation within the flow of materials. Within the cartographic mapping of the forest, Tinks participated in the unfolding of Mundy Park, rather than tracing determinant representations of flora or fauna, and was entangled within the most complex and multifaceted assemblages within the cartography.

In this example, representation was predominantly a nomadic and intra-active process that cut across typical disciplinary and bodily boundaries, disrupting standard renderings of the forest. Knowing and becoming were not contained within any one individual, but were entangled between human and more-than-humans, producing emergent and fluid understandings and identities, as well as empowering connections. Drawings, photos, and discussions stabilized knowledge, but only temporarily, and it continued to unfold as materials disassembled and reconfigured. Conceptualizing literacy as an unbounded, embodied, entangled, and aesthetic performance rather than as an individual competency produced novel representations, more

Representation: Being and Becoming 169

FIGURE 9.5 Becoming with Peach the tree

FIGURE 9.6 Peach the Tree in Mundy Park and her sister tree in fairyland

ethical human-tree relationships, as well as an inclusive learning environment in which who/what was becoming literate was broadly constituted.

The Problem and Potential of Representation

Representation is not a mirroring between the subject and object, but rather an entangled indeterminate process: "Writing has nothing to do with signifying. It has to do with surveying, mapping, even realms that are yet to come" (Deleuze & Guattari, 1987, pp. 4–5). In these ways, traditional notions of meaning making espousing the written word as truth and a penultimate agent of our being take on a lesser role as they entangle with the process of writing within an assemblage of other, that we also acknowledge as contributor. Herein we might ask: Who are we being and becoming, and with whom or what do we come to know? This is an ontologically different stance than that of an objective worlding of words for the purposes of responding to pre-set questions or reifying or validating knowledge already traced and territorialized. Here, learners are teachers and teachers are learners, but even this presumably interactive relationship exceeds its limits in collective assemblages of the learner-teacher with material in time and space.

Thinking and writing differently, we can envisage collective assemblages with DeLanda (2016), in ways that go beyond human beings as the *only* agents. This avoids what he refers to as *micro-reductionism* through the concept of *emergent properties* whereby "the properties of a whole [are] caused by the interactions between [and among] the parts" (DeLanda, 2016, p. 9). As explained by DeLanda (2016), "if a social whole has novel properties that emerge from the interactions between [and among] people," this acts to effectively block an aggregated unification of that experience, thus allowing the new assemblage to possess both the original identity and the novel identity created by the union (p. 9).

Honouring what is emergent and opening up (noticing our posthuman ways of becoming with materials), we begin to recognize that, through a heterogeneity of intra-actions, we can embrace the idea of one and both and the myriad. In this practice, although delimitations are possible, they are avoided when new avenues begin to emerge so that we are not bound in limiting representations. From these possibilities, new insights and questions also emerge that help to re-create our language and literacy pedagogical practices and transcend the boundedness and determinacy of disciplines like mathematics, early childhood education and nature-based education, and, even more broadly, the boundedness and determinacy of subject and object. For example, the singularity of disciplines makes it difficult to imagine what occurs at home, outside the school or nature classroom, and outside the rootedness of a discrete topic. When might learning yield learning rather than perennially and in a linear way only privileging learning that yields from direct teaching or assessment? When might mathematics intra-act with our orientations towards objects or objects intra-act with orientations towards mathematics? And when, in our crossings between home/school/nature classrooms, do spaces for learning emerge or disappear and re-appear as an ontology?

In this chapter, we have looked for ways to re-imagine and re-orient self to practice and practice to self. We believe that this can move pedagogy forward in other sensory, emotive, diffractive, and organic ways. In this work, our hope is to yield new knowledge and ideas rhizomatically rather than in a reproduction of truncated pathways that strictly adheres to the sign and signifier and representations of both what and how we teach and learn, and what and how we document (and research).

172 Margaret MacDonald, Cher Hill, and Nathalie Sinclair

FIGURE 9.7 Being and becoming

Rather than considering the languages of mathematics, early childhood education, or nature-based education as representations of thought, we might consider instead language as a fluid and moveable part of material entanglements of human and non-human agencies, to see these representations as part of an assemblage of our knowing (holding power in the moment of that coming together), and in the moments of being shared out or holding meaning for others, we can shake off the "fixedness" of representation. Here, representation isn't the telos or ultimate end in meaning making. It doesn't stand as knowledge and truth in and of itself. Instead, representation, Deleuze and Guattari's *tracings*, may be seen as a useful part of the continual (ongoing) learning journey, the map, a way to reach a new level of understanding but not to arrive at a destination. In this way, the representation is part of the assemblage (created within the assemblage) *and* is flattened and folded so that it also becomes a product of the assemblage. It is both subject *and* object, tracing learning in that moment of coming together, yet also standing as a temporary placeholder as we navigate and move forward in the learning journey.

Note

1 Tinks is short for Tinkerbell Rainbow, which was a name bestowed on her at birth by her brother. Although not her formal given name, it is what she is commonly called, and appears to be a generative force within this learning assemblage. Tinks was five years old at the time this chapter was drafted.

References

Barad, K. (2007). *Meeting the universe halfway: Quantum physics and the entanglement of matter and meaning*. Durham, NC: Duke University Press.
Barad, K. (2014). Diffracting diffraction: Cutting together-apart. *Parallax*, 20(3), 168–187. doi:10.1080/13534645.2014.927623.
Bennett, J. (2010). *Vibrant matter: A political ecology of things*. Durham, NC: Duke University Press.
Braidotti, R. (2011). *Nomadic theory: The portable Rosi Braidotti*. New York: Columbia University Press.
Braidotti, R. (2013). *The posthuman*. Cambridge: Polity Press.
Cheverie, C. & Wallace, A. W. (2016). *The Peel Project* (Motion Picture). Canada: The Canadian Wilderness Artist Residency & Studio 110. https://vimeo.com/ondemand/thepeelproject.
Colebrook, C. (2002). *Understanding Deleuze*. Crows Nest: Allen & Unwin.
Colebrook, C. (2014). *Sex after life: Essays on extinction*, vol. 2. Retrieved May 20, 2019, from http://hdl.handle.net/2027/spo.12329363.0001.001.
Cutler, A., & MacKenzie, I. (2011). Bodies of learning. In L. Guillaume & J. Hughes (Eds.), *Deleuze and the body* (pp. 53–72). Edinburgh: Edinburgh University Press.
Davies, R. (1985). *What's bred in the bone*. Toronto, ON: Macmillan.
De Freitas, E., & Sinclair, N. (2014). *Mathematics and the body: Material entanglements in the classroom*. Cambridge: Cambridge University Press.
DeLanda, M. (2016). *Assemblage theory*. Edinburgh: Edinburgh University Press.
Deleuze, G., & Guattari, F. (1987/2005). *A thousand plateaus: Capitalism and schizophrenia*. (B. Massumi, Trans.) Minneapolis: University of Minnesota Press.
Flowers, M., Lipsett, L., & Barrett, M. J. (2014). Animism, creativity, and a tree: Shifting into nature connection through attention to subtle energies and

contemplative art practice. *Canadian Journal of Environmental Education*, 19, 111–126. Retrieved May 20, 2019, from https://cjee.lakeheadu.ca/article/view/1301.

Haraway, D. (1985/1991). A cyborg manifesto: Science, technology, and socialist-feminism in the late twentieth century. *Simians, cyborgs, and women: The reinvention of nature* (pp. 149–182). New York: Routledge.

Hayles, K. (1999). *How we became posthuman: Virtual bodies in cybernetics, literature, and informatics*. Chicago, IL: University of Chicago Press.

Hill, C. M. (2017). More-than-reflective practice: Becoming a diffractive practitioner. *Teacher Learning and Professional Development*, 2(1), 1–17. Retrieved May 20, 2019, from http://journals.sfu.ca/tlpd/index.php/tlpd/article/view/28.

Hill, C. M., & Piersol, L. (2018). The transformative becomings of a nature-based educator. In E. R. Lyle (Ed.), *Fostering a relational pedagogy: Self-study as transformative praxis* (pp. 56–70). Boston, MA: Sense.

Ingold, T. (2011). *Being alive: Essays on movement, knowledge and description*. London: Routledge.

MacDonald, M. (2007). Toward formative assessment: The use of pedagogical documentation in early elementary classrooms. *Early Childhood Research Quarterly*, 22, 232–242. doi:10.1016/j.ecresq.2006.12.001.

MacDonald, M. (2015). Early childhood education and sustainability: A living curriculum. *Childhood Education*, 91(5), 332–341. doi:10.1080/00094056.2015.1090845.

MacDonald, M., Bowen, W., & Hill, C. (2017). Using engaged philosophical inquiry to deepen young children's understanding of environmental sustainability: Being, becoming and belonging. *Journal of Philosophy in Schools*, 4(1), 50–73. doi:10.21913/JPS.v4i1.1419.

Olsson, L. M. (2012). Eventicizing curriculum: Learning to read and write through becoming a citizen of the world. *Journal of Curriculum Theorizing*. 28(1), 88–107. Retrieved May 16, 2019, from http://journal.jctonline.org/index.php/jct/article/view/173/08olsson.pdf.

Oxford English Dictionary (n.d.). Retrieved May 20, 2019, from https://en.oxforddictionaries.com/.

Shaviro, S. (2009). *Without criteria: Kant, Whitehead, Deleuze and aesthetics*. Cambridge, MA: MIT Press.

Sinclair, N. (2018). An aesthetic turn in mathematics education. In E. Bergqvist, M. Österholm, C. Granberg, & L. Sumpter (Eds.), *Proceedings of the 42nd Conference of the International Group for the Psychology of Mathematics Education* (vol. 1, pp. 51–66). Umeå: PME.

Smythe, S., Hill, C., MacDonald, M., Dagenais, D., Sinclair, N., & Toohey. K. (2017). *Disrupting boundaries in education and research*. Cambridge: Cambridge University Press.

Snaza, N., Applebaum, P., Bayne, S., Carlson, D., Morris, M., Rotas, N., Sandlin, J., Wallin, J., & Weaver, J. (2014). Toward a posthuman education. *Journal of Curriculum Theorizing*, 30(2), 39–55. Retrieved May 20, 2019, from http://journal.jctonline.org/index.php/jct/issue/view/23.

Whitehead, A. N. (1933/1967). *Adventures of ideas*. New York: Free Press.

Whitehead, A. N. (1929/1978). *Process and reality*. New York: Free Press.

Wolfe, C. (2009). *What is posthumanism?* Minneapolis: University of Minnesota Press.

10

EXPLORING AFFECT IN STOP FRAME ANIMATION

Gabriele Budach, Dimitri Efremov, Daniela Loghin and Gohar Sharoyan

About This Chapter

Writing this chapter has been a collective endeavour, unfolding upon a meandering path, full of discovery and surprise, filled with moments of hesitation, uncertainty and frustration, and with feelings of energy, excitement, and deep connection. We experience this, and hope Deleuze and Guattari might agree, as a process of "becoming," which is still ongoing and "not yet" fully known (Spinoza, cited in Gregg and Seigworth, 2010, p. 3). When we started, we had no previous experience of working together on such a project; we had not experienced thinking and discussing intensely as a group, giving shape and substance to ideas, or articulating experiences that were difficult to put into words. Nor had we collaboratively produced a text that dealt with an experience that was shared but was interpreted differently. We had no concrete plan or pre-meditated path along which we might travel, no image of what the finished product would look like. There were no explicit rules guiding our process. The design of this chapter emerged as we moved forward together, talking about our experience, immersing ourselves in readings about affect, and responding to others' ideas, of others' ways of seeing, feeling, and thinking, as they became apparent and gained importance as forces shaping the process and unfolding within a timespan of seven months.

What we did have at the outset was our enthusiasm for a shared learning experience that was extraordinary and captivating to the extent that we wanted to explore, learn about it more and share it with others, in our effort to communicate what had us affected so deeply. Our belief in this project emerged from the intensity of our experience that had us bonding as a group, stronger than before, trusting in the process that lay ahead of us.

It started with a summer school workshop titled "Multilingual Identities in the Making," organized within the Master in Learning and Communication in Multilingual and Multicultural Contexts programme in which we were all involved at the University of Luxembourg. Under the guidance of filmmakers and digital artists Bo Chapman and Zoe Flynn from Salmagundi Films, London, we joined a week-long workshop on "animating objects." As we set out to investigate "identities in the contact zone" (Pratt, 1991), the workshop involved selecting a personally meaningful object that each participant was then invited to animate with hands and camera lenses, using a tablet mounted on a tripod, with a stop motion application installed upon it.

Stop frame animation making unfolded as a process that none of us could have anticipated, predicted, or pre-designed. It seemed governed, to a significant extent, by forces that lay beyond our control, but still producing something new, surprising, unique, and, we felt, very valuable. What emerged seemed less to be products of our will alone than to have been shaped by all the elements involved in the process, human and non-human (objects, technology and furniture, stories emerging from the concrete actions performed *in situ*, and memories mixed in with images produced in front of the camera lens). All these elements became part of co-creating movement, motions, gestures, and actions involved in animation making. While animation can be done, these days, entirely on a computer using specific software, we opted for the analogue procedure of literally moving objects manually, in tiny increments, step-by-step, in front of a camera lens. This involved placing an object – taking a shot – moving the object a tiny bit – taking another shot – moving the object yet again – taking another shot – and so on. In this way, animation making revolves primarily around the co-production of movement, a process oriented towards movement rather than stasis (Massumi, 2002). In co-producing movement, all elements – human and non-human – play a role and have a place engaging with each other in intensive intra-play. Ultimately, this process produces an animation and exerts a deeply affective and transformative power on all the entities involved.

Looking back, we therefore agree that animation making is an extraordinary field of experimentation with important pedagogical potential that we explore in this chapter. The analogue approach we adopted to animating objects taught us something new, exciting, and important about the power of affect; this was indeed a deeply affecting experience for us, resonating with what Spinoza (1959) has called *affectus* – the bigger or lesser modification of the mind or of the body, either taken in isolation or together. We experienced affect, which Deleuzian-Spinozan-inspired work describes as the capacity "to affect and to be affected" (Gregg & Seigworth, 2010, p. 2), in manifold manifestations during the animation making process. However, making sense of this proved equally intriguing, challenging, and difficult. We hope to share with our readers some of the insights about our experience that we have been able to distil so far.

The fascination for us lay in the fact that each of us felt affected and also experienced animation making differently. We brought different ideas, connections, sensitivities, and abilities to affect and to be affected by the task, and creating very different things from it. We believe that this is what makes animation such a rich terrain for exploring and understanding affect and processes of learning as fundamentally rhizomatic (Deleuze and Guattari, 1987). We felt that the process resembled a rhizomatic plant whose roots do not produce one single plant (unlike a tree) but rather spread out in all the available soil and produce multiple plants in multiple locations, that are all connected. In our case, such possibilities for connection were offered by the object each of us selected (what it could do), the film setting and the possibilities it provided, our imagination, the stories (already thought of and present in our head), and those emerging from the immediacy of animation making. This space – made up of different elements whose configuration and abilities to bond or disconnect changed throughout the process – looked different for each of us. While variation is a very common feature in any process of learning, interpreting, and problem solving, we felt that the openness and freedom of choice and exploration we experienced throughout the process added to the range and shape of difference that could be seen in our animation pieces.

Preparing for Animation Making in Summer School

Our process began with reading a text – the highly inspirational *Arts of the Contact Zone* by Mary Louise Pratt (1991). It helped us to select an object that would embody a "contact zone" for each of us individually. Dimitri selected a portable music player, the object longest in his possession, connecting him with the world when travelling was difficult for him. Daniela selected a bookmark given to her by her grandfather at the age of four that spurred her imagination about books and her interest in reading, at a time when that ability for her was "yet to become." Gohar chose a carrot, called *gazar* in Armenian, that had gained some importance for her recently, bringing to the fore the relatedness of the Armenian language to a wider range of other languages and cultures. Selecting an object proved very easy for Dimitri and Daniela who decided almost instantaneously while reading the text. It took more time for Gohar to decide on an object that would carry important meaning for her. We started to see how the space we would be sharing during Summer School was bound to open up as a "simultaneity of stories – so far" (Massey, 2005, p. 24) with the prospect of moving, evolving, and transforming through what was yet to come. The space, as it was building even before we met for the Summer School workshop, became shaped by our individual interpretations of the reading, the choices made to select our objects, the stories the objects brought with them, and the intensity with which we felt bonded to each other, to the objects and to the stories.

Initially situated within a "book space" (Lankshear & Knobel, 2006), our exploration of Pratt's (1991) text turned quickly into a "bloom-space" (Gregg & Seigworth, 2010) where affect reigned, with the text moving gradually and rather quickly in the background, out of sight, as individual projects started to unfold between hands and moving objects in front of a camera lens. Resonating with scholarly critiques of the multiliteracies approach proposed by the New London Group (1996), the process took us away from doing literacy in ways that centre on text (Lankshear & Knobel, 2006) towards a world of literacy that is much broader than the materiality, organization, and (sequential) structuration inherent to printed texts, and the affordances required to (re)produce them. Making an animation challenged our ideas on how to engage with texts, textual planning and production; our habitual and rehearsed ways of going about text design seemed, to some extent, problematic. Recourse to existing (textual) grammars, their rules and modes of application (about how to structure a storyline, for instance) failed, or were fundamentally challenged by a process that seemed to be guided by different forces, defying predictability and structured planning. The aim of our exploration of this process here is therefore not to suggest another model or set of rules for making a "good animation." On the contrary, we learned to appreciate the possibility of working outside a matrix of grammar rules, evading the corset of static and fixed positions, such as the ones that underlie ideas of design, as theorized in systemic functional grammar (Halliday, 1978; Halliday & Matthiessen, 2014; for a fuller discussion, see Leander & Boldt, 2012, p. 31). Traditionally, design has been understood as a pre-planned, systematic approach to creation that is based on principles attached to functions and values within a system. In this view of creation, elements of a system are (re)combined according to pre-existing rules that are both knowable and teachable. Hence, creation can be imagined and anticipated, based on an in-depth knowledge of the system and its modes of operation. In regard to our own experience of animation making, an anticipatory imagining of the kind described above failed, or was at least difficult, as the design seemed to be suggested by the process itself, and not by a pre-determined idea of a pre-conceptualized potential product. Animation work was leading us along an unknown path, destabilizing at times, but ultimately liberating. It was not "projected toward some textual end point, but [unfolded] as living its life in the ongoing present, forming relations and connections across signs, objects, and bodies in often unexpected ways," a process that "generat[ed] intensity and the excitement of emergence" (Leander & Boldt, 2012, p. 26).

In retrospect, we agree with the critique expressed by Leander and Boldt (2012) describing the effect of models that pre-structure creation, learning, and, in their context, literacy activity, as a "domestication [of learners and learning][1] that subtracts movement, indeterminacy, and emergent potential" (p. 24). What made our experience unique and valuable resided precisely in these elements: movement, indeterminacy, and emergent potential.

When Summer School began, we first shared our objects and stories in ways that resonated with Johnson Thiel's (2015) idea that "materials offer new reference points" (p. 129) and that sharing stories around materials and objects to which we feel affectively and emotionally connected "[make it possible] to create listening spaces for students ... that can shift understandings of communities, identities, and neighborhoods" (Pahl & Rowsell, 2010, as cited in Johnson Thiel, 2015, p. 123). In our case, the topics in focus were the challenges and opportunities of living in contact zones, where different cultures meet and mingle. Sharing the objects and listening to the stories affected some of us more deeply than others. Some could recognize themselves in the stories that others told. Others felt less engaged by the group sharing and turned quite quickly towards their own object, eager to explore its potentialities. This pattern of some connecting more strongly with some aspects than with others within the general assemblage of the classroom was present throughout. How these dynamics unfolded, in varying ebbs and swells of intensity, we attempt to sketch, at least in a very broad manner, in the following sections of the chapter.

While seated together in the same classroom – on chairs positioned in a circle, holding our objects in our hands, surrounded by other stuff, technical equipment, paper, pencils, props for filming, and so on – each of us started entering into our own individual assemblage around animating a personal meaningful object. We use the term "assemblage" here to refer to what Coleman and Ringrose (2013) call the "temporary grouping of relations" which, for us, became established at that particular instance of animation making, and dissolved, at least physically, after the project was finished. The assemblage included mobile objects, technical apparatus, locations, the objects we chose, the camera with the application, and the spot for filming, inside or outside of the classroom. The forming of the assemblage, and how we experienced it, happened in different ways for each of us. Variation derived from the (already existing, but always becoming) animators' relationships with the focus objects, additional materials, the environment and film setting, and people intervening in the process. All of these elements interacted as parts of the assemblage, and determined how conversation unfolded between the different parts, and how affective flows built up or lessened in the "swells and ebbs of intensities that pass between bodies"

(Gregg & Seigworth, 2010). In what follows, student co-authors share individual reflections on their personal experiences of the animation making process. We consider these narratives that emerged from the recollection of experience built on readings about new materialism to be our primary data.

Rethinking Our Experience after Reading and Discussing Affect

Dimitri

At the same time as attending the Summer School workshop, I was also actively involved in another project. In the mornings, I was working on my stop-motion film, and in the afternoons, I was participating in another project, which was a youth exchange.

The activities were the opposite of each other: the youth exchange was a fast-paced, active social event, while the Summer School project was slow, monotonous, almost menial – but at the same time very intimate. Given the opposite nature of these two projects, I began to treat my filmmaking time as "me" time, the time when I could relax, focus on myself, and isolate myself from the world around me. The monotonous nature of the work on my film also made it therapeutic for me.

The Summer School project was supposed to be personal from the start, since the idea was to work with a personal object. The selection process to pick an object I would subsequently work with was quick and intuitive. I chose a music player, the object longest in my possession (over ten years), and one that I still use on a daily basis. I never thought too much about it; from the beginning of my involvement in the Summer School project, I decided that I would go with the flow, and for the whole duration of it. I wanted to try to approach the project from a different, more creative angle.

In my opinion, a creative process should not be tamed by rules and restrictions. I was not very engaged into the preparatory stages of the project, when all the participants were sharing their ideas, talking about their objects, and thinking aloud about the way they planned to approach the work on their film. I wanted to have a very personal experience; in retrospect, I feel that I purposefully restricted my communication with everything and everyone around me for the duration of the summer school workshop.

I was waiting to jump into the creative process. I skipped the scenario-creating stage completely (I am now struggling to remember the word that was used to describe the six-panel format we were supposed to use to compile our scenarios[2]). Once I gained access to the filming equipment, I set the "stage" and began working.

To reiterate, throughout the whole project I was going with the flow. I did not think my next steps through, I did not analyze what I was doing; furthermore, I ignored the urge to structure my efforts. In my everyday life, I am an organized person, I think ahead, I strategize, I plan, because, at this current stage in my life, I have to. But, within the scope of this project I did not have to be as methodical. This is the main difference with the angle that I took for this project.

Another decision that I made dealt with my use of materials. I purposefully did not introduce any external objects to the environment in which I was working, except for the music player, which ended up being the centrepiece of the film. I sourced all the other materials from the room in which we were working. In retrospect, I was trying to establish a more meaningful communication between the main object (the music player), myself and the environment around us in this way.

In my selection of materials, I relied on only a few items, namely some sheets of coloured paper, a paper knife, some adhesive tape, and coloured pens. I like minimalism in art; maybe that was the reason for my selection of objects. The other reason could have been that I was trying to attempt to create a more meaningful interaction between the few objects that I used. An image that comes to mind is a party with a room full of people in which everybody is talking. The level of noise in the room is very high; one cannot expect to create a meaningful relationship with another person in these conditions. However, if the room is occupied by a small group of people, the likelihood of the development of deeper relationships is much more likely.

I isolated myself from almost all human contact while working on my film. The state I was in was reminiscent of a trance; I did not want anyone to interfere in my communication with my object. I refused help and guidance from the leaders of the project; my verbal interaction with other participants was minimal, even though we were all working in the same room. I enjoyed that.

I also enjoyed the tangibility of the work that I was doing. The monotonous, tactile movement of an object ever so slightly, taking a picture of the scene, another slight rearrangement of the scene, another photo ... The process was very soothing. It also felt meaningful. I was talking to my scene, and it was talking back to me – and, sometimes, it was talking back *at* me as well. It was a negotiation, a live discussion, a debate with no prearranged roles, assigned opinions or moderation. It was equally exciting for everything and everyone involved to see where all this was going. All decisions were made instantaneously, like the arguments that one comes up with in a heated discussion on a personal topic.

When it was time to stop filming, I knew it even though I did not plan it. It just felt right to stop. The conversation was over. I received cues from the object, from the scene, from the environment, and I responded to them.

I did some very simple editing; all the decision-making that I did for this part was effortless, as it had been during the filming.

What I want to emphasize is that not at no point during the making of my film did I think about the need to show my work to the other participants at the end of the project. What is more, I was very reluctant to show and explain the result to anyone else. To me, the process was the most important part. The result mattered very little to me. It matters very little to me even now. Merely elaborating on this experience in the textual format feels unnatural. The beauty of the process was its "unconsciousness," the feeling of going with the flow, letting go, doing what I felt was right at that particular moment in time.

Daniela

Every object has a story to tell, be it the objects we feel specifically connected to or the ones that end up in our trash bin. However, there are objects in our lives that we cherish more than others. Objects that, like the *madeleine* in Proust,[5] awaken memories and emotions that are deeply buried within ourselves. Turkle (2007) calls them *evocative*. The object I chose to animate fits very well in this category.

FIGURE 10.1 [3] Dimitri deeply immersed in conversation and co-creation
Note: To see Dimitri's movie,[4] please visit https://vimeo.com/335556188 (password: affect1).

The bookmark came into my life and I came into its life more than twenty years ago, when my grandfather gave it to me. I remember feeling very excited when I received it, and I promised to take good care of it, making sure, every day, that I did not lose it. Also, it generated a very deep interest in books, and I could not wait to learn how to read and to be able to place the bookmark in *my* own books. A multitude of stories, relationships, and life events have built and strengthened our connection since then and all of them came back to me the moment I brought the bookmark to class. Therefore, it is safe to say that, during the filmmaking, I was highly emotionally engaged.

The choice of the object was relatively easy, and mainly driven by the memories that connected me to it. As my grandfather passed away 15 years ago, I wanted to take advantage of this time and do something that would celebrate our relationship.

Before starting to work on our movies, we brought the objects to the classroom and shared their story with the others. We sat in a circle and exchanged stories about the objects, and ideas on how to animate them. We could immediately see how our stories and objects connected as we were sharing them, even though our relationships with them varied greatly. I could almost instantly relate to Dimitri's object and his story. Like him, I grew up with limited opportunities to travel. So, it was through music and movies that a window opened for me on "the outside world." Sharing stories also provided a great source of new knowledge for me. One of the participants chose a gift she received while travelling to India. This led to a group conversation about Indian culture and traditions and gave me the chance to learn something new about this country.

When we started with the filming work, we were given complete freedom. The only instructions we received were to create a digital story based on the object we had chosen. There were no limits or restrictions when it came to how or what we wanted to show in our movies. This was both liberating and destabilizing. Liberating because I felt free and completely in control of my story. Destabilizing because of the highly emotional and evocative load that my object was carrying. The multitude of events and stories that my bookmark had been involved in made it difficult to choose, develop, and represent a storyline. I remember creating, cancelling, and re-creating storyboards. Every time I thought that I had found the best solution, some new memory would come up and make me change my ideas. I felt that eventually I settled on a story that I wanted to tell, but, after starting to film, I ended up changing it again.

One of the most difficult decisions was how to create the set for my movie. At first, I considered doing it in the classroom, using white wallpaper as a background. However, this did not feel right. The bookmark spurred my interest and love for books, and I felt that it belonged in the middle of books. This is why I chose the new university library as a location for filming. However, deciding on the perfect spot for my object within this space turned out to be more complicated than I thought. It felt like it was not just me working with the bookmark, but also the bookmark working with me. In the end, I had the impression that my object decided on its own what the best spot would be, which, in turn, influenced and changed my decisions.

The intensity of emotions involved in the making of the movie fluctuated during the process. One of the main reasons for this is the fact that the location I chose as a film set is frequented by many students during the day. This led to the activity of filming often being interrupted by people passing by and stopping to enquire about the movie and the summer school workshop. Those were moments when I felt that the connection between my object and me was weaker and the intensity of emotions lower.

On the contrary, the part of the film that shows me learning the alphabet was the most intense in terms of emotions. This was mainly because it was filmed entirely in the classroom, and my engagement with the bookmark was not disturbed for the whole time I was working there. The intensity of emotions was amplified by the many memories connected to this particular moment. This was the moment when my hands were mechanically moving the bookmark and taking the photos, while my mind wandered back to my grandparents' living room, to those winter evenings by the fireside when they patiently showed me every letter of both the Latin and the Cyrillic alphabet. At certain points, I could almost smell the burned wood and mint tea that was so characteristic of my grandparents' house in wintertime and hear my grandfather's favourite composer playing quietly on the record player. This was also the moment where I felt that I needed to use one of those songs as a background soundtrack for my movie.

The music was the last piece of the puzzle and, once added to the movie, I felt that my picture was complete. When assembled together, the bookmark, the books, and the music made me relive some of the most vivid memories of my childhood.

To conclude, I would say that, in addition to the fact that it was extremely enjoyable, this experience taught me many new things. First, I developed a higher level of empathy towards my colleagues. As we all shared a similar path in making our movies and faced similar challenges, we grew to understand each other better and develop a deeper appreciation for each other's work.

Second, as I come from a long tradition of learning by following instructions, I learned how to work when there are no instructions at all. As I mentioned above, it was destabilizing at first, because I did not know where to start, or how to proceed. But, as time passed, I learned how to orient myself in a rule-free context, how to make my own decisions, and how to trust them.

Exploring Affect in Stop Frame Animation 185

FIGURE 10.2 Daniela with her bookmark learning how to read
Note: To see her movie, please visit https://vimeo.com/335557806 (password: affect2).

Gohar

Looking back, my process of animation making unfolded in phases. These, however, did not emerge in a linear way. In fact, the whole making of the animation happened in a rather rhizomatic fashion. Saying this, I feel inspired by how Deleuze and Guattari (1987) refer to life as emergent, as having no natural directions of growth, boundaries, or barriers.

Initially, I was filled with hesitation and uncertainty about the object I had to animate. I was not sure whether a carrot would provide a lot of space and possibilities to work with or to tell a personal story. Little by little, my perspective changed as I tried to look beyond what I thought was a limit. I managed to overcome the boundaries that I had created for myself. I embraced the challenges and difficulties that seemed to be in my way, hindering the progress of my project, and I invested myself in the creative space. The openness and flexibility of this kind of creative space was one of the most motivating factors I based my work on.

I spent a lot of time experimenting, repurposing, and redefining the object I was working with. I set myself the task to animate a carrot – a type of vegetable that had gained a certain significance for me at a certain point. It was that object which opened up for me a new understanding of the world in general, and of my home country in particular. Consequently, the object also gained an emotional connotation for me.

Hence, my goal became to put together the emotions and the newly acquired meanings that the carrot carried for me, and to share them through a story. To achieve that, I had to go through an intensive process of repurposing. The carrot ceased to be merely a vegetable that I might use to cook with or to eat raw. It was no longer a product sitting on the counters of grocery stores. Throughout the process of working with it, the carrot kept transforming and changing.

First, it started to obtain some anthropomorphic features while I was playing with it. Of course, I arrived at this understanding later, once I reached the stage of reflecting back on my experience. It was only after I gave it deep thought that I realized the extent to which I was making the carrot behave in a human-like way. For instance, I made it have hands and feet. I made it *unterhaken* [6] with other carrots. I made it dance in order to express happiness, joy, and excitement. On the whole, this kind of contact with the carrot made me treat it as one of my own kind. At one point, we became one entity, as the film will show. Inspired by Lenz Taguchi (2014), I feel that, in our shared experience, both the carrot and I were holding and exercising agency and had the capacity to transform each other.

Second, I started to relate more and more to the carrot in the sense that my imagination went wild, and I totally integrated into the creative space and process. This integration manifested itself in all the ways I used the carrot in order to tell my story. I cut it into pieces, then into even smaller pieces, I grated the carrot, decomposing its boundaries and recomposing the material in new ways. Immersed in this doing, the boundary between bodies – the carrot and me – became invisible and less and less tangible.

Then, there was another aspect of the process that created physical contact between the object and me. The haptic nature of animation making gave it another dimension: taking shot – after shot – after shot. I can refer to it as a meditative and contemplative process. It gave a space for my body and mind to be in harmony and balance. Each touch and movement were accompanied by a sensation, a feeling, an emotion. I was experiencing some sort of cleansing of the mind and relaxation of the body while performing these constantly repetitive actions such as moving the object, pressing the button, placing the objects in a new position, pressing the button again, and so on.

Feeling empty for some time while doing the moves, the process would then turn into some sort of reflective practice, developing into a chain of thoughts about myself. As this new dynamic starting to flow, I remember asking myself a number of questions: why had I had chosen that object? What did I think now about carrots? Did it have a new meaning in my life?

Exploring Affect in Stop Frame Animation 187

What was it? Through these questions, I was trying to understand things about myself. It was, in some sense, an exploration of my identity. Speaking with an image, I felt like I was on a hiking tour to a place I had already been to, but this time it was a different season, and therefore the landscape looked different.

Finally, what remains memorable for me is the screening of our animated films, and the moment of sharing them with the other participants. After experiencing the role of the author-creator of a film, my perspective and relationship with the audience shifted dramatically. I saw personal stories; I saw the emotions of others, their memories, all that while thinking about my own experience. All these spoke to me in a strong and more intimate way, since I could relate to them based on what I had been through myself.

FIGURE 10.3 Gohar exploring carrots.
Note: To see her movie, please visit https://vimeo.com/335567239 (password: affect3).

Three Stories: A Summary

Three different stories, three different processes of becoming, starting from different points in an individual course of life and leading to different points at the end of a summer school workshop.

Ready to dive into something new, an experiment of creative process, Dimitri did not bring any plans or pre-meditated ideas to the task. This seemed to make it easier for him to establish an affective relationship with things immediately at reach, to make space for the forming of an assemblage, and to generate a workflow. Isolating himself from human contact seemed to intensify communication with his objects (and not thinking or worrying about the result). Experiencing the process seemed to help him to immerse himself and stay intensely immersed in the process.

Hoping to celebrate the relationship with her grandfather to whom Daniela feels strongly emotionally connected through her object, she brought a goal and pre-existing design, filled with memory, to the animation project. Carrying a complex, long-time experience to the animation stage turned out to be difficult, as memories and scripted ideas seemed to resist transformation into animation work. Expanding possibilities emerged from choosing a location outside the classroom – the library – allowing the project and affective connection to intensify, as pieces of furniture, books, and magazines suggested themselves into the assemblage. Other forces seemed to pull her away from the project and to decrease the affective intensities sustaining it, as people interrupted her work by watching and asking questions. It is noteworthy that the strongest connection and greatest affective intensity unfolded in the classroom, when, undisturbed, the most simple design, involving the bookmark and a few letters written on a piece of paper, created the scene. This happened at the end of the entire process, provoking a kind of synesthetic revival of childhood memories, filled with strong emotions, images, and senses – smells and sounds.

An object of knowledge, rather than one of human bonding, was what Gohar brought to the task. Making sense of that connection and struggling with the affordances of her object, it took time for her to find her way into the assemblage, affective relationship, and workflow. It seemed that exploring the object – and giving up on what it conventionally meant and was used for – began to open up new possibilities to connect with and understand the world, her country, and, ultimately, herself. It seemed that through the process of exploring, abandoning conventional meaning and repurposing, an emotional relationship began to grow that enabled her to ask new questions. Interestingly, swells followed ebbs of intensity; periods of emptiness gave way to periods of reflection, connecting body and mind in ways that enabled new perspectives and the revisiting of places that she could now see from a different viewpoint.

Expanding the Assemblage: Beginning to Think-With Theories of Affect

Writing this chapter has been a complex experiment. It began with the summer school workshop, the first-hand *experience of affect* that we explored in this chapter. At that point, affect as a focal point of theoretical reflection was still unknown to us, the student co-authors. Together in the same classroom, we shared our stories, and soon, as we began filming, a flow of energy – that we now call affect – moved through the assemblages of our projects and those of our colleagues, working next to us. The experiment then became about testing what creating movement and inter-acting with materials would do for us, and how it would stimulate learning for us under these conditions.

The experiment and assemblage expanded when we decided to embark on a process of thinking and writing collectively about our experience as co-authors. Reading about and discussing affect, we learned a new language of description. Finding a way into the literature, we practiced what MacLure (2013) advises: that the qualitative researcher should take a fresh look at data, and that the value of an affective approach is that it can help to slow us down and sit with that which in the data sparks "fascination or exhilaration .... incipience, suspense or intensity" (p. 173). She also suggests that qualitative researchers should spend more time considering data "hot spots"– those affective relations to data that both "disconcert" and create a sense of "wonder" – where data "glows" for the researcher in various moments of fieldwork, analysis, and beyond (pp. 172–173). During monthly meetings, we discussed the progress of our thinking-with affect and of our experience in the process of animation making. To feed this reflection, we read a selection of articles individually (Pahl & Rowsell, 2011; Johnson Thiel, 2015; Leander & Boldt, 2012; Gregg & Seigworth, 2010), and highlighted quotes and excerpts that became significant for each one of us, as they seemed to resonate in a particular way with our experience. These collections of quotes and excerpts were shared from one group session to another. This practice helped us to share our experience on a more reflective level and to better understand terms such as assemblage, affect, and affective intensities. Feeling an imprecise force of attraction at first, we gradually discovered deeper levels of meaning through our discussions, and we gradually adopted a new language of description to talk about our experience. Dimitri felt attracted to quotes such as these found in Gregg and Seigworth (2010): "Sigmund Freud once claimed ... that affect does not so much reflect or think; affect acts (1966: 357–59)" (p. 2); and "affect [is] the prime 'interest' motivator that comes to put the drive in bodily drives (Tomkins)" (p. 6). He pointed out that this was precisely what he felt during the animation making. Daniela felt very much attracted to a quote from Pahl and Rowsell

(2011) highlighting the fact that "artifacts give power to meaning makers" (p. 134). She also felt very strongly about Turkle's (2007) notion of "evocative objects" which helped her to make sense of the strong emotional connection and relationship that her bookmark symbolized for her. After her exploration, Gohar kept insisting on how important the process and idea of transformation had been for her; first, the transformation of her object; and then, her own transformation, the transformation of her relation to the object and the revealing of things "not yet known" to her, that exploring the object had laid open. Her experience resonated strongly with Lenz Taguchi's (2014) idea that "both humans and objects hold the capacity of agency and co-constitutively transform each other" (cited in Johnson Thiel, 2015, p. 115). Through our readings, we were able to distil these aspects of the process that, we agreed, had become important for us all during animation making. We felt that working on the animation was an intensive process. Being focused on an object, touching, handling, exploring, and moving it over a long period of time created an unusual, and unusually intense contact, that, we believe, played an important part in creating affect in our context. We noted that the *haptic*, the prolonged physical engagement with one or more objects also had a strong – and often soothing – affective impact, similar to a deeply immersive and meditative practice. Even though the intensity of the experience varied across time, space, and individuals, haptic engagement, we felt, was fundamental for all of us. Two more dimensions we discussed and distilled as central in shaping individual experience of animation making were *emotions* and the impact of *memory*. We agreed that all three dimensions could have a shaping and driving force in the process, but that the haptic – the power of touch – was the strongest in creating affect, for all of us.

What We Learned from Our Experience and What We Wish to Share

By sharing our experience, we wish to recommend animation making as a valuable experience to be lived by others too. We experienced affect as a force that stimulates learning through the deep and prolonged engagement with materials. Thinking about and in terms of affect taught us about the forces that may enhance or hinder motivation, exploration, and experimentation, nurturing the flow of process or cutting us off from it. We learned about the value of engaging in and giving oneself up to an experimental process of which the outcome is not pre-designed.

Experiencing this process also taught us new ways of learning that decentred us from language and linguistic textual norms. Making stop motion animated film does not focus on language or language learning in particular. But it can open a space for language learning in which flexible multilingualism has room to thrive (see Daniela's movie using English and Romanian). While ideologies of monolingualism often prevail in regular classroom settings, creative processes such as animation making can undermine their power of persistence and enable new forms of communication and multilingualism.

In our Master's programme, we strive to build an environment where diversity is the norm and where diverse positioning has room to be constructed and expressed. We feel that animation making can provide such a safe space inviting exploration, experimentation, and the unfolding of the unknown. This is because animation making forces us to unlearn some of the rules that are characteristic of the type of behaviour demanded in the monolithic systems we have been educated in, and that we have embodied to the point that at first it may feel difficult or uncomfortable to unlearn them. In broader terms, we appreciated animation making as an approach that forced us, to a certain extent, to engage with materials, experiencing the benefits of "vital materialism" that, as Bennett (2010) defines it, "set[s] up a kind of safety net for those humans who are now ... routinely made to suffer because they do not conform to a particular (Euro-American, bourgeois, theocentric, or other) model of personhood" (p. 13). As Bennett further points out, we also felt that there was an "ethical aim ... to distribute value more generously, to bodies as such" (p. 13).

Although we do not think that it is possible (or desirable) to teach affect, we believe in the possibility of creating conditions in which affect can emerge and thrive, giving space for "life forces" to unfold (Coleman & Ringrose, 2013; Hickey-Moody & Malins, 2007). Such spaces allow learners to explore the vital capacity of life, its *agencements*, and its potential for becoming (Wallin, 2011). This should invite us to rethink curriculum in ways that consider and make space for a different kind of learning, one that does away with determining pre-conceptions, and that happens in relations of immanence and in-between-ness. "Life force" became tangible for us in animation making, most intensely, when objects took the lead, suggested the next move, provided the next fresh idea, behaving in an unruly fashion, folding in the curve of the hand, and thus blurring the fine line between humans and objects.

We also wish to offer animation making as a terrain to introduce thinking-with new materialist theories, with students, teacher, and teacher trainees, as an alternative way of approaching curriculum design and learning. We recommend our approach as we see value in the fact that it had us engaging in first-hand experience before exploring, experimenting, and thinking-with affect theory. Since we were rather eclectic in our choice of sources, we do not wish to suggest (another) affect theory, but rather to show how elements of theories of affect (in the plural) resonated with our experience. This process helped us to gain a deeper understanding of the processes we lived, while learning about movement – and how animation making mobilizes the body and the mind – about the materiality of things – and how we connect with them. It also taught us to pay attention to the environment in a new way, as it became part of the assemblage of our project. Finally, we learned about ourselves, by observing what happened to us as we joined the assemblage, and by noticing, more or less consciously, how the process affected us, and, ultimately, changed us. Finally, we wish to say that none of the fourteen participants in the summer school workshop has been left unaffected by the experience, and that all reported on the experience as intensive, powerful, empowering, liberating, and carrying intensity in some way or another, while deeply involving learning. We agree with Latour (2004) who states that learning happens best – and only really – if it happens in the midst of affected bodies: "there is no life to expect apart from the body …. to have a body *is to learn to be affected*, meaning 'effectuated,' moved, put into motion by other entities, humans or non-humans" (p. 205, emphasis in the original). Creating, thinking, and building this piece of work together has been an exciting journey and a strong, bonding experience. Coming out of it, we feel invigorated, more knowledgeable and empathic towards our peers, having experienced the process, its flow and affective intensities. Looking back, we wish to say, happily and proudly, "we have been there together."

Notes

1 Added by the authors of this chapter.
2 Dimitri is referring here to the storyboards provided to students.
3 Copyright of the images in this chapter is owned by the first author. Written consent was obtained from the co-authors prior to the summer school workshop.
4 Copyright of the films referred to in this chapter is co-owned by the first author and the respective co-authors.
5 See Marcel Proust (2001) *A la recherche du temps perdu*.
6 The verb *unterhaken* is German for "to link arms." It emerged from one of our group discussions that took place in English, although none of us were native speakers of that language. At the time, no one could think of the term in English, so Gabriele suggested the German term, and we stayed with it throughout our discussion, repeating the term and the moves it suggests, and sharing a lot of laughter and fun around *unterhaken*.

References

Bennett, J. (2010). *Vibrant matter: A political ecology of things*. Durham, NC: Duke University Press.
Coleman, B., & Ringrose, J. (2013). *Deleuze and research methodologies*. Edinburgh: Edinburgh University Press.
Deleuze, G., & Guattari, F. (1987). *A thousand plateaus: Capitalism and schizophrenia* (B. Massumi, Trans.). Minneapolis: University of Minnesota Press.

Gregg, M., & Seigworth, G. J. (Eds.). (2010). *The affect theory reader.* Durham, NC: Duke University Press.
Halliday, M. A. K. (1978). *Language as social semiotic.* London: Edward Arnold.
Halliday, M. A. K., & Matthiessen, C. M. I. M. (2014). *Halliday's Introduction to functional grammar* (4th ed.). London: Routledge.
Hickey-Moody, A., & Malins, P. (2007). *Deleuzian encounters: Studies in contemporary social issues.* London: Palgrave Macmillan.
Johnson Thiel, J. (2015). Vibrant matter: The intra-active role of objects in the construction of young children's literacies. *Literacy Research: Theory, Method, and Practice,* 64(1), 112–131. https://doi.org/10.1177/2381336915617618.
Kress, G. R., & Van Leeuwen, T. (2006). *Reading images: The grammar of visual design* (2nd ed.). New York: Routledge.
Lankshear, C., & Knobel, M. (2006). *New literacies: Everyday practices and classroom learning* (2nd ed.). Maidenhead: Open University Press.
Latour, B. (2004). How to talk about the body? The normative dimension of science studies. *Body & Society,* 10(2–3),205–229. doi:10.1177/1357034X04042943.
Leander, K., & Boldt, G. (2012). Rereading "A pedagogy of multiliteracies": Bodies, texts, and emergence. *Journal of Literacy Research,* 45(1), 22–46. doi:10.1177/1086296X12468587.
Lenz Taguchi, H. (2014). New materialisms and play. In L. Brooker, M. Blaise & S. Edwards (Eds.), *The SAGE handbook of play and learning in early childhood* (pp. 79–90). London: SAGE Publications.
MacLure, M. (2013). Classification or wonder? Coding as an analytic practice in qualitative research. In B. Coleman & J. Ringrose (Eds.), *Deleuze and research methodologies* (pp. 164–183). Edinburgh: Edinburgh University Press.
Massey, D. (2005). *For space.* Thousand Oaks, CA: Sage.
Massumi, B. (2002). *Parables for the virtual: Movement, affect, sensation.* Durham, NC: Duke University Press.
Pahl, K. H., & Rowsell, J. (2010). *Artifactual literacies: Every object tells a story.* New York: Teachers College Press.
Pahl, K. H., & Rowsell, J. (2011). Artifactual critical literacy: A new perspective for literacy education. *Berkeley Review of Education,* 2(2), 129–151. doi:10.5070/B82110050.
Pratt, M. L. (1991). Arts of the contact zone. *Profession,* 33–40. Retrieved August 30, 2019, from www.jstor.org/stable/25595469.
Proust, M. (2001). *A la recherche du temps perdu.* Paris: Gallimard.
Spinoza, B. (1959). *Ethics: On the Correction of Understanding* (A. Boyle, Trans.). London: Everyman's Library.
The New London Group (1996). A pedagogy of multiliteracies: Designing social futures. *Harvard Educational Review,* 66(1), 60–92. Retrieved August 30, 2019, from https://www.hepg.org/her-home/issues/harvard-educational-review-volume-66-issue-1/herarticle/designing-social-futures_290.
Turkle, S. (Ed.). (2007). *Evocative objects: Things we think with.* Cambridge, MA: MIT press.
Wallin, J. J. (2011). What is curriculum theorizing: For a people yet to come. *Studies in Philosophy and Education,* 30(3), 285–301. doi:10.1007/s11217-010-9210-y.

INDEX

Aboriginal perspectives *see* Indigenous perspectives
actualize/actualization 85, 139, 141, 143, 145, 147, 157, 165
affect: affective capacity 13, 59, 92, 139–142, 148, 176–177; affective flows 4, 5, 11, 12, 92, 98–99, 123–124, 129, 132, 137, 179; affective forces 8, 9, 10, 57, 58, 69, 92, 93, 97, 121, 123, 133, 136, 139–140, 143–147, 163, 176–177, 179, 188–191; affective intensity/-ies 12, 58–60, 64, 65, 69–70, 92, 98, 99, 125; affective pedagogies 11, 100; affect theory 13, 59–60, 78, 91–92, 100, 123, 137–143, 145, 147–149, 175, 191
agencement 106, 191
agency/-ies: agency from a posthuman/new materialist/sociomaterial perspective 3, 18, 40, 58, 92, 99–100, 123–124, 127, 148, 164, 186; agency from an Indigenous perspective 35, 40, 45–46; distributed agency 140–141, 143–144, 147–149, 186, 190; human agency 45, 138, 155; relational agency 41, 46–47, 92, 100, 107, 172, 190
agential cut(s) 123, 126–128, 131
agential realism 40, 123
Ahmed, S. 59–60, 68
anthropocentric perspective *see* human-centred perspective

assemblage(s) 2, 9, 10, 11, 12, 13, 32, 36, 44, 57, 59, 65, 66, 67, 69, 92, 93, 99, 105–107, 110–111, 113–116, 122–123, 127, 138–141, 144–145, 147–149, 153–154, 159, 162–163, 165, 168, 170–173, 173n1, 179, 188–189, 192; classroom assemblage 146–148, 150; research assemblage 141–143

Barad, K. 3, 7, 19, 28–29, 40, 41, 48–49, 91–93, 98–100, 105–106, 123, 127–128, 156, 164, 168
Baylor, B. & Parnall, P. 43
becoming(s) 3, 5, 6, 9, 10, 11, 12, 29, 32, 36–37, 39, 41, 43, 49, 50, 58, 59, 70, 74–76, 78, 92, 97–99, 104–106, 110, 121–125, 129–130, 138, 141–142, 145, 150n1, 154, 160–161, 163, 165, 168–172, 175, 191
Benesch, S. 136, 139, 145, 146
Bennett, J. 165, 191
Berlant, L. 8, 66–67
binary/-ies *see* dualism(s)
body/-ies 55, 58, 78–79, 82, 84, 92, 99, 138–141, 145, 147, 156, 162–163, 164–165, 168, 178–179, 186, 191–192; student-bodies 11, 139, 141, 145, 149; teacher-bodies 11, 139, 141–142, 145, 149; text-bodies 11, 139, 141–142, 144–145, 147–149
Boldt, G. 2, 108
Boler, M. & Davis, E. 139

Bonta, M. & Protevi, J. 138
Borg, S., 140
boundaries 1, 12, 13, 25, 49, 92, 141, 154, 159, 168, 185–186
Braidotti, R. 59, 153–154

Cartesian thinking 3, 74, 77, 127, 138
cartography 12, 154, 163–170
causality 91, 111; cause and effect 8, 9, 91, 99; relational causality 91–92, 96, 98–100, 143
Colebrook, C. 2, 5, 140, 158
Coleman, D. 35, 38, 43, 44
Coleman, R. & Ringrose, J. 179
collaboration 24, 25, 26, 30, 43, 108, 111, 128, 130–132, 175
collaborative inquiry 54, 69
colonialism 3, 8, 33, 93, 95
Comber, B. 38
community/-ies 55, 56–57, 60, 62, 120, 132, 179
concept(s) 19, 158
contact zone 176–177, 179
Cottom, T. M. 2
critical praxis 8, 55
critical thinking 10, 57, 104, 108, 112, 116
curriculum 26, 32, 38, 39, 55, 56, 69, 107, 109, 136, 145–146, 160, 161, 163, 191

data 55, 58, 61, 104, 109–110, 121, 123, 124–126, 133, 137, 141–143, 149, 189
Davies, B. 39, 44
de Freitas, E. 3
de Freitas, E. & Sinclair, N. 157
DeLanda, M. 2, 171
deterritorialization 12, 108, 115, 153
Deleuze, G. & Guattari, F. 2, 7, 10, 11, 12, 13, 19, 23, 26, 69, 104–107, 120, 123, 137–140, 145–146, 150n1, 153, 159, 162, 163–165, 170, 173, 175, 177, 185
Deleuze-Guattarian (or DeleuzoGuattarian) 23, 26, 137–142, 145, 148–149
Deleuzian 11, 23, 30, 147, 149, 176
desire 23, 30, 99, 100, 108, 130
desiring(s) 7, 26, 30, 123, 129–130
deterritorialization 13, 108, 115–116, 142, 153
dichotomy/-ies *see* dualism(s)
diffraction 2, 13, 124, 168, 171

digital tools 18–19, 57, 60–61, 64–65, 75, 94, 122, 133
displacement 54, 57, 65
disrupt(ion) 7, 13, 32, 69, 91, 96, 98, 100, 114–115, 142–143, 163
Doucet, A. 123–124
dualism(s) 55, 58, 59, 74, 77, 85, 127, 138, 145, 153, 159, 163, 165

early childhood education 72, 73, 74, 75, 77, 80, 85–87, 132, 158–159, 171–172
educational change 10, 29, 38, 48, 67, 70, 99–100, 104, 111
embodiment: embodied act(s) 153; embodied affect 141, 145; embodied becoming 163; embodied engagement 123, 154, 159; embodied feelings 127; embodied knowledge 161; embodied literacy 168; embodied memory 93; embodied reaction(s) 138, 139, 140; embodied reality 36; embodied representation(s) 164; writing as embodied 38, 47
emotion(s) 11, 59–60, 81–83, 85–86, 127–128, 136–137, 139–141, 143–145, 147–149, 163, 171, 179, 182–184, 186–188, 190
encounter(s) 1, 11–12, 24, 41, 47–48, 59, 67, 69–70, 75, 91, 99, 139–140, 142, 147, 159
entanglement(s) 3, 5, 9, 26, 28, 39, 40, 55, 59, 75, 91–92, 97–98, 100, 120–121, 123, 125–128, 132, 153, 159, 163–165, 168, 170, 172
environmental perspectives 41–42, 44, 46, 56, 65, 67, 69, 159–160, 168
Erdrich, L. 37
ethics 3, 19, 29, 40, 41, 60, 99, 141, 150, 154, 156
ethico-onto-epistemology/ies 28–29

feeling(s) 4, 13, 130, 144–146, 157, 161, 163, 175, 186
Feminism 68, 156
First Nations' perspectives *see* Indigenous perspectives
Fitzpatrick, K. 2
fluidity 18, 24, 25, 105, 154, 164, 168, 172

genocide 34, 51n2
geometry 12, 154, 155–158
Golembeck, P. & Doran, M. 140

Goodchild, P. 30
Gregg, M. & Seigworth, G. J. 180, 189
Grosz, E. 5, 6, 9, 60, 70, 76–80, 82, 84, 85
Guo, Y. 136

haeccities 2
haptic 13, 186, 190
Haraway, D. 36, 37, 39, 44, 155
hope 1–2, 4, 8, 48–49, 69, 96, 122, 171
Honan, E. & Bright, D. 13
human-centred perspective(s) 58, 68, 122, 138, 140–141, 148, 155

identity/-ies 18, 36, 45, 79, 100n2, 106, 123–124, 156, 168, 171, 176, 179, 187
idealism 73–76, 77–78, 80, 82, 85, 87, 87n2, 155
imagination 9, 11, 146, 154, 157–159, 165, 171, 177, 186
immanent/immanence 12, 138
in-between(ness) 105, 160, 191
incorporeal 9, 58, 59, 78–79, 82, 158–159, 162–163
indeterminacy 12, 32, 57, 96, 98, 107, 123, 131, 143, 154, 158, 170, 179
Indigenous perspectives 3, 33–34, 35, 37, 39, 41, 48, 50, 67, 68, 93–95, 100–101n2, 123
inequality/-ies 1, 65, 67, 93–95, 112–113, 116
Ingold, T. 3, 4
injustice *see* inequality/-ies
in process 161, 163
instructional coaching 104, 106, 109, 116, 117n1
intensity/-ies 8, 10, 12, 13, 14, 44, 57, 58, 70, 92, 99, 125, 127, 132, 161, 175, 179, 184, 189–190, 192
interpretation 5, 11, 12–13, 58–59, 67, 88n6, 128, 132, 142, 154, 158, 160, 175, 177–178
interviews 60–62, 125–126
intra-action(s)/intra-active 5, 8, 9–10, 38, 40, 41, 48, 75, 91–92, 97–99, 122–124, 126–127, 129, 133, 164, 171

Jackson, A. & Mazzei, L. 36
Johnson Thiel, J. 179

Kalman, J. & Street, B. 94
Kimmerer, R. W. 44

knowledge(s)/knowing 12, 29, 40, 49, 50, 54, 63, 66, 68, 69, 78, 85, 105, 143, 154, 159–161, 163–164, 168, 171–173
Kuby, C. R. 11, 19, 125, 141
Kuby, C. R. & Gutshall Rucker, T. 95, 97
Kuby, C. R. & Rowsell, J. 11

land 5, 8, 34, 35, 37, 40, 50, 67
land acknowledgment 33–34
language 9, 57, 58, 73, 74, 75, 79, 81, 84–86, 162, 171–172, 190–191
language education 9, 49, 55–56, 57, 58, 69, 136–138, 143, 145, 148, 150, 191
Lather, P. 2
Latour, B. 192
Leander, K. & Boldt, G. 13, 32, 98, 179
learn(ing) 4, 5, 7, 8, 10, 12, 13, 21, 23, 32, 34, 39–41, 43, 44, 48, 49, 50, 55, 57–58, 61, 63, 64, 65, 69, 73–74, 80–81, 94–95, 98, 100, 107–108, 111, 122, 130–132, 145, 158–161, 163, 165, 170–171, 175, 177, 184–185, 190, 192
Lekta 78–80, 82, 85–86, 87n4
Lenz Taguchi, H. 190
Lenz Taguchi, H. & St. Pierre, E. 38
line(s) of flight 10, 13, 69, 107–109, 114–116, 153, 160–161
listening 43–44, 48, 50, 66
literacy/-ies: family literacy/-ies 54–55, 60, 63, 64, 68, 94–95; literacy desiring 6–7, 18–19, 21–23, 24, 25, 26, 27–28, 29–30, 97; literacy practices 9, 13, 18–20, 23, 26, 28, 29, 35, 42, 49, 55–56, 57, 66, 69, 74, 85, 91–93, 96, 99, 164, 170–171, 178; literacy research 40, 91, 122, 125, 132, 138, 178–179; literacy skills 1, 8–9, 73, 81–82, 94; phonics literacy approach 73, 80; whole language literacy approach 73–74, 80

MacLure, M. 9, 75, 76, 143, 189
maker education 11, 75, 120–122, 131–132
Malone, K. 67
map(ping) 5–6, 110, 160, 163–165, 170, 173
Masny, D. 142
Massey, D. 38, 177
Massumi, B. 100
mathematics: mathematical concepts 156, 158; mathematics education

155–156, 171–172; mathematical objects 157
materialism 74–76, 77–78, 82, 85, 87, 87n2, 137–141, 145–146, 156, 191
materiality/-ies 3, 5, 9–10, 23, 28, 29, 39, 40, 55, 57, 58, 69, 76–77, 79, 86–87, 100, 107, 111, 121–123, 124, 127–128, 132–133, 161, 164, 168, 178, 181, 186, 191–192
material-discursive 23, 99, 105, 128, 133
Mazzei, L. 3
method(s) 13, 51n3, 58, 65, 87n6, 109–110, 125, 141–142
methodology/-ies 55, 87n1
molar lines 107–109, 112–113, 115
molecular lines 107–108
more-than-human(s) 18, 23, 26, 30n1, 40, 164, 168
Morton, T. 66
movement 12–13, 20, 58, 70, 153, 158, 161, 176
multimodality 12, 123, 125–126, 130, 133
multiplicity/-ies 5, 26, 48, 107, 110, 153–154, 157

nature-based education 40, 44, 47, 59, 164, 171–172
new materialism 5, 55, 57, 58, 74, 75, 120, 122, 124, 127, 136, 138, 180, 191
Nichols, T. P. & Campano, G. 138
nomadic: nomadic literacy 163, 168; nomadic thought 154
non-human(s) (or nonhuman(s)) 3, 5, 7, 11, 18, 23, 26, 30n1, 35, 40, 42, 47, 48, 58, 66, 106–107, 116, 120, 122, 123, 125, 128, 130, 138–139, 141, 155, 156, 159, 172, 176, 192
non-linear(ity) 10, 19, 99–100, 185
non-representational 11, 30n1, 67–68, 75, 125, 133
Nxumalo, F. & Rubin, J. C. 13

object(s): evocative objects 182, 190; hyperobjects 66; objects and affect 57–59; objects in assemblages 55, 60, 67, 105–106, 127, 138, 154; objects in intra-actions 92, 123, 171; objects in stop-frame animation 12–13, 176–191; ontology of objects 155–158, 165
Olsson, L. M. 82, 161

onto-epistemology 11, 137–138, 146
ontology/-ies 28, 123, 156, 161, 168, 170–171
ontoethics 6, 8, 57, 87n3
optimism: politics of 1–2; cruel optimism 2, 8, 66–67
Organization for Economic Cooperation and Development 95
Ormiston, N. T. L. 48

Pahl, K. & Rowsell, J. 179
Pearce, L. 8, 68
pedagogy/-ies 6, 7, 19, 22, 26, 29, 32, 36, 38, 39, 48, 49, 57, 63, 67, 69, 73, 96, 98–100, 104, 108–109, 111, 113, 116, 136–137, 139–150, 154, 160–161, 164, 171, 176
Pedagogical Documentation (PD) 12, 56, 154, 158–165
performativity 7, 40
place: critical place inquiry 32, 36, 38, 39, 40, 43, 49; ethics of 4, 7, 35, 37; place-thought 7, 32, 35, 36–37, 38, 40, 43, 47; understanding of 37, 38, 39, 56
plateau(s) 2, 13
play 20, 24, 47, 75, 76, 78, 80, 154, 159, 176
plugging into 19
posthumanism 5, 10, 18, 58, 59, 92, 93, 120–125, 127, 132, 138, 150n1, 154–156, 158, 171
poststructuralism 18
power 8, 33, 37, 47, 68, 95, 107, 113, 142, 149, 159, 163
privilege 8, 33, 58, 138
Professional Development (PD) 104–105, 109, 116
provocation 38, 122, 143, 161

questionnaire(s) 141, 143, 149

realism 73–75, 80, 85, 87
reflection 11, 186–187, 189
relationality/-ies 5, 19, 23, 32, 37, 38, 40–41, 44, 48, 55, 59, 91–93, 100, 107, 125, 130, 139–140, 145, 154, 158
relational ontology 55, 58, 60, 66, 69, 138, 140, 143, 164
relationship(s) 7, 10, 12, 18, 19, 21, 23, 25, 26, 28, 29, 34, 35, 37, 40, 41, 50, 70, 108, 122, 123, 159, 171, 179, 181, 183, 187–190

representation(s) 12, 40, 55, 73, 79, 81, 126, 153–155, 158–159, 161, 164, 168, 170–171–173
representational practices 2, 33, 58, 67, 73, 75, 80, 123, 125, 158, 159–160, 163
response-ability/-ies 3, 29, 41, 44, 99
rhizoanalysis 142–143, 149
rhizomatic 10, 18, 22, 25, 27, 38, 104–106, 110–111, 114, 116, 142, 153–154, 159, 164–165, 171, 177
rhizome 105, 107, 153, 177
rhythm(s) 92–93, 96, 98, 99

St. Pierre, E. A. 3
St. Pierre, E. A., Jackson, A. Y. & Mazzei, L. 74, 75
Sedgwick, E. K. 58, 59
sense 8–9, 73, 75–82, 84–87, 143, 148
settler colonialism 34, 49
Sinclair, N. J. & Carriou, W. 34, 37, 38
Sinclair, N. & de Freitas, E. 3
Smith, D. 7, 23
smooth spaces 154
Smythe, S. 4
social-material (or sociomaterial) perspectives 60, 138–139, 141, 144–145, 148–149
socio-constructivism 40, 73, 80, 122, 140, 155, 158
sociocultural theory 10, 57–58, 104, 108, 140
Spinoza, B. 6, 13, 77, 92, 139, 175–176
standardized practices 5, 9, 10, 12, 24, 56, 65, 69, 93, 104, 107, 113–114, 154, 159–160, 163, 191
The Stoics 8–9, 77–78, 86, 87n3
stop frame animation (or stop-motion) 12–13, 20, 30n1, 176–192
story/-ies 4, 8, 13, 20–21, 25, 27–28, 33, 37, 39, 43, 44, 47–48, 50, 55–56, 58, 67–68, 91–93, 95–99, 128, 141, 177–179, 183, 187, 189
storytelling 9, 92–93, 99, 123
striated spaces 9, 10

Strom, K. & Martin, A. D. 107–108
Styres, S. 50
subjectivity 3, 26, 58, 59

technology 131–132, 159, 163, 176
territorialization 12, 106–108, 114, 116, 153–154, 159, 171
theory and practice (or theory-practice) 19–20, 22
thinking 139–140, 142–146, 148–149, 153–154, 161, 171, 175, 180, 189
think(ing)-with 2, 6, 11, 12, 14, 19, 36, 40, 100, 106, 122, 123–124, 132, 189, 191
Thomas-Muller, C. 41
Tierney, R. D. 141
Todd, Z. 4
Tomlinson, B. 148–149
Toohey, K. 75, 143, 149–150
transform(ation) 1, 8, 10, 48, 55, 57, 67, 69–70, 78, 81–82, 84–85, 98, 105–106, 108, 116, 124, 138, 143, 145, 157–158, 162–163, 177, 186, 188, 190
tree(s) 5, 35, 42, 45, 47, 49, 54, 58–59, 105, 165–170, 177
Tsing, A. L. 44
Tuck, E. & Gaztambide-Fernández, R. A. 35
Tuck, E. & McKenzie, M. 37, 38, 39, 40, 41, 49

vignette(s) 11–12, 28, 141–142, 144–147

Wagamese, R. 41
Watkins, M. 140
Watts, V. 35
Western perspectives 33, 49, 67, 76, 105
Whitehead, A. N. 156–157
whiteness 3, 34
writing 7, 18–19, 21–22, 24–25, 26, 27–29, 30n1, 32, 36–37, 38, 39, 42, 49, 54, 170–171, 189; place-writing: 40, 43–44, 45, 46, 47, 48, 49, 50
Wyatt, J., Gale, K., Gannon, S., Davies, B., Denzin, N. & St. Pierre, E. A. 44